COMMUNISM IN FINLAND

A History and Interpretation

COMMUNISM IN FINLAND

A HISTORY
AND INTERPRETATION

JOHN H. HODGSON

PRINCETON, NEW JERSEY

PRINCETON UNIVERSITY PRESS

1967

Publication of this book has been aided by
the Whitney Darrow Publication Reserve Fund
of Princeton University Press.

Composed and Printed in the United States of America
by Princeton University Press, Princeton, New Jersey

1918

TO K. H. WIIK

"A Man of Honor"

—Väinö Tanner
January 17, 1963

PREFACE

In Finnish there are few scholarly analyses of Finnish Communism, and, quite naturally, the topic has received even less attention in English. This study focuses on events which seem most important to the author; those questions which do not receive extensive treatment here will, hopefully, be dealt with in future research by other scholars.

The first three chapters deal with the development of the left wing in the Finnish Social Democratic Party from the turn of the century until the formation of the Finnish Communist Party in Moscow, in 1918, by former Social Democrats who had fled to Soviet Russia following defeat in the Civil War. In the fourth and fifth chapters Communism within Finland in the 1920s and early 1930s is discussed. The sixth chapter deals with Soviet Karelia, an experiment in autonomy led by Finnish Communists, which was to be national in form and Socialist in content. With the Great Purges this experiment came to an abrupt halt. On the eve of the Second World War Finnish Communism in Soviet Russia, as in Finland, was a negligible force. Soon, however, the Finnish Communist Party was transformed from a small, illegal band of conspirators into a large, legal organization. This metamorphosis is the subject of chapter seven. In the concluding chapter there is a recapitulation of my general thesis that the strength of Finnish Communism, past as well as present, is in large measure a reflection of the nature of Finnish Social Democracy. The history of independent Finland has been more turbulent than that of the neighboring Nordic countries, and many Finnish workers have consequently sought a radical, non-Scandinavian variety of Socialism. In its absence, there has been an acceptance of the obvious alternative.

For many reasons two figures, Otto Wille Kuusinen and Yrjö Sirola, play a prominent role in this study. They represented the main current in the left wing of the Finnish Social Democratic Party up to the Civil War; they were the principal figures on the Red side in the armed conflict of 1918; and it was due to their efforts that the Finnish Communist Party was founded. It should also be noted that both men were active in Comintern work. Sirola was a Comintern emissary in the United States among Finnish-Americans, who accounted for approximately one third of the membership of the American Workers' (Communist) Party in the early 1920s when it was organized on the basis of language groups, as well as in Scandinavia. Kuusinen occupied prominent positions in the highest organs of the Comintern during most of that organization's existence and at different periods was concerned with Scandinavian, English, and Asian affairs. Kuusinen was also a key figure in the Communist Party of the Soviet Union. From 1957 until his death in 1964, Kuusinen was a member of both the Presidium and Secretariat of the C.P.S.U. Central Committee.

I wish to express my gratitude to the many people interviewed in connection with this project. I also wish to thank my wife, Sirkka-Liisa, for her aid in translating documents from Swedish to Finnish and for her encouragement and advice. My "secretary," Hilja Riuska, has been a constant source of vital information about contemporary Finnish politics. Chapter seven owes much to the assistance graciously provided by the offices of the Finnish Social Democratic Party. This study, further-more, could not have been completed without the financial support of the Russian Research Center, Harvard University, and the Ford Foundation. Finally, I wish to thank Edward Surovell of Princeton University Press for his careful job of editing and for his well-founded, but temperate, criticism of a manuscript which at times must have seemed unruly in form and unfamiliar in content.

Syracuse, New York   JOHN H. HODGSON
June 17, 1966

CONTENTS

COMMUNISM IN FINLAND
A History and Interpretation

CHAPTER ONE

The Rise of Finnish Socialism and the Emergence of a Left Wing

THE RISE of Finnish Socialism depended only partly upon the existence of an industrial proletariat, which began to emerge in the 1860s with the introduction of steam power in the sawmill industry.[1] It depended also upon the pleasure of the Tsar, since Finland had been incorporated into the Russian Empire as an autonomous unit in 1809. In 1883 St. Petersburg gave Finnish authorities the power to permit the establishment of labor associations, and the next year an employer-led Workers' Association was set up in the capital, Helsinki, and soon afterward in other key cities.[2] In 1893 delegates from the associations gathered for a First Congress of Workers' Associations, which adopted a program reflecting the views of Viktor Julius von Wright,[3] who, as owner of a small factory and chairman of the Helsinki Workers' Association, hoped to prevent the spread of Socialism by improving labor conditions.[4] He cherished

[1] R. H. Oittinen, *Työväenkysymys ja työväenliike Suomessa* (Helsinki: Tammi, 1954), p. 33. In 1880 the industrial proletariat accounted for 6.6 per cent of Finland's total population. Göran von Bonsdorff, *Suomen poliittiset puolueet* (Helsinki: Tammi, 1957), p. 11.

[2] Oittinen, *op.cit.*, p. 94. [3] *Ibid.*, pp. 95-96.

[4] Hannu Soikkanen, *Sosialismin tulo Suomeen* (Porvoo: WSOY, 1961), pp. 21-22, 27; Carl Erik Knoellinger, *Labor in Finland* (Cambridge, Mass.: Harvard University Press, 1960), p. 42. Wright was also, to some degree, motivated by humanitarian feelings.

3

the idea of bringing employers and employees together, but workers initially resisted the employer-led labor associations.[5]

At the Second Congress of Workers' Associations, held in 1896, Wright and his conservative bourgeois colleagues chose to abandon the labor movement, which they felt had become too radical.[6] Into the leadership void stepped more liberal members of the bourgeoisie, the Young Finns, but with the formation three years later of the Finnish Labor Party they too withdrew from the labor movement.[7] With this new party Democratic Socialism took root in Finland, some ten years behind Norway and Sweden, twenty behind Denmark.[8]

Shortly before the formation of the Finnish Labor Party and of the utmost importance for the development of Finnish Socialism was the launching of a vigorous Russification campaign. In February 1899 the Tsar issued a manifesto designed to increase Russian control over Finnish affairs by undermining the power of the Finnish Diet. The February Manifesto was followed by decrees which made Russian the language for Finnish civil servants and which abolished the Finnish army as a separate unit. In 1903, climaxing the Russification program, St. Petersburg gave the Governor-

[5] Oittinen, *op.cit.*, p. 98. In the 1880s trade union sections were established in the workers' associations. Membership in the trade union sections—in contrast to membership in the associations—was made up almost exclusively of employees. *Ibid.*, pp. 100, 109.

[6] R. H. Oittinen, "Suomen työväenliikkeen synty," in *Suomen sosialidemokraattinen työväenliike 1899-1949* (Helsinki: KK:n kirjapaino, 1949), p. 22; Y. K. Laine, *Suomen poliittisen työväenliikkeen historia*, I (Helsinki: Tammi, 1951), pp. 90, 92, 102, 137.

[7] Yrjö Sirola, in *Työmies* (Superior, Wisconsin), August 29, 1928, p. 3. Hereafter cited as *Työmies* (Sup.).

[8] Hannu Soikkanen, "Sosialististen aatteiden sisältö ja leviäminen," *Historiallinen Aikakauskirja*, No. 4 (1961), pp. 282, 284.

General of Finland—the Tsar's chief representative in the Grand Duchy—dictatorial powers. The Finnish response to Russification was in one respect unanimous. All strata of society sought to safeguard Finnish constitutional rights. There was, however, disagreement over the means to achieve this end. In bourgeois circles a group known as the Constitutionalists, composed of Young Finns and Swedish-speaking Finns, favored a policy of passive resistance, whereas a second group, the Old Finns, sought to preserve Finnish autonomy through conciliatory measures.[9]

This split among members of the bourgeoisie had its counterpart in the Social Democratic Party. In 1903, the year when the Finnish Labor Party was renamed the Finnish Social Democratic Party, two distinct lines began to form.[10] The city of Tampere became a center for Social Democrats who, led by Yrjö Mäkelin, favored cooperation with the Constitutionalists.[11] The Social Democrats in Helsinki, on the other hand, clung to a concept of class warfare and demanded a struggle against Russification independent from that of the bourgeoisie.[12] The banner raised in Helsinki by Edvard Valpas included a cautious attitude toward Russia,[13] thus giving rise to the charge that Social Democrats in

---

[9] A third group was satisfied neither with passive resistance nor with conciliation. Members of the Activist Movement wanted military action against Tsarism. For further details in English on these three groups, see John H. Hodgson, "Finland's Position in the Russian Empire, 1905-1910," *Journal of Central European Affairs*, Vol. xx, No. 11 (July 1960), pp. 158-160.

[10] Soikkanen, *Sosialismin*, p. 133.

[11] *Ibid.*, pp. 110, 134, 166; Yrjö Sirola, in *Työmies* (Sup.), October 16, 1928, p. 3.

[12] Soikkanen, *Sosialismin*, pp. 134, 165; Sirola, in *Työmies* (Sup.), October 16, 1928, p. 3.

[13] Soikkanen, *Sosialismin*, p. 165.

the capital supported the conciliatory policy of the Old Finns.[14] In reality, however, sympathy on the part of the Valpas group for the Old Finns was more in the nature of an endorsement of the latter's harsh attitude toward the Swedish-speaking minority in Finland.[15]

An open clash between the Valpas and Mäkelin groups occurred in 1904 over the attitude to be taken in the fall election of the four-estate Diet. Social Democrats in several cities agreed with Mäkelin that in order to safeguard Finnish autonomy there should be cooperation with the Constitutionalists. Valpas, however, made cooperation with any bourgeois party conditional upon that party's acceptance of the Social Democratic demand for an electoral reform which would include universal and equal suffrage.[16] A congress of the Social Democratic Party supported Valpas. When Social Democrats in four cities proceeded to cooperate with the Constitutionalists in the fall election, the Valpas group, pointing out that the Constitutionalists as a body had not found the proposed electoral reform satisfactory, charged that the decision of the party congress had been violated.[17] The new Diet, which included three Socialists elected on lists of the Constitutionalists, met in December 1904 and was faced with the suffrage problem. Socialist hopes for reform were dashed when the Diet, under pressure from the nobles and the burgesses, tabled the matter and declared the end of Russification a prerequisite for settlement, in the autumn, of the suffrage question.[18]

Revolution in Russia provided an unexpected catalyst

---

[14] *Ibid.*, p. 137; Laine, *op.cit.*, I, 171.

[15] Sirola, in *Työmies* (Sup.), October 16, 1928, p. 3.

[16] Soikkanen, *Sosialismin*, pp. 104-105, 107, 109.

[17] *Ibid.*, p. 107; Laine, *op.cit.*, I, 176.

[18] Laine, *op.cit.*, I, 194-195, 203.

for reform. On October 31, 1905, duplicating events in Russia, a general strike was organized in Finland. The major role was played by Finnish Socialists, who, for the first time, were making a significant public showing.[19] Joined by members of all political parties, they sought to restore Finnish constitutional rights. Membership in the Social Democratic Party surged, increasing from 16,610 to 85,027 between 1904 and 1906. The general strike meant, moreover, a decisive breakthrough for the labor movement in the countryside, among agricultural workers as well as in industrial and commercial centers located in the countryside.[20] The strike also brought into the Social Democratic movement a large number of young intellectuals. Among the latter, the so-called November Socialists, were men who became leading personalities in both the left and right wings of the party: O. W. Kuusinen, Yrjö Sirola, Eero Haapalainen, Kullervo Manner, Edvard Gylling, Karl Wiik, and Väinö Tanner.[21]

The majority of the November Socialists, including Otto Kuusinen, had belonged to the party of the Old Finns before joining the Socialists. The social radicalism of the Old Finns in the early years of the twentieth century acted as a bridge to Socialism, and in the atmosphere created by the general strike it was relatively easy to cross from the bourgeois camp of the Old Finns to the

[19] Oittinen, *Työväenkysymys*, p. 123.

[20] Soikkanen, *Sosialismin*, p. 343; Knoellinger, *op.cit.*, p. 50.

[21] Soikkanen, *Sosialismin*, pp. 272-273. Yrjö Sirola, Eero Haapalainen, and Karl Wiik were active in the labor movement before the events of 1905, although they are generally referred to as November Socialists. For further details on Väinö Tanner, who has represented the right wing in Finnish Social Democracy for some sixty years, see Marvin Rintala, "Väinö Tanner in Finnish Politics," *The American Slavic and East European Review*, Vol. xx, No. 1 (February 1961), pp. 84-98.

7

labor movement. For members of the Constitutionalists, however, it was difficult to switch allegiance to the labor movement owing to the stress put by their group on individualism, national feeling, and the concept that laws are absolute.[22] A notable exception was Yrjö Sirola. Sirola began his political activity as a Young Finn,[23] the more liberal element in the bourgeois Constitutionalist group, but chose to leave the Young Finns because he was prejudiced against the Swedish-speaking minority in Finland—a fact which had caused him, upon becoming a university student in 1896, to adopt a Finnish surname in place of his original Swedish surname Sirén—and could not embrace the Young Finns as they became more closely allied in the Constitutionalist group with Swedish-speaking Finns.[24] Sirola found his niche in the Tampere wing of the Social Democratic Party. In 1904 he joined forces with Yrjö Mäkelin, as an editor for the newspaper *Kansan Lehti*, and together the two men sought to justify cooperation with the Constitutionalists.[25]

Tampere became the center of activity during the general strike. On November 1, 1905, a manifesto, first printed on red paper and thus known in history as the Red Manifesto, was drawn up in that city.[26] The mani-

[22] Soikkanen, *Sosialismin*, pp. 214-215.

[23] Yrjö Sirola, in *Työmies* (Sup.), October 13, 1928, p. 3.

[24] Yrjö Sirola, "Sosialistiherrasta herrassosialistiksi," *Työväen Arkisto*: (Sirola 92 III); Yrjö Sirola, in *Proletaari*, No. 6 (69), October 1933, p. 7. The language struggle in Finland between the Swedish-speaking minority and the Finnish-speaking majority has had, particularly during the first decade of the twentieth century, a great impact on Finnish politics.

[25] Sirola, "Sosialistiherrasta." Sirola states in *Työmies* (Sup.), October 13, 1928, p. 3, that he became a member of the Social Democratic Party late in the summer of 1903.

[26] Yrjö Sirola, "'Punaisen julistuksen' päiviltä," in *Suurlak-*

festo, in effect the work of Mäkelin,[27] called for the resignation of the Finnish Cabinet *(Senaatin talousosasto)*, the election by universal and direct suffrage of a national assembly, and the formation of a provisional government to rule until a national assembly could meet and promulgate a constitution.[28] On November 4 a mass meeting of workers in Helsinki elected Constitutionalists, Old Finns, and Social Democrats to a provisional government.[29] This move was, however, out of step with the march of events. Early in the morning a manifesto prepared by the Constitutionalists, a number of whom had supported but then rejected the Red Manifesto,[30] had been signed by the Tsar. Legislation aimed at the Russification of Finland was suspended, and the Finnish Cabinet was given the task of drawing up a new Diet order and an electoral law based on universal and equal suffrage.[31] When news of the manifesto reached Finland, the desired effect was achieved. Fearing that a continuation of the general strike would cause an armed clash with Tsarist forces, leaders of the Social Democratic Party decided to halt the strike. At the Social Democratic Party congress held shortly thereafter, Yrjö Sirola—elected party secretary at the congress—stated

---

kovuosi 1905 (Kuopio: Kansankulttuuri, 1955), p. 31. Sirola was secretary of the Tampere strike committee.

[27] Yrjö Sirola, in *Työmies* (Sup.), October 20, 1928, p. 3.

[28] For the complete text, see Sigurd Roos, *Suomen kansallislakko*, Vol. II (Helsinki: Alex. F. Lindberg'in kirjapaino, 1907), pp. 391-393.

[29] Social Democrats, with eight representatives in the Provisional Government, were in the minority. Roos, *op.cit.*, II, 599; Laine, *op.cit.*, I, 245.

[30] Laine, *op.cit.*, I, 237; Roos, *op.cit.*, I, 136-137, II, 387.

[31] The full text can be found in *Seimovyi ustav Velikogo kniazhestva Finliandskogo*, s prilozheniiami (St. Petersburg: 1913), pp. 188-190; Roos, *op.cit.*, II, 751-752.

that in practice, not principle, the workers would have to retreat from the demands made in the Red Manifesto.[32] When Mäkelin saw that revolution would not occur in Russia, he too was willing to retreat in favor of the new Parliament.[33]

When the demands of the Red Manifesto were not met, Finnish workers turned their backs on Mäkelin and looked for leadership to Valpas, whose emphasis was on uncompromising class struggle.[34] At the party congress held in 1906 moderates were shunted aside, and Valpas was elected chairman of the party. Siltasaari—a section of Helsinki where *Työmies*, a newspaper edited by Valpas, was located—became the hub of Finnish Social Democracy. Thus began what is known as the Siltasaarelaisuus period of the Finnish Social Democratic Party.

In accordance with the provisions of the manifesto issued by Tsar Nicholas in November 1905, the Finnish Cabinet established a fourteen-member committee, including three Socialists,[35] to draft a Diet reform and a new electoral law. Within three months of its first meeting, the committee had completed its recommendations. The Finnish Cabinet, after making some changes, for-

---

[32] *Suomen sosialidemokraattisen puolueen neljännen edustajakokouksen pöytäkirja* (Tampere: Työväen puoluehallinto, 1906), pp. 42-49.

[33] Laine, *op.cit.*, I, 244.

[34] Soikkanen, *Sosialismin*, pp. 258, 263; Hannu Soikkanen, "Työväenliike ja oikeustaistelu," in Päiviö Tommila, ed., *Venäläinen sortokausi Suomessa* (Porvoo: WSOY, 1960), p. 126.

[35] The three Social Democrats were Edvard Valpas, Yrjö Sirola, and Heikki Lindroos. The presence of Socialists on the committee was soon criticized by Otto Kuusinen on the grounds that it enhanced the prestige of a reform which fell short of the mark. O. W. Kuusinen, "Eduskuntakomitean ehdotus valtiopäiväjärjestykseksi," *Sosialistinen Aikakauslehti*, No. 5 (March 1), 1906, pp. 100-101, 103.

warded these proposals to St. Petersburg, where they were reviewed by Finns and Russians sitting on a mixed committee. In May 1906 the Tsar submitted to the Finnish Diet a reform bill which, for the most part, conformed with the proposals transmitted to St. Petersburg by the Finnish Cabinet.[36] On July 20 the Tsar ratified a new Organic Law of the Diet for Finland, and the old four-estate system passed out of existence. Finland was henceforth to have a unicameral legislature elected every three years and meeting in three-month sessions, with the Tsar reserving the right of dissolution. Elections to Parliament would be on the basis of universal suffrage for all men and women who had reached the age of twenty-four; the vote would be equal, secret, and proportional.

The left wing in the Social Democratic Party, the Siltasaarelaiset, considered the parliamentary reform a step forward. Otto Kuusinen stated that the Finnish Parliament was beginning to resemble a democratic institution.[37] He was pessimistic, however, about the fate of social legislation. Opposition would come from the bourgeoisie,[38] and even if Social Democrats should control Parliament, reforms emanating from Finland would be negated by Russian authorities.[39] Yrjö Sirola shared Kuusinen's view that the only real guarantee of social reform in Finland would be an extension of par-

[36] Atte Pohjanmaa, "Suurlakosta Venäjän vallankumoukseen," in *Suomen sosialidemokraattinen*, pp. 59-60; Laine, *op.cit.*, I, 337.

[37] O. W. Kuusinen, "Eduskuntauudistuksen viimeiset vaiheet," *Sosialistinen Aikakauslehti*, No. 11-12 (June), 1906, p. 246.

[38] O. W. Kuusinen, "Anarkia ja vallankumous," *Sosialistinen Aikakauslehti*, No. 17-18 (October), 1906, p. 396.

[39] O. W. Kuusinen, "Venäjän vallankumousliike ja Suomen sosialidemokratia," *Sosialistinen Aikakauslehti*, No. 14 (August), 1906, p. 320.

11

liamentary prerogative and power.[40] For Kuusinen an attempt to expand parliamentary power and achieve real democracy legally, through Parliament, was a hopeless venture; it would be like trying to lift oneself from a swamp by one's own hair.[41] The prerogatives of Parliament must, he insisted, be expanded in conjunction with a victorious Russian revolution.[42] Kuusinen warned, however, that Finland's rights would not necessarily be respected by a new government in Russia. Such a government would be bourgeois, not Socialist. He urged that Finland press for genuine democracy during, not after, a revolutionary crisis in Russia. Only then could Finnish rights be secured. Kuusinen advocated, moreover, the use of force against the Tsar in case of dire necessity.[43] Sirola was not so radical as Kuusinen on the question of force, although he too considered some secret activity essential.[44] Violence and undercover measures were opposed by the older generation of Social Democrats,[45] but Kuusinen felt that the views of the older and younger generations could be reconciled.[46] Armed conflict with Tsarist troops was a possibility, but he did not consider weapons necessary in the struggle at home against the bourgeoisie.[47] The Siltasaarelaiset

[40] *Suomen sosialidemokraattisen puolueen viidennen edustajakokouksen pöytäkirja* (Helsinki: Sosialidemokratinen puoluetoimikunta, 1906), pp. 121, 130.

[41] Kuusinen, "Anarkia," p. 397.

[42] Kuusinen, "Venäjän," p. 320.

[43] *Suomen sosialidemokraattisen puolueen viidennen*, pp. 320-321.

[44] *Suomen sosialidemokraattisen puolueen kuudennen edustajakokouksen pöytäkirja* (Kotka: Kyminlaakson työväen kirjapaino, 1909), p. 36.

[45] Soikkanen, *Sosialismin*, pp. 252, 275.

[46] *Suomen sosialidemokraattisen puolueen viidennen*, p. 320.

[47] Kuusinen, "Venäjän," pp. 323-324.

viewed revolution in Finland as an historical phenomenon that would occur without artificial stimulation.[48]
Revolution in Finland would be born, not made.[49]

In the summer of 1906 Kuusinen looked to the Red
Guard—an organization nominally subordinate to the
Social Democratic Party which had arisen to preserve
order when police left their posts during the general
strike, but whose image had suffered from clashes with
the bourgeoisie—for armed support in a confrontation
with Tsarism.[50] Participation by members of the Red
Guard in a revolt of Russian soldiers stationed on an
island fortress outside Helsinki dealt a mortal blow, however, to this paramilitary group. On August 3, 1906, the
Finnish Cabinet sought to stem social unrest in Finland with a decree ordering the Red Guard to disband.
Formal dissolution came later that month when the
Guard was disbanded by a Social Democratic Party
congress, with words of praise for services rendered during the previous year.[51]

Following this party decision, Kuusinen and other
left-wing Socialists met for clandestine talks. The result
of these deliberations was the formation of a secret
organization to replace the Guard. All activities of the
new organization were to be directed against the Tsarist
government in cooperation with Russian Social Democrats. Members of the organization were instructed to
oppose anarchism, which had begun to capture the

48 Yrjö Sirola, "Suomen sosdem. puolue hallinnon suhtautumisesta
Viaporin kapinaan," in V. N. Sokolov, *Viapori. Sotilaskapina v. 1906*
(Petroskoi: Kirja, 1935), p. 215.

49 Kuusinen, "Anarkia," pp. 391, 393.

50 Kuusinen, "Venäjän," pp. 322-323.

51 *Suomen sosialidemokraattisen puolueen viidennen*, pp. 394-395.
For further information in English about the Red Guard and the
Viapori Revolt, see Hodgson, "Finland's," pp. 160-162.

fancy of some Finnish workers, and to observe the principles of Social Democracy.[52] Kuusinen began to edit a newspaper for the young radicals, but Finnish authorities quickly discovered and confiscated the printing press.[53] Flight to America by the chairman delivered the *coup de grâce* to this revolutionary organization.[54] A belief that revolution in Russia was imminent had been the inspiration for Kuusinen and like-minded Social Democrats,[55] but the swift restoration of reaction in St. Petersburg forced them to acknowledge the futility of their endeavors. Russification, not freedom, was on the horizon.

In the spring of 1908 three interpellations dealing with the "Finnish question" were debated in the Russian State Duma. Finland's representative in St. Petersburg—the Minister State Secretary for Finnish Affairs—was accused of having deliberately sacrificed Imperial for local Finnish interests, and Finland was described as a hotbed of revolution. The actual purpose of the interpellations was to be found in the demand that extensive legislation giving Russia tight control over Finnish affairs be considered urgent business.[56] On May 18 the President of the Council of Ministers, P. Stolypin, answered the interpellations. In a patriotic speech he

[52] Timo Korpimaa, *Salaisilla poluilla* (Rauma: O. Y. Länsi-Suomen kirjapaino, 1934), pp. 70-71, 75-76. Korpimaa, a November Socialist, was present when the radical organization was founded.

[53] Yrjö Sirola, "Suomen vv. 1905-1906 opetuksista," *Kommunisti*, No. 10 (147), October 23, 1935, p. 467; Sirola, in Sokolov, *op.cit.*, p. 221.

[54] Korpimaa, *op.cit.*, p. 74.

[55] Kuusinen, in *Suomen sosialidemokraattisen puolueen seitsemännen edustajakokouksen pöytäkirja* (Helsinki: Sosialidemokraattinen puoluetoimikunta), pp. 80-81.

[56] Material presented in this paragraph is treated more extensively in Hodgson, "Finland's" pp. 166-171.

proclaimed the need for legislation which would give to Russo-Finnish relations a new, correct perspective. In June 1908 the Tsar supported the Council of Ministers in its view that the Council—not the Minister State Secretary for Finnish Affairs—should determine what matters were of Imperial importance, to be dealt with by Russian legislation, and what matters were of local significance, to be dealt with by the Finnish Parliament. Two years later, by order of the Tsar, legislation was introduced in the State Duma and State Council. Nineteen categories, including schools, the press, customs, railways, public assembly, and internal administration, came under Imperial jurisdiction. At the discretion of the Tsar the prerogatives of the Finnish Parliament could, moreover, be limited still further. The bill was passed in the Duma, evoking from one right-wing deputy the exclamation *finis Finlandiae!* and it went through the State Council with no amendments and no revisions. On June 30, 1910, the bill was signed by the Tsar and became law.

The executive council of the Finnish Social Democratic Party gathered the following month, and the issue of cooperation with bourgeois parties was, in the face of renewed Russian oppression, once again debated. At this meeting Yrjö Sirola opposed the type of cooperation which the bourgeoisie wanted—mass meetings, run by the bourgeoisie, which would issue protests—and he rejected the notion that one can separate political and social matters, cooperating with the bourgeoisie in the former but adhering to a class struggle in the latter.[57] Otto Kuusinen, at a party congress, noted the existence of two distinct groups within the labor movement. One saw no difference between Russian oppression and op-

[57] *Työmies*, July 20, 1910, p. 1.

pression by the Finnish bourgeoisie; the other was more "patriotic" and urged cooperation with the bourgeoisie against Russification. Kuusinen's own position was that man cannot be divided into two parts. Man cannot cooperate with the bourgeoisie one day and fight them the next. When one is a good friend with the bourgeoisie on the question of Russia (*ryssänpolitiikka*), one is also a good friend with them in other matters.[58] Kuusinen told the party congress that he opposed all radical measures, which, he felt, were based on a false expectation of revolution in Russia. He argued against letting an event which might occur in some ten or fifteen years dictate contemporary party tactics. Finnish Social Democrats were exhorted to discount the Russian factor and move along on their own, struggling against Russian reaction through Parliament.[59]

Finnish Social Democracy during this period was characterized by concern with ideals and a rejection of practical work,[60] a fact which, for at least one leading figure in the party, posed a serious dilemma. Yrjö Sirola did not want to join the revisionists,[61] but as a member of the Social Democratic parliamentary group he was often inclined toward their point of view.[62] He was not entirely satisfied with the Marxism of the Siltasaarelai-

---

[58] *Suomen sosialidemokraattisen puolueen seitsemännen*, pp. 74-76, 79.

[59] *Ibid.*, pp. 80-83.

[60] Väinö Hupli, in *Suomen Sosialidemokraatti*, March 24, 1926, p. 2.

[61] Yrjö Sirola, in *Työmies* (Sup.), November 2, 1928, p. 5.

[62] Yrjö Sirola, in *Työmies* (Sup.), October 30, 1928, p. 3. It is interesting to note that in May 1909, at a meeting of the executive council of the Social Democratic Party, Sirola supported Väinö Tanner—called by Sirola the party's best revisionist theoretician—for election to the executive committee.

suus group in view of its failure to provide answers to questions of everyday practical importance. Sirola was also troubled by Marx's pronouncements that the state would wither away and that the proletariat had no fatherland. To solve these problems and to see first hand an advanced capitalist society, Sirola departed for America in the fall of 1910.[63]

Sirola settled in Duluth, Minnesota, where, as instructor and rector of the Finnish-American Workers' College, he was intimately associated with industrial unionism.[64] Among certain segments of the American proletariat the notion was becoming widespread that governmental organs, although important, should not be the focus of labor's attention, and direct, self-sustaining action by workers was assuming greater significance.[65] Strikes had become, at least for Sirola, the ultimate weapon.[66] Sirola was convinced, moreover, that in the United States only a general strike could be effective due to the power wielded by trusts.[67] In his eyes, and in the eyes of others, the attractiveness of the general strike was enhanced by two circumstances. In the United States class-conscious Socialists—the vanguard of revolution— did not hold high government office, and militarism— the bulwark of conservatism—was in its infancy.[68]

[63] Sirola, in *Työmies* (Sup.), November 2, 1928, p. 5. Other factors, such as indebtedness and the means by which he was elected a Parliamentary Trustee of the Bank of Finland, also contributed to Sirola's decision to leave Finland.

[64] Yrjö Sirola, in *Työmies*, July 8, 1913, p. 6.

[65] Y. S., "Millä tavoin vallankumous on tapahtuva?" *Säkeniä*, Vol. 8, No. 7 (July 1914), p. 281.

[66] Yrjö Sirola, "Valtiokäsitteen selvittelyä," *Säkeniä*, September 1912, p. 323.

[67] Sirola, in *Työmies* (Sup.), November 2, 1928, p. 5.

[68] Y. S., "Industrialismista-kommunismiin," *Kumous*, No. 14 (October 26, 1918), p. 150.

Instructors at the Workers' College were labeled sabotage-syndicalists.[69] Sirola was accused of being more concerned with tearing down the old order, through use of the general strike, than with constructing a new one.[70] He did not conceal his belief that it would be utopian to sketch in detail the building of a distant Socialist society,[71] but he rejected the allegation that one who supports a general strike is a syndicalist.[72] He found much of interest in syndicalism, yet he could not subscribe to all of its doctrines.[73] What the syndicalist movement did for Sirola was to push him further to the left. He had departed from Finland under the spell of revisionism, but in December 1913[74] he returned home with more radical ideas.[75]

Sirola had become convinced that with the development of a revolutionary Socialist spirit and with the emergence of a strong, economically unified organization, unions would be the center of labor's struggle against capitalism.[76] His experiences abroad had led him to examine anew the concept of revolution. In America he saw revolution as freedom from the bourgeoisie, whereas in Finland it had meant liberation from Tsarist oppression.[77] Finnish Social Democracy had not been able to cope simultaneously with class struggle and a struggle for national independence, and neither had

[69] Sirola, in *Työmies*, July 8, 1913, p. 6.

[70] *Säkeniä*, January 1913, p. 16.

[71] Y. S., "Millä," pp. 274, 279.

[72] Yrjö Sirola, "Valtion säilyttäjät," *Säkeniä*, December 1912, p. 446.

[73] Y. S., "Millä," pp. 279-280; Sirola, in *Työmies* (Sup.), November 2, 1928, p. 5.

[74] Yrjö Sirola, in *Työmies* (Sup.), November 10, 1928, p. 3.

[75] Y. S., in *Proletaari*, No. 6 (69), October 1933, p. 7.

[76] Y. S., "Millä," p. 279.

[77] Sirola, in *Työmies* (Sup.), November 2, 1928, p. 5.

been effective.[78] But with the outbreak of the First World War, Finnish Social Democrats suddenly found themselves in a situation which sharpened class struggle to the point of civil war and which permitted the realization of Finnish independence.

[78] Yrjö Sirola, in an introduction to "Rabochaia revoliutsiia v Finliandii v 1918 g.," *Proletarskaia revoliutsiia*, No. 8 (79), August 1928, p. 169.

CHAPTER TWO

From Parliamentary Socialism to Revolutionary Socialism

AFTER the First World War had begun, strategic considerations became a major determinant in Russian policy toward Finland. It was feared that Germany would attack Petrograd through Finnish territory,[1] and, as a precautionary measure, troops were sent into the Grand Duchy. Within a year Russian forces numbered some 50,000, and by August 1917 troops numbered approximately 125,000.[2] The outbreak of hostilities between Russia and Germany was also responsible for an abrupt halt to social reform.[3] The Finnish Parliament, moreover, was not called into session for almost three years. It appeared that time was on the side of Russification. Many Finns became convinced that it would be only with German support that the Russian yoke could be overthrown. Those who grasped at this straw wanted to send recruits to Germany, where, circumventing the restrictions imposed by Russification legislation, they could

[1] Carl Enckell, *Poliittiset muistelmani*, Vol. 1 (Porvoo: WSOY, 1956), pp. 64, 68; Colonel U. V. Rauanheimo, "Venäläiset joukot Suomessa maailmansodan 1914-18 aikana," *Tiede ja Ase*, No. 8, 1950, pp. 168-169. Enckell was Minister State Secretary for Finnish Affairs.

[2] Rauanheimo, "Venäläiset," pp. 157, 165, 167. Land forces accounted for about four fifths of the total.

[3] R. H. Oittinen, *Työväenkysymys ja työväenliike Suomessa* (Helsinki: Tammi, 1954), p. 147.

receive military training. These Finnish Jägers would then return home and, with German aid, lead Finland in a revolt against Russia.[4] Although it was civil war in which the Jägers finally distinguished themselves, their original objective had, unquestionably, been Finnish independence.[5] The Social Democratic Party felt, therefore, a need to define its attitude toward the Jäger movement.

K. H. Wiik, a member of the executive committee of the Social Democratic Party, traveled to Germany in the summer of 1915 to learn more about the Jäger movement. Expressing his conclusions at a meeting of leading party figures, Wiik stated that to support the Jäger movement would be the same as supporting Germany. In terms of theory, a bourgeois Germany was no different from any other bourgeois country. Wiik added that success of the Jägers was predicated upon uncertain German victory in the World War, and he cautioned against staking everything on one card. The executive committee agreed, on the whole, with Wiik.[6] The party apparatus was not to support the Jägers.[7] There was, however, to be no opposition to the Jäger movement, for it might achieve the desired goal of Finnish independence.[8] The door was to be kept open for future cooperation by permitting party members to work within the movement as individuals.[9]

[4] K. H. Wiik, in *Suomen Sosialidemokraatti*, July 20, 1929, p. 6.

[5] V. Tanner, in *Suomen sosialidemokraattisen puolueen kahdennentoista edustajakokouksen pöytäkirja* (Helsinki: Tampereen työväen kirjapaino, 1920), p. 98.

[6] Wiik, in *Suomen Sosialidemokraatti*, July 20, 1929, p. 6.

[7] Karl Wiik, *Aktivismen och socialdemokratin*, p. 6.

[8] Karl H. Wiik, "Mistä johtui vuoden 1918 Suomen sota," in *Kuoleman kentiltä* (Hämeenlinna: Osakeyhtiö Hämeen Kansan kirjapaino, 1924), pp. 12-13.

[9] Wiik, *Aktivismen*, p. 6.

21

A substantial number of workers—many of whom were motivated by the feeling that Germany, in contrast to Russia, belonged to "Europe" and had the world's most powerful labor movement[10]—joined the Jägers.[11] The Jägers also drew support from highly placed party functionaries.[12] Yrjö Mäkelin, whose son was a Jäger, is reported to have praised the movement and to have looked forward impatiently to a German attack on Petrograd.[13] Yrjö Sirola has acknowledged his connections with the Jägers,[14] and, according to a prominent figure in the movement, Sirola believed that Finland would have to shed blood for her independence.[15] But the March Revolution in Russia put an end to the dilemma in which many Finnish Social Democrats found themselves. They could now turn their backs on Germany and hope for the best from a new Russian government.[16]

Negotiations between Finland and Russia concerning the former's status in the emerging Russia of the Provisional Government began immediately after the collapse of the Tsarist regime. On March 18, 1917, a parliamentary delegation traveled to Petrograd with two sets of proposals, one reflecting the views of the Finnish bourgeoisie, the other the hopes of Social Democrats.

[10] Wiik, in *Suomen Sosialidemokraatti*, July 20, 1929, p. 6.

[11] Wiik, *Aktivismen*, p. 6.

[12] Iurii Sirola, *Kommunisticheskaia partiia Finliandii* (Moscow-Leningrad: Moskovskii Rabochii, 1929), p. 20; Yrjö Sirola, in *Työmies* (Sup.), August 31, 1928, p. 3.

[13] Herman Gummerus, *Jääkärit ja aktivistit* (Porvoo: WSOY, 1928), pp. 401-402.

[14] Yrjö Sirola, in *Työmies* (Sup.), November 10, 1928, p. 3; *Suomen työväen vallankumous 1918: Arviota ja itsekritiikiä* (Leningrad: Kirja, 1928), pp. 162-164; *Suomen Kansanvaltuuskunnan Tiedonantoja*, April 3, 1918, p. 1.

[15] Kai Donner, Th. Svedlin, and Heikki Nurmio, eds., *Suomen vapaussota*, Vol. I (Jyväskylä: K. J. Gummerus Oy, 1921), p. 309.

[16] Wiik, "Mistä," p. 14.

There was agreement in the delegation on the importance of overturning Russification measures of the past eighteen years, but the Social Democrats pressed harder than the bourgeoisie for social reform.[17] When the Provisional Government let it be known that only one set of proposals would be considered, those of the bourgeoisie were submitted.[18] A manifesto based on these recommendations was then issued by the Provisional Government. Various laws and decrees which impinged upon Finnish rights, including the legislation passed in 1910, were annulled. There was also reference to the Provisional Government's decision to call into session the Finnish Parliament,[19] where, as a result of an election held the previous year, Social Democrats would occupy 103 of the 200 seats. To those who negotiated the manifesto it was evident that the Provisional Government had one major objective, to repeal the legal injustices perpetrated under Tsarist rule and thereby induce Finns to support the war effort.[20]

The formation of a new government enjoying the confidence of the population, a Finnish demand to which Petrograd had voiced no objection, was soon an issue debated at a meeting of the Social Democratic Party executive council, a body which met infrequently —between party congresses—and which looked to the party's executive committee, a smaller group, for the conduct of daily business. Otto Kuusinen opposed the formation of a Red government, feeling that a govern-

[17] Juhani Paasivirta, *Suomen itsenäisyyskysymys 1917*, Vol. 1 (Porvoo: WSOY, 1947), pp. 63-65, 68. The Socialist members of the delegation were Otto Kuusinen, Kullervo Manner, Edvard Gylling, Karl Wiik, and Matti Paasivuori.

[18] *Ibid.*, I, 69; Väinö Tanner, *Kuinka se oikein tapahtui* (Helsinki: Tammi, 1957), p. 18.

[19] Paasivirta, *op.cit.*, I, 70.

[20] *Ibid.*, I, 62-63.

ment composed of Social Democrats would face insurmountable difficulties. He found a bourgeois government objectionable also because it could hinder the passage of important reforms. Therefore, in spite of its revisionist nature, Kuusinen supported a temporary coalition government.[21] A satisfactory government would include, in addition to at least two members of the Agrarian Party (a party which had emerged in 1906 with a program of extensive social reform designed to reach primarily the small farm owners), an equal number of Social Democrats and radical (*villi*), preferably nonparty bourgeois ministers.[22] Oskari Tokoi, chairman of the Finnish Trade Union Organization, a confederation of labor unions strikingly political in nature owing to the fact that since its birth in 1907 affiliated unions generally belonged to the Social Democratic Party, began to inquire in bourgeois circles about the possibility of forming such a government. His efforts, however, came to naught.[23] Radical members of the bourgeoisie willing to enter a coalition government with Social Democrats and Agrarians could not be found.[24] Kuusinen responded by calling for an end to negotiations and the formation of a bourgeois government. Edvard Gylling, on the other hand, argued successfully for further negotiations with the bourgeoisie. But so slim was his margin of victory that Gylling expressed a will-

[21] *Suomen sosialidemokraattisen puolueneuvoston pöytäkirjat*, March 19-23, 1917, pp. 52, 60, 65, 81. In 1906 Kuusinen had demanded that J. K. Kari be expelled from the Finnish Social Democratic Party for entering a bourgeois government.

[22] Otto Kuusinen and Kullervo Manner, in *Työmies*, March 29, 1917, p. 7.

[23] *Suomen sosialidemokraattisen puolueneuvoston*, March 19-23, 1917, p. 87.

[24] Kuusinen and Manner, in *Työmies*, March 29, 1917, p. 7.

ingness to withdraw his proposal. The executive council then proceeded to endorse the position taken by Kuusinen.[25] The following day this decision was overruled by the higher executive committee,[26] and agreement with the bourgeoisie was reached on the formation of a government headed by Oskari Tokoi. On March 26, 1917, the new government, which included six right-wing Social Democrats and six moderate bourgeois, was recognized in Petrograd.[27]

High on the work agenda of this government was the question of whether in Finnish affairs the Provisional Government was heir to the powers which had been wielded by the Tsar. The question became more pertinent when the Provisional Government sent its Minister of Justice, Alexander Kerenskii, to Helsinki in an effort to gain Finnish support for the war effort. Leading Finnish Social Democrats contacted Kerenskii and sought to ascertain the attitude of the Provisional Government toward internal independence for Finland. At Kerenskii's request, a memorandum which presented in written form the views of the Finnish Social Democratic Party was drawn up by Otto Kuusinen, Edvard Gylling, and Karl Wiik. It was a trial balloon leaving only foreign affairs under Russian control. On April 9 Petrograd replied. Gylling and Wiik were notified by the Governor-General's aide that the Provisional Government had rejected the memorandum.[28]

[25] *Suomen sosialidemokraattisen puolueneuvoston,* March 19-23, 1917, pp. 87-89, 94-96.

[26] Kuusinen and Manner, in *Työmies,* March 29, 1917, p. 7.

[27] Paasivirta, *op.cit.,* I, 77-78. The six Socialists were Oskari Tokoi, Väinö Tanner, Väinö Voionmaa, Wäinö Wuolijoki, Matti Paasivuori, and Julius Ailio.

[28] *Ibid.,* I, 90-91, 94, 96, 130. A typed copy of the memorandum can be found in *Syyttäjistön arkisto* F k 1: Y. Sirolan ja O. Tokoin

Two days before Finnish Socialists knew the fate of their memorandum a decision had been made to send to the Provisional Government a proposal, prepared by the Finnish Cabinet, urging that the jurisdiction of the Provisional Government, the Governor-General, and the Finnish Cabinet be clearly defined. It was at this time, however, that there developed in Petrograd a conviction that only a constituent assembly could solve matters of great import, and the Finnish Cabinet was so informed.[29] Clarification of the Provisional Government's position came at the fall session of an organ which had been established soon after the March Revolution in the hopes of solving various legal problems. One view presented was that open conflict with Finland was preferable to submission. If Finland should achieve independence and Russia be defeated in the war, the Finnish question would no longer have meaning. If, on the other hand, Russia should be victorious, she could, after the cessation of hostilities, deal with Finland as one would with a rebellion. Concessions were rejected on the grounds that one must wait for the constituent assembly and avoid setting a precedent.[30]

The intransigent stand of the Provisional Government was a bitter disappointment for Finnish Socialists. Suspicion and hostility increased. The Socialist speaker of Parliament, Kullervo Manner, stated in April 1917 that Finland should not recognize the authority of the Provisional Government. Otto Kuusinen, who with Yrjö

---

papereita (Valtionarkisto). See also Työväen Arkisto: 327 (47:471) "1917."

[29] Paasivirta, *op.cit.*, I, 114, 155, 158.

[30] "Iz istorii natsional'noi politiki Vremennogo Pravitel'stva," *Krasnyi arkhiv*, Vol. 5 (30), 1928, pp. 68, 70-71.

Mäkelin shaped the party's demands for independence, was of the same opinion.[31] At the insistence of Kuusinen and Mäkelin the Committee on Constitutional Affairs soon issued a memorandum stating in clear language that the prerogatives of the Provisional Government were not the same as those of the Tsar. Mäkelin wanted Parliament to assume the Tsar's powers and then, when the political situation should become favorable, issue a declaration of independence.[32] Kuusinen agreed that Finland must be free from Russia, must have full internal autonomy,[33] but in terms of tactics he was more cautious than Mäkelin. Kuusinen sought the support of the Russian people. Opinions on the Finnish question were aired by other leading Social Democrats. Speaking before Parliament, Oskari Tokoi, head of the Finnish government, pointed to sovereignty as the ultimate policy objective.[34] Yrjö Sirola and Karl Wiik, presenting a memorandum to an international Socialist conference, proclaimed that autonomy for Finland was not enough.[35] Full independence could, however, wait in view of the war.[36] Finnish Social Democrats in the spring of 1917 were striving for complete internal independence.[37]

[31] Paasivirta, *op.cit.*, I, 131, 133; I. I. Siukiiainen, *Revoliutsionnye sobytiia 1917-1918 gg. v Finliandii* (Petrozavodsk: Karel'skoe knizhnoe izdatel'stvo, 1962), p. 82.

[32] Paasivirta, *op.cit.*, I, 132, 135.

[33] Siukiiainen, *op.cit.*, p. 82.

[34] Paasivirta, *op.cit.*, I, 136-137, 201.

[35] Karl Wiik, in *Suomen Sosialidemokraatti*, December 6, 1927, p. 8; Passivirta, *op.cit.*, I, 186-187; Juhani Paasivirta, "Sosialidemokraattinen puolue ja Suomen itsenäistyminen," in *Suomen sosialidemokraattinen työväenliike 1899-1949* (Helsinki: KK:n kirjapaino, 1949), pp. 132-133.

[36] Reference by Gummerus, *op.cit.*, pp. 404-405, to the memorandum.

[37] Paasivirta, *op.cit.*, I, 137; Wiik, *Aktivismen*; Gummerus, *op.cit.*;

A significant event for Finnish independence occurred in June 1917 when the All-Russian Congress of Soviets of Workers' and Soldiers' Deputies met in Petrograd. At this congress Mensheviks and Social Revolutionaries, members of the Provisional Government, reversed their position on the Finnish question. They supported a resolution which demanded full internal independence for Finland. Only foreign policy and military affairs were placed outside the jurisdiction of the Finnish Parliament. This declaration had a profound effect on politics in the Grand Duchy. The Finnish Social Democratic parliamentary group considered it a sign that the question of supreme power could at last be settled.[38]

The Socialist members of the Committee on Constitutional Affairs drew up a proposal, the *valtalaki*, which reflected the sentiment expressed at the Congress of Soviets. With the exception of foreign affairs and defense, all powers formerly exercised by the Tsar were to be assumed by the Finnish Parliament. On July 18, 1917, in a 136 to 55 vote, this bill was endorsed by the Finnish Parliament. Socialists, Agrarians, and a small bourgeois group known as Independence Men had joined in a declaration of internal independence.[39]

The *valtalaki* became, however, merely an expression of desire. The Provisional Government proceeded to dissolve the Finnish Parliament. Promulgation of the Russian order received majority support in the Finnish Cabinet when the Governor-General, as titular head of that organ, voted with the bourgeois ministers to break

Siukiiainen, *op.cit.*, pp. 81-82; Seikko Eskola, "Suomen kysymys vuonna 1917 Ruotsin sisäpolitiikassa," in *Uusi Suomi*, February 7, 1966, p. 4.

[38] Paasivirta, *Suomen itsenäisyyskysymys*, I, 179, 192-193, 204-205.
[39] *Ibid.*, I, 209, 211, 213; II, 15.

a tie.[40] A step of unforeseen magnitude had been taken. Class conflict in Finland intensified. Social Democrats saw the act of dissolution as a joint maneuver of the Finnish bourgeoisie and the Provisional Government,[41] and when a bourgeois majority was elected to Parliament in October 1917, following a united campaign against the Socialists, the proletariat began to lose faith in the efficacy of parliamentary action.[42]

Two other factors heightened unrest in Finland. In March 1917, when the Tsarist regime collapsed, extensive fortification work in the Grand Duchy—at one point employing some forty thousand unskilled Finnish laborers—came to an end.[43] Throughout the year these

[40] In protest over the dissolution of Parliament, four of the six Socialist ministers resigned. Two, Väinö Tanner and Matti Paasivuori, remained in the government until early September 1917, stating that only the Provisional Government could release them from their duties. Väinö Tanner, *op.cit.*, pp. 116, 120.

[41] Paasivirta, *Suomen itsenäisyyskysymys*, II, 24; "Me vaadimme," in *Toiset valtiopäivät 1917 pöytäkirjat*, I (Helsinki: Valtioneuvoston kirjapaino, 1918), p. 15. In the opinion of Oskari Tokoi, all the misfortunes which later befell Finland can be traced to Parliament's dissolution. *Suomen Sosialidemokraatti*, June 16, 1927, p. 4.

[42] Otto Kuusinen, in *Suomen sosialidemokraattisen puolueneuvoston*, October 28-30, 1917, p. 3; Karl H. Wiik, *Kovan kokemuksen opetuksia* (Helsinki: Työväen kirjapaino, 1918), p. 47. A marginal notation made by Wiik in his personal copy of *Kovan kokemuksen opetuksia* indicates that at least one leading Socialist, Oskari Tokoi, also lost faith in legality as a means of achieving reform.

[43] O. T[oko]i, in *Kansan Lehti*, January 22, 1918, p. 2; Oskari Tokoi, *Maanpakolaisen muistelmia* (Helsinki: Tammi, 1959), pp. 158, 179; Matti Turkia, in *Suomen Sosialidemokraatti*, January 29, 1933, p. 6; Wiik, "Mistä," p. 18; Sirola, in *Työmies* (Sup.), November 10, 1928, p. 3. The number of Finns in fortification work is estimated as high as 100,000 by one Communist source. SKP:n KK, "Suomen työväen vallankumous v. 1918," *Kommunisti*, No. 1 (37), January 15, 1928, p. 8. In the province of Uusimaa there were, according to Einar W. Juva, *Suomen kansan aikakirjat*, IX (Helsinki: Otava, 1937), p. 614, about 14,000 fortification workers.

unemployed workers had been an unorganized, dangerous element.[44] Their mood was revolutionary,[45] and
much of the hooliganism that plagued Finland at the
time could be traced directly to this group.[46] The March
Revolution also created a stampede for membership in
labor associations.[47] The Finnish Trade Union Organization tripled in size within six months, jumping from
about 50,000 to 156,000; these new members, most of
whom were riding the crest of a revolutionary wave,
brought into the trade union movement a new perspective.[48] They believed that society could be changed at a
moment's notice.[49]

Late in October 1917 Kullervo Manner, chairman of
the Social Democratic Party,[50] expressed uncertainty
about the possibility of keeping the masses under control.[51] He called attention to the fact that workers, particularly in Helsinki, had begun to act outside the party.
For Manner it was sad but apparently true that revo-

[44] Wiik, *Kovan*, pp. 17-18.

[45] Sirola, in *Työmies* (Sup.), November 10, 1928, p. 3.

[46] Tokoi, *Maanpakolaisen*, p. 158; E. Eloranta, in *Suomen kansanvaltuuskunnan pöytäkirjat*, March 5, 1918.

[47] Tokoi, *Maanpakolaisen*, p. 179.

[48] Oskari Tokoi, in *Suomen Metalliteollisuustyöntekijäin Liiton kahdeksannen Helsingissä joulukuun 4-11 p:nä 1917 pidetyn eduustajakokouksen pöytäkirja* (Helsinki: Työväen kirjapaino, 1919), p. 8.

[49] *Ibid.*, p. 8; Matti Paasivuori, in *Suomen Sosialidemokraatti*. November 22, 1927, p. 6.

[50] In the summer and fall of 1917 other full members of the party executive committee were: Edvard Gylling (vice-chairman), Matti Turkia (secretary), Otto Kuusinen, Yrjö Sirola, Karl Wiik, and Jussi Pietikäinen. At the turn of the year Pietikäinen, also a member of the executive committee of the Finnish Trade Union Organization, was replaced by Ev rt Eloranta.

[51] Karl H. Wiik, *Dagboksanteckningar från åren 1917 och 1918*, October 27, 1917.

lution was rapidly approaching.[52] Another party stalwart, Kuusinen, was convinced that revolution in Russia was only a few days off and that it would render impossible the task of controlling the masses.[53] He saw in the existence of Finnish Red Guard units—formed in October as a counterweight to the bourgeois Civil Guards, and under the auspices of the executive committees of the Finnish Trade Union Organization and the Social Democratic Party—one measure which would help prepare the party for any eventuality. In the same spirit he mentioned that a reform bill had been drafted by leading Social Democrats.[54] In final form this bill, *Me vaadimme*, demanded alleviation of the critical food shortage; work for the unemployed; municipal reform; resignation of the Finnish Cabinet; the disbanding and disarming of the "Butcher Guards" (Civil Guards); an eight-hour workday; emancipation of the peasantry; old age, disability, and health insurance; a general tax reform; approval of the *valtalaki*; negotiation of an agreement with Russia which would guarantee Finland internal independence; the election and convocation of a national assembly to enact further reforms.[55]

What the workers were demanding was, in short, "Bread and Justice."[56] Finland's foreign commerce with the West had declined substantially as a result of the World War, and an already serious food shortage became drastic when trade with Russia evaporated during the chaotic months following the overthrow of the Tsar.

[52] *Suomen sosialidemokraattisen puolueneuvoston*, October 28-30, 1917, p. 23.

[53] *Ibid.*, pp. 3-4; Wiik, *Dagboksanteckningar*, October 27, 1917.

[54] *Suomen sosialidemokraattisen puolueneuvoston*, October 28-30, 1917, pp. 4, 6.

[55] *Toiset valtiopäivät*, I, 15-18.

[56] *Ibid.*, I, 15; Siukiiainen, *op.cit.*, p. 114.

Yrjö Sirola was perhaps correct when he stated that the greatest single cause of ferment in Finland was the shortage of food.[57] Another member of the executive committee, Karl Wiik, declared that Finnish workers would turn against even a Social Democratic government if it failed to give them more food.[58] On numerous occasions Russian troops had demonstrated for the reforms demanded by the Social Democratic Party,[59] and many Finnish workers began to feel that food could be obtained from the bourgeoisie only with the aid of Russian troops.[60] By mid-autumn the situation in Finland was explosive. On November 7 a spark creating the prerequisites for civil war was produced.[61] The Bolshevik Revolution appeared to give the Finnish proletariat a chance of dealing at long last with the ruling class.[62] No longer was it a question of Social Democratic leaders pulling the workers forward. The party was rolling down tracks, like a heavy train, and the leaders had only to avoid being crushed.[63]

[57] *Työmies*, November 11, 1917, p. 1.

[58] Karl Wiik, in *Syyttäjistön arkisto*: Sos.-dem. järjestöt, marraskuun v. 1917 puoluekokous, p. 28. For a discussion of the attempts made by the Finnish government to obtain foodstuffs from other countries in 1917-1918, see Juhani Paasivirta, *Ensimmäisen maailmansodan voittajat ja Suomi* (Porvoo: WSOY, 1961), pp. 74-105.

[59] V. Smirnov, *Iz revoliutsionnoi istorii Finliandii 1905, 1917, 1918 gg* (Leningrad: Leningradskoe oblastnoe izdatel'stvo, 1933), p. 87.

[60] K. H. [Wiik], in *Työmies*, December 15, 1917, p. 3.

[61] Turkia, in *Suomen Sosialidemokraatti*, January 29, 1933, p. 6; [Karl Wiik], in *ibid.*, February 19, 1928, p. 9; Kullervo Manner, in *Työväenjärjestöjen Tiedonantaja*, November 8, 1927, p. 4; K. Wiik, in *Suomen Sosialidemokraatti*, November 15, 1927, p. 5.

[62] Yrjö Sirola, "Työväen Vallankumouksellisen Keskusneuvoston toiminta," *Vapaussodan arkisto* I A 2, p. 2 (Valtionarkisto).

[63] Matti Turkia, in *Suomen Sosialidemokraatti*, August 30, 1922, p. 3.

The Bolshevik Revolution also had a profound effect on Finland's bourgeois parties. Those parties that had voted against the *valtalaki*, i.e. against increasing the powers of the Finnish Parliament to such an extent that only foreign affairs and defense would come under Russian control, now felt that the question of supreme power could be settled irrespective of Russian wishes. Given the new situation, bourgeois circles, with the exception of some Agrarians, began to advocate that a special organ, or the Finnish Cabinet, assume those powers which had been exercised by the Tsar. On November 8 a proposal transferring the Tsar's powers to a three-member board of regents (*Valtionhoitajakunta*) was laid before Parliament. This special organ would counterbalance broad parliamentary power. In the opinion of its sponsors a board of regents would also limit the influence of Socialists and ensure that social development not be directed along radical lines.[64]

Two bourgeois groups, the Independence Men and the Agrarian Party, objected to the proposal. They sought a solution which would win Socialist support. The Agrarian Party consequently proposed that Parliament approve the *valtalaki*, not a board of regents. On the same day the Social Democratic parliamentary group voted to offer for adoption the program which had been outlined in *Me vaadimme*.[65] Oskari Tokoi announced in Parliament that only an endorsement of this program could prevent the nightmare of revolution.[66] On November 9 Parliament made its choice. Two votes were taken. On the first, between the *valtalaki* and *Me vaa-*

64 Paasivirta, *Suomen itsenäisyyskysymys*, II, 120, 133-134, 136-137.
65 *Suomen sosialidemokraattisen eduskuntaryhmän pöytäkirjat*, November 8, 1917.
66 *Toiset valtiopäivät*, I, 20.

dimme, some proponents of a board of regents supported the Socialists in order to defeat the moderate Agrarian proposal. On the second, the Agrarians, who found *Me vaadimme* too radical, felt obliged to cast their ballots for the only other alternative. Both Agrarians and Socialists considered dishonest the voting tactics of the opposition,[67] and together they managed to have the conservative proposal sent to the Committee on Constitutional Affairs. Election of the three regents was made dependent upon the report of this committee.[68] Before an opinion could be delivered, however, a board of regents became an anachronism.

A Central Revolutionary Council which, with the addition of nine representatives from the Social Democratic parliamentary group, included twenty-seven members[69] had been formed on November 8 by the executive committees of the Social Democratic Party and the Finnish Trade Union Organization.[70] At this meeting of the executive committees it was proposed that the bourgeois Parliament surrender its powers to the Socialist one dissolved by the Provisional Government, the so-called Manner Parliament, and there was

[67] Kalle Lohi, in *ibid.*, p. 85; Wiik, in *Suomen Sosialidemokraatti,* November 15, 1927, p. 5.

[68] *Toiset valtiopäivät,* I, 88.

[69] Wiik, *Dagboksanteckningar,* November 8, 1917; Tokoi, in *Suomen Ammattijärjestön v. 1917 pidetyn edustajakokouksen pöytäkirjaluonnos,* November 12 [Työväen Arkisto 331.88 (471) (063) "1917"]. Membership appears to have remained fixed at twenty-seven until November 16, 1917, although some personnel changes took place during the first week of the council's existence. These changes brought several representatives of the Red Guard and the Helsinki Council of Workers' Organizations into the Central Revolutionary Council.

[70] *Työmies,* November 9, 1917, p. 5; Tokoi, in *Suomen Ammattijärjestön v. 1917,* November 12; Sirola, "Työväen," p. 8.

talk of Finnish workers taking power with the support of the Manner Parliament. Edvard Gylling, a moderate member of the party executive committee, suggested that the workers take power until a national assembly—called for in *Me vaadimme*—could meet.[71] He was convinced that the party would lose control over its followers unless there was a firm commitment to the program put forth in *Me vaadimme*. Otto Kuusinen stated that Social Democrats planned to take power that week, and, appearing before the Central Revolutionary Council the next day, he expressed fear that relations between Finnish Social Democrats and Russian Bosheviks in Helsinki might become greatly strained—the Bolsheviks might even disarm Finnish workers—if Finnish workers did not act. Sirola told the Central Revolutionary Council on November 10 that Finland had to have a government which could negotiate with Russian troops.[72] Attempts by the bourgeoisie to negotiate would result in complete chaos.[73] To save the situation, if it could be saved, and to keep the number of victims down to a minimum, Sirola favored the formation of a workers' government. Sirola noted also that the internal situation in Finland was such that there would be lawlessness in various parts of the country regardless of what the Russians did. Finnish workers, particularly in Helsinki, wanted to seize power. To hold these forces in check Sirola urged that workers' councils be formed throughout Finland and that supreme power be vested in the Central Revolutionary Council until a national

[71] *Suomen sosialidemokraattisen eduskuntaryhmän*, November 8, 1917.

[72] Wiik, *Dagboksanteckningar*, November 8-10, 1917.

[73] Sirola, cited in *ibid.*, November 10, 1917; [Karl Wiik,] "Suomen työväenliikkeen kohtalokkailta hetkiltä," in *Suomen Sosialidemokraatti*, February 4, 1928, p. 7.

assembly could be convened.[74] The question of seizing power was not, however, settled by the Central Revolutionary Council at this time.[75]

On November 12 the Finnish Trade Union Organization gathered for its fourth congress in a charged atmosphere. The delegates were told by Oskari Tokoi, chairman of the Trade Union Organization, that it was up to the congress to decide whether the workers should seize power or whether they should only try to pressure a bourgeois government into granting reforms. Eero Haapalainen, who was to become head of the Red Guard on the eve of the Finnish Civil War, advocated an armed struggle to either victory or death. One delegate proclaimed that the prospect of death in battle should not deter the workers, because the alternative was death from starvation.[76] Late in the evening delegates from the Trade Union Organization met with the Central Revolutionary Council for guidance. The council ruled that decisive action should be undertaken quickly but that the workers should first give Parliament one more opportunity to enact their demands.[77] An immediate seizure of power was rejected on the grounds that there was still hope of forcing the bourgeoisie to accept the program presented in *Me vaadimme*.[78] In line with this decision the Trade Union

[74] Wiik, *Dagboksanteckningar*, November 10, 1917. Juhani Paasivirta, referring to the workers' councils, is in error in his distinguished work *Suomen itsenäisyyskysymys*, II, 129, when he states that Sirola sought to carry out a *coup d'état* with Bolshevik assistance. See chapter three for a discussion of the attitude taken by Sirola and other leading Social Democrats toward Russian aid.

[75] Oskari Tokoi, in *Suomen sosialidemokraattisen eduskuntaryhmän*, November 10, 1917.

[76] *Suomen Ammattijärjestön v. 1917*, November 12.

[77] J. Lumivuokko, in *ibid.*, November 13.

[78] Sirola, "Työväen," pp. 14-15.

Organization threatened the following day to call a general strike if Parliament in its afternoon session refused to order publication by the Cabinet of legislation enacted during the summer by the Manner Parliament: the *valtalaki*, a law establishing an eight-hour workday, a municipal reform bill, a law giving Parliament the right to pass on the legality of actions taken by the Cabinet, and other laws ratified by Parliament on the basis of the *valtalaki*.[79] The bourgeois members of Parliament were not intimidated, and the Central Revolutionary Council voted later that day, November 13, to declare a general strike.[80]

The Agrarian Party attempted a reconciliation. If Social Democrats would agree to enter a government with Agrarians and, possibly, several radical Independence Men, the Agrarian Party would support passage of the *valtalaki*.[81] The Social Democratic parliamentary group was advised by the Central Revolutionary Council to state in its reply to the Agrarians that since Parliament had been unable to act on long-standing demands for reform, the workers would take matters into their own hands.[82] At a subsequent meeting the Social Democratic parliamentary group voted to inform the Agrarians that it would support any proposal transferring supreme power to Parliament, a stand which was backed by the Central Revolutionary Council,[83] but that it could not commit itself on a new government.[84]

79 *Toiset valtiopäivät*, I, 98-99; Tanner, *op.cit.*, p. 133.

80 Wiik, *Dagboksanteckningar*, November 13, 1917.

81 Sirola, "Työväen," pp. 26-28; *Toiset valtiopäivät*, I, 120.

82 Sirola, "Työväen," pp. 28-29.

83 *Ibid.*, p. 31. It is not correct to state, as does Juhani Paasivirta in *Suomen itsenäisyyskysymys*, II, 142, that the Central Revolutionary Council and the Social Democratic parliamentary group were at loggerheads on this point.

84 Sirola, "Työväen," pp. 30-31; *Toiset valtiopäivät*, I, 120.

On November 15 conservatives proposed that Parliament temporarily entrust the Tsar's former powers to the Finnish Cabinet until the Committee on Constitutional Affairs could pass judgment on the board of regents.[85] The Agrarian Party, acting with Social Democrats, countered with the proposal that supreme power be vested in Parliament. The forces which on July 18 had cooperated to achieve passage of the *valtalaki*— Agrarians, Socialists, and Independence Men—once again cast ballots together. Supreme power passed to Parliament.[86] Under the new law it was not clear where jurisdiction in foreign affairs and defense lay, in Petrograd or Helsinki, but on December 6 a formal declaration of independence did away with this ambiguity.[87] One month later, following visits to Petrograd by a bourgeois and Socialist delegation, Finland received *de jure* recognition from the Soviet government.[88]

After the Finnish Parliament proclaimed itself heir to the Tsar's powers on November 15, it was proposed that Parliament hold a night session to consider bills providing for an eight-hour workday and municipal reform. Edvard Valpas announced that those who were leading the general strike, which was now in its second

---

[85] *Toiset valtiopäivät,* I, 119.

[86] Paasivirta, *Suomen itsenäisyyskysymys,* II, 143.

[87] Proposals calling for Finnish independence had been introduced in Parliament by both the Social Democrats and the bourgeoisie. The former wanted independence to be achieved through agreement with Soviet Russia, whereas the latter, triumphant, rejected the concept of negotiation.

[88] The Social Democratic delegation, sent by the party executive committee with instructions to gain Bolshevik support for Finnish independence, included Kullervo Manner, Edvard Gylling, and Karl Wiik. These men were informed by the Bolsheviks that the Soviet government would do nothing without the knowledge and approval of Finnish Social Democrats. K. H. Wiik, *Miten Suomen itsenäisyys saatiin tunnustetuksi,* Työväen Arkisto: 327 (47:471) "1917."

day and had paralyzed the entire country, had lost confidence in their ability to control the masses. Some workers felt that once again they would be deceived by Parliament. Valpas urged Parliament to meet in a late session and prove itself capable of enacting social reforms.[89] The most prominent Agrarian saw armed conflict as a possible alternative,[90] and Parliament was persuaded. At a post-midnight session a municipal reform bill was passed and an eight-hour workday established. The general strike had been effective.[91] In the revolutionary atmosphere which then prevailed, however, these long-awaited reforms no longer satisfied all workers.[92]

Leaders of the Social Democratic Party had miscalculated when they thought it possible to keep the proletariat within the framework of a peaceful general strike. The situation was more critical than even they realized.[93] Isolated acts of violence demonstrated that discipline could not be maintained in all instances.[94] Party leaders could not control the Red Guard.[95] Many of its members, new to the labor movement, were more familiar with weapons than with the party program.[96]

89 *Toiset valtiopäivät*, I, 151-152.

90 Santeri Alkio, in *ibid.*, p. 152.

91 Tanner, *op.cit.*, p. 141.

92 Oittinen, *op.cit.*, p. 156.

93 Yrjö Sirola, in *Toiset valtiopäivät*, I, 222. Sirola was secretary of the strike committee. Wiik, *Dagboksanteckningar*, November 13, 1917.

94 Yrjö Sirola, in *Syyttäjistön arkisto*: Sos.-dem. järjestöt, marraskuun v. 1917 puoluekokous, p. 86. In March 1956, addressing Parliament after the third general strike in Finnish history, Prime Minister Fagerholm noted how difficult it is to control the forces unleashed by a general strike. *Valtiopäivät 1956 pöytäkirjat*, Vol. I (Helsinki: Valtioneuvoston kirjapaino, 1957), pp. 177, 180.

95 Paasivirta, *Suomen itsenäisyyskysymys*, II, 149-151.

96 E. Huttunen, in *Työ*, January 11, 1918, p. 2.

The masses, once they had begun to move, did not want to turn back; for the first time serious consideration was given to the proposal that workers seize power violently.[97] The Helsinki branch of the Red Guard notified the Central Revolutionary Council that if an order to act were not forthcoming, the Red Guard would seize power on its own.[98] The Helsinki Council of Workers' Organizations, formed in March 1917, and of great importance for law enforcement because of its ties with the city militia, backed the Red Guard.[99] On November 16, at 3:00 A.M., the Central Revolutionary Council came to grips with the question.

All members of the Central Revolutionary Council agreed that it was time to end the general strike, but this consensus did not obviate the necessity of a lengthy debate culminating in two very different proposals. Edvard Gylling urged the council to end the strike on the condition that a coalition government of Socialists and several Agrarians be formed. Supporting Gylling's proposal, Yrjö Sirola stipulated that a coalition government would be satisfactory only if Social Democrats should, as soon as possible, take control of the government in the province of Uusimaa, where Helsinki is located, take over the Board of Administration of the Finnish State Railways, and disperse the bourgeois Cabinet. Together

[97] [Wiik,] in *Suomen Sosialidemokraatti*, February 4, 1928, p. 7.
[98] Wiik, *Dagboksanteckningar*, November 16, 1917.
[99] [Wiik,] in *Suomen Sosialidemokraatti*, February 4, 1928, p. 7; Sirola, "Työväen," pp. 33-34; Siukiiainen, *op.cit.*, pp. 124-125. The minutes of the Helsinki Council of Workers' Organizations are located in the Karelian branch of the Academy of Sciences of the USSR. To date only Siukiiainen has had access to them. See I. I. Siukiiainen, "Gel'singforsskii seim rabochikh organizatsii v 1917-1918 gg.," in *Skandinavskii sbornik*, Vol. v (Tallinn: Estonskoe gosudarstvennoe izdatel'stvo, 1962), pp. 115-134.

these views became the Gylling-Sirola proposal. The second major proposal also called for an end to the strike, but only on the condition that the workers seize power immediately. In a 14 to 11 vote, with Otto Kuusinen abstaining, the revolutionary path was chosen.[100] However, the matter was not yet settled. The Central Revolutionary Council was informed several hours later by J. Lumivuokko, father of the revolutionary proposal, that the Trade Union Organization, of which he was vice-chairman, could not assume the responsibility involved in a seizure of power. Opposition within the Central Revolutionary Council had been too great. Representatives of the Trade Union Organization shifted their support to the position taken by Sirola. Kullervo Manner, chairman of the strike committee, then stated that if a government could be formed in accordance with Gylling's proposal and if Sirola's addendum were enforced, the Social Democrats could extricate themselves from a difficult situation.[101]

100 Wiik, *Dagboksanteckningar*, November 16, 1917; Erkki Räikkönen, "Suomen kohtalonyö 1917," *Helsingin Sanomat*, November 7, 1959, p. 10; Sirola, "Työväen," pp. 34-36; Sirola, in *Syyttäjistön arkisto*: Sos.-dem. järjestöt, marraskuun v. 1917 puoluekokous, p. 86; *Suomen työväen vallankumous*, p. 170. Following the decision to seize power, the Central Revolutionary Council was reduced in size. It now included six members of the party executive committee (Y. Sirola, O. Kuusinen, K. Manner, M. Turkia, E. Gylling, K. Wiik), six members of the executive committee of the Trade Union Organization (O. Tokoi, J. Lumivuokko, M. Aaltio, E. Elo, A. Lehto, V. Perttilä), three members of the Social Democratic parliamentary group (J. Vuoristo, M. Airola, H. Välisalmi), and one representative chosen by the executive committee of the Red Guard (E. Laiho-Louhikko). A five-man executive committee was also set up at this time. Sirola, "Työväen," pp. 37, 40-41; Wiik, *Dagboksanteckningar*, November 16, 1917; *Työväen Vallankumouksellisen Keskusneuvoston Tiedonantolehti*, November 17, 1917, p. 1.

101 Sirola, "Työväen," p. 38; Wiik, *Dagboksanteckningar*, November 16, 1917.

41

The Central Revolutionary Council renewed discussion of the general strike the following day. All representatives were of the opinion that the strike should be ended, but there was disagreement, again, over the prerequisites for such a step. Some members of the Social Democratic Party executive committee, in particular Otto Kuusinen, and of the parliamentary group, opposed any plan to take power and wanted the workers to save their strength. Threatened with a strike, the bourgeoisie would be forced to grant concessions, so these moderates thought. Most members of the Trade Union Organization executive committee felt, however, that the formation of a Socialist, or at least a Socialist majority, government should be the prerequisite for ending the strike. Parliamentary support for such a government would be sought but was not essential.[102] The workers would take power by either legal or revolutionary means.[103] In agreement with the trade union position,[104] Yrjö Sirola was willing to enter a temporary revolutionary workers' government.[105] He considered the formation of such a government imperative since Finland was without a Cabinet and there was no indication that Parliament, whose prerogative it was to select a new government, would be called into session in the near future.[106]

[102] Wiik, *Dagboksanteckningar*, November 17, 1917; Sirola, "Työväen," pp. 43-48.

[103] *Suomen Ammattijärjestö*, No. 11-12 (November-December), 1917, p. 175.

[104] Wiik, *Dagboksanteckningar*, November 17, 1917.

[105] *Ibid.*, November 18, 1917; Sirola's notes, referred to in *Suomen vapaussota vuonna 1918*, Vol. III (Helsinki: Otava, 1922), pp. 170-171.

[106] Sirola's notes, referred to in *Suomen vapaussota*, III, 171; Sirola, in *Syyttäjistön arkisto*: Sos.-dem. järjestöt, marraskuun v. 1917 puoluekokous, p. 87; Wiik, *Dagboksanteckningar*, November 18, 1917. The bourgeois Cabinet had submitted its resignation to

Sirola hoped that a temporary revolutionary government would help save the country from anarchy. At the same time it might pave the way for the formation in Parliament of a government which would be acceptable to the workers.[107] The Central Revolutionary Council did not, however, commit itself to one line of action. Whether or not the workers should take power was to be left an open question until the opinion could be sought of the Social Democratic parliamentary group, the Helsinki Council of Workers' Organizations, and the Association of Railway Workers.[108]

The parliamentary group and, presumably, the Helsinki Council of Workers' Organizations[109] opted for the formation by parliamentary means of a Social Democratic government.[110] The Central Revolutionary Council then voted to halt the general strike and delegate to the parliamentary faction the job of forming a Red, Social Democratic government.[111] Announcement of this decision came the same day, November 18, and was followed by a return to work first in Helsinki and then

---

the Finnish Parliament on November 16, and it was not until November 21, after an interval of five days, that Parliament again convened in full session. On November 27 a new government was formed.

[107] Wiik, *Dagboksanteckningar*, November 18, 1917; Sirola, in *Syyttäjistön arkisto*: Sos.-dem. järjestöt, marraskuun v. 1917 puoluekokous, p. 87.

[108] Wiik, *Dagboksanteckningar*, November 17, 1917; Sirola, "Työväen," pp. 48-49.

[109] Siukiiainen, *Revoliutsionnye sobytiia*, pp. 126-127.

[110] Wiik, *Dagboksanteckningar*, November 18, 1917; Sirola, "Työväen," pp. 49-50.

[111] Sirola, "Työväen," p. 50; *Suomen työväen vallankumous*, p. 171; Wiik, *Dagboksanteckningar*, November 18, 1917. Yrjö Sirola abstained on the final vote. Since he had been out of the country most of the summer, Sirola did not consider himself well enough informed to cast a ballot.

in other parts of the country.[112] There was hope among party leaders that the second task, the formation of a temporary Social Democratic government, which might be transformed into a coalition government,[113] could be accomplished by bringing pressure to bear in Parliament.[114] But insurmountable obstacles lay ahead. The five-day strike had caused the prestige of Socialists to plummet in liberal bourgeois circles. Agrarians and Independence Men drew closer to the other bourgeois parties and were no longer so eager to solve political problems jointly with Social Democrats.[115] Many workers, moreover, were demanding that the revolution be continued.[116]

On November 21 debate in the Social Democratic parliamentary group focused on the question of political power. Otto Kuusinen, noting that heretofore he had opposed a seizure of power, proclaimed that in the name of order the workers would have to take power to control the forces of anarchy.[117] Yrjö Sirola confessed that he had been confused by recent events. He had been uncertain as to the correct path to be followed, although

[112] *Työ*, November 20, 1917, p. 7; *Helsingin Sanomat*, November 20, 1917, p. 10.

[113] Yrjö Sirola, in *Suomen sosialidemokraattisen eduskuntaryhmän*, November 19, 1917, 8:00 P.M. As late as mid-January 1918, Sirola supported the formation of a coalition government. Yrjö Sirola, "Kehittyykö tilanne vallankumoukselliseksi?" in *Työmies*, January 12, 1918, p. 5.

[114] Kullervo Manner, in *Suomen sosialidemokraattisen eduskuntaryhmän*, November 19, 1917, 12:15 A.M.

[115] Paasivirta, *Suomen itsenäisyyskysymys*, II, 151, 155; Anton Huotari, in *Syyttäjistön arkisto*: Sosialidemokraattiseen puolueeseen kuuluvia, vangittuja kansanedustajia koskevia kuulustelu pöytäkirjoja, p. 17 (Valtionarkisto); Tanner, *op.cit.*, p. 151.

[116] Sirola, "Työväen," pp. 55-56.

[117] *Vapaussodan arkisto* II B 192 a:-Sekalaisia asiakirjoja: Sos.-dem. eduskuntaryhmän asiakirjoja; Wiik, *Dagboksanteckningar*, November 21, 1917.

now he knew what had to be done. Since Finland still did not have a government, Sirola proposed that the workers establish a temporary Cabinet to remain in power until the Manner Parliament, dissolved by the Provisional Government, could gather and choose a successor.[118] Anton Huotari, around whom the most moderate elements in the parliamentary faction rallied, countered with a proposal that the extraordinary party congress, which had just been summoned by the executive committee in response to the prevailing turmoil,[119] resolve the question of party tactics.[120] Occupying intermediate positions were the proposals made by Emil Saarinen and the faction's preparatory committee. The preparatory committee wanted action first and then a decision by the party congress.[121] Saarinen, on the other hand, thought that the emphasis should be reversed. In his proposal, finally adopted by the parliamentary group, it was the party congress which received primary stress, although provision was made for the formation, in case of necessity, of a temporary government.[122]

---

[118] Wiik, *Dagboksanteckningar*, November 21, 1917.

[119] *Suomen sosialidemokraattisen puolueen kymmenennen edustajakokouksen pöytäkirjaselostus* (Turku: Sosialistin kirjapaino Osakeyhtiö, 1925), p. 11; *Suomen työväen vallankumous*, p. 171.

[120] Wiik, *Dagboksanteckningar*, November 21, 1917; *Vapaussodan arkisto* II B 192 a:-Sekalaisia asiakirjoja: Sos.-dem. eduskuntaryhmän asiakirjoja.

[121] The preparatory committee included, among others, the following: K. Manner, J. Mäki, J. Kohonen, V. Jokinen, Y. Sirola, O. Tokoi, and Y. Mäkelin. Santeri Saarikivi, in *Syyttäjistön arkisto*: Sosialidemokraattiseen puolueeseen kuuluvia, vangittuja kansanedustajia koskevia kuulustelu pöytäkirjoja.

[122] Wiik, *Dagboksanteckningar*, November 21, 1917; *Vapaussodan arkisto* II B 192 a:-Sekalaisia asiakirjoja: Sos.-dem. eduskuntaryhmän asiakirjoja. Four ballots were cast. A complete record of the third vote, Sirola versus Saarinen, and the fourth vote, Saarinen versus the preparatory committee, can be found in *Vapaussodan*

Four days later the Extraordinary Congress of the Social Democratic Party convened. In his report on party tactics Otto Kuusinen noted that a fundamental division had taken place within the party during and after the general strike. Some members emphasized nonparliamentary methods and use of the Red Guard; others did not want to go beyond parliamentary action. Kuusinen pointed out that if the revolutionary wing in the party should be followed and then defeated by the bourgeoisie, the labor movement would be crushed so thoroughly that the process of rebuilding it would take at least twenty years. On the other hand, Social Democrats would run the risk of losing their class consciousness, of becoming slaves to the bourgeoisie, if they should limit themselves to parliamentary methods.[123] In the discussion which followed, two groups, about equal in size and accounting for most of the delegates, emerged. One group, led by Eero Haapalainen, urged that the workers take power by any means. A second group, headed by Seth Heikkilä, supported parliamentary action and the formation of a coalition government.[124]

Haapalainen asserted that the masses had gone on strike in the name of revolution and that for this reason

---

arkisto II B 192 a:-Sekalaisia asiakirjoja: Sos.-dem. eduskuntaryhmän asiakirjoja. The fourth voting sheet can also be found in *Suomen sosialidemokraattisen eduskuntaryhmän*, December 4, 1917, 8:00 P.M. Some additional detail is contained in E. Huttunen, *Sosialidemokraattinen puoluejohto ja kansalaissota* (Helsinki: Kansanvalta, 1918), pp. 75-78, but it should be noted that this account is not wholly accurate.

[123] *Suomen sosialidemokraattisen puolueen kymmenennen*, pp. 19-20.

[124] A. H. [Anton Huotari], in *Kansan Lehti*, December 14, 1917, p. 5; "Humu-Pietari" [Matti Turkia], in *Suomen Sosialidemokraatti*, September 22, 1929, p. 8.

46

it was difficult to halt their movement. The struggle should be continued; the workers should seize power. With half a battalion of Red Guards Haapalainen claimed he could conquer all of southern Finland.[125] The revolutionary wing was bolstered by Stalin, who, appearing personally at the congress, promised Russian aid and urged Finnish Social Democrats to seize power. In an atmosphere of world war, impending revolution in the West, and Bolshevik power in Russia, the only admissible tactic was one which called for courage and daring.[126] Revolutionary fervor mounted when the Helsinki Red Guard threatened to force the assembly to seize power if the congress did not of its own volition make the appropriate decision.[127]

Heikkilä, on the other hand, considered it impossible to establish a dictatorship of the proletariat in Finland because of the country's economic backwardness. He warned that if Finnish workers should seize power, the fate of their government would be identical with that of the Paris Commune. Heikkilä proposed that a coalition government dominated by Social Democrats be established. Disturbed by irresponsible acts of the Red Guard, the parliamentary wing of the party also incorporated in its proposal a demand that the Red Guard be turned into a trustworthy party organ. Heikkilä stopped short of asking the congress to disband the Red Guard, no doubt because, as one delegate had pointed

[125] *Syyttäjistön arkisto*: Sos.-dem. järjestöt, marraskuun v. 1917 puoluekokous, pp. 44-45, 48-49.

[126] The full text of Stalin's speech is cited in Smirnov, *op.cit.*, pp. 217-219; also in *Työ*, November 29, 1917, p. 5.

[127] *Suomen sosialidemokraattisen puolueen kymmenennen*, p. 21; [Wiik,] in *Suomen Sosialidemokraatti*, February 4, 1928, p. 7; I. I. Siukiiainen, *Revoliutsiia 1918 goda v Finliandii. Avtoreferat dissertatsii* (Petrozavodsk: 1958), p. 28.

out, it would be impossible to enforce such a decision.[128]

On a test vote the revolutionary wing of the party was defeated.[129] The two proposals were then sent to a policy committee, where, under the direction of Otto Kuusinen, a compromise solution was worked out.[130] The committee's recommendations, defended by Kuusinen on the basis of party unity,[131] were approved. Violence was to be used only to meet violence; the Red Guard was to be brought into line with the principles of Social Democracy; situations might occur which would make it imperative that the workers join a coalition government, or even seize temporary control of the government. The power to act during an emergency was placed

[128] *Syyttäjistön arkisto:* Sos.-dem. järjestöt, marraskuun v. 1917 puoluekokous, pp. 54, 71, 115.

[129] *Ibid.,* p. 101; *Suomen sosialidemokraattisen puolueen kymmenennen,* p. 28.

[130] Paasivirta, *Suomen itsenäisyyskysymys,* II, 153.

[131] Wiik, *Dagboksanteckningar,* November 27, 1917. Party unity in this instance was not supported by Yrjö Sirola. He urged the left wing of the party to form a revolutionary, Marxist, group. The task of such a group would be to inform the workers that the necessary conditions for revolution did not yet exist but that the Social Democratic Party would, at the right moment, be with the workers. A parallel is sometimes drawn between Sirola's support for a new party, or group, and the Bolshevik-Menshevik controversy in the Russian Social Democratic Labor Party. Sirola, however, has stated that the question of Bolshevism and Menshevism was considered strictly a Russian matter of no concern to the Finnish labor movement. Before the Civil War, January–May 1918, Finnish Social Democrats were barely acquainted with the writings of Lenin. *Ibid.,* November 21, 1917; *Syyttäjistön arkisto:* Sos.-dem. järjestöt, marraskuun v. 1917 puoluekokous, pp. 36, 88-89; Sirola, in M. Maizel', *Stranitsy revoliutsionnoi istorii finliandskogo proletariata* (Leningrad: "Priboi," 1928), p. 141; Yrjö Sirola, "Miksi ei Suomessa ollut bolshevikkipuoluetta?" *Kommunisti,* No. 1 (37), January 15, 1928, p. 35; O. W. Kuusinen, *Suomen työväenliikkeen opetuksia* (Lappeenranta: SKP:n puoluetoimikunta, 1949), p. 11; TsK KPF, "40 let rabochei revoliutsii v Finliandii," *Novaia i noveishaia istoriia,* No. 2, 1958, p. 125.

in the hands of the executive council and the parliamentary group.[132] While the Social Democratic Party was defining its position on tactics in general and the formation of a government in particular, Parliament rejected a Socialist bid for power and approved a bourgeois Cabinet headed by P. E. Svinhufvud.

The Social Democratic Party executive committee, in accordance with the wishes of the November congress, soon called for a meeting of Red Guard units in an attempt to define their relationship to the party.[133] At this meeting, held in Tampere, a majority of the delegates agreed that the power of decision in Red Guard affairs should rest with the party. Those who opposed party control promised to respect the will of the majority, although delegates from Helsinki soon began to act independently.[134] On December 20 Yrjö Sirola and Oskari Tokoi were sent to a meeting of the Helsinki Red Guard in order to defend the party point of view.[135] Sirola was shouted down,[136] and, shortly before Christmas, he felt certain that the Finnish labor movement was heading toward inevitable destruction.[137] Tokoi noted that the Social Democratic Party had been turned

[132] *Suomen sosialidemokraattisen puolueen kymmenennen*, pp. 29-30, 33.

[133] T. Lekhen, "Proletariat Finliandii v bor'be za vlast'," *Istoriia proletariata SSSR*, sbornik 3 (19), 1934, p. 24.

[134] *Kansan Lehti*, January 15, 1918, p. 4; *Työmies*, January 11, 1918, p. 4; M. T[urki]a, in *Suomen Sosialidemokraatti*, May 11, 1927, p. 6. Turkia represented the party executive committee at the Tampere meeting.

[135] Wiik, *Dagboksanteckningar*, December 20, 1917; A. Taimi, *Sivuja eletystä* (Petroskoi: Karjalais-Suomalaisen SNT:n Valtion kustannusliike, 1954), p. 234. Taimi mentions Tokoi by name but refers to Sirola only as "a member of Parliament."

[136] Wiik, *Dagboksanteckningar*, December 20, 1917.

[137] Huttunen, *Sosialidemokraattinen*, p. 97; Tanner, *op.cit.*, p. 201.

from a leader into a follower,[138] and by the end of the year the party clearly could not control the Red Guard. The situation became even more serious when the Red Guard came under the influence of its most unruly elements.[139] At a meeting held on January 6, 1918, the Helsinki branch adopted a resolution formally proclaiming its independence from the party.[140] Red Guards in the capital demanded that the Governor of the province of Uusimaa resign and, threatening violence, seized the former residence of the Governor-General. K. Rovio, head of the militia in Helsinki,[141] stated that he was helpless before the Red Guard. He demanded that the Helsinki Council of Workers' Organizations investigate the activities of the Red Guard and define the relationship between that body and organized law enforcement. A committee, which included members of the Helsinki Council of Workers' Organizations, the party executive committee, the trade union executive committee, and the Red Guard, was established to deal with this question.[142]

Attention was now riveted on the problem of preserving law and order, a task which, since the abolition of the Tsarist police force in March 1917, had first devolved upon a Finnish militia enjoying the confidence

[138] W. Ström, "Kun suomalainen jääkäri varoitti punaisten pääjohtajia tarttumasta miekkaan isänmaata vastaan," *Suomen vapaussota*, No. 5, May 16, 1934, p. 88.

[139] [Wiik,] in *Suomen Sosialidemokraatti*, February 19, 1928, p. 9.

[140] Siukiiainen, *Revoliutsionnye sobytiia*, p. 167.

[141] In the summer of 1917, while hiding in Finland, Lenin stayed with Rovio, and completed *State and Revolution*. From 1929 to 1935 Rovio was first secretary of the Karelian *Obkom* of the Russian Communist Party (b). See chapter six.

[142] *Työmies*, January 9, 1918, p. 3.

of labor organizations. The Cabinet had intended to replace the militia with municipal organs of law enforcement, but in many localities, particularly Helsinki,
strong militia opposition prevented this transfer of
power.[143] Faced with an expanding strike movement,
riots caused by the food shortage, and a lack of discipline
among Russian troops on Finnish soil, the bourgeoisie in
the summer of 1917 had established a Civil Guard.[144]
This had been followed by the formation of a Red
Guard.[145] There was, however, no official Finnish
police force or army. Consequently the bourgeois Cabinet of P. E. Svinhufvud, troubled by anarchy and grow-
ing social unrest, urged Parliament at the turn of the
year to grant it the power to organize a force capable
of restoring order. It was generally understood that the
government wanted to legalize the Civil Guards,[146] and
so Social Democrats considered the Cabinet's request an
attempt to raise a class army to be used against the
workers.[147] Edvard Gylling warned that if the government should receive the power which it was seeking,
civil war would follow.[148] Another Social Democrat
charged that some of the bourgeoisie already considered
civil war a certainty and thus wanted to be prepared

143 Paasivirta, *Suomen itsenäisyyskysymys*, I, 100.

144 *Ibid.*, II, 110-111; Juhani Paasivirta, *Suomi vuonna 1918*
(Porvoo: WSOY, 1957), pp. 177-178.

145 The formation in October 1917 of a Red Guard, or, as it was
then formally called, an Order Guard, was opposed by Edvard
Gylling and Karl Wiik. *Suomen sosialidemokraattisen puolueen
kymmenennen*, p. 8.

146 K. W. [Karl Wiik], in *Suomen Sosialidemokraatti*, January
28, 1938, p. 4.

147 J. Vuoristo, in *Toiset valtiopäivät*, I, 944.

148 *Ibid.*, I, 918. Other members of Parliament also feared civil
war.

for the inevitable.[149] Parliament, turning a deaf ear to the opposition, granted Svinhufvud's Cabinet the authority to establish an armed force. After January 12 civil war no doubt was, as Yrjö Sirola has asserted,[150] inevitable.

[149] P. Leppänen, in *ibid.*, I, 913.
[150] Yrjö Sirola, in *Sosialisti*, March 12, 1918, p. 7.

CHAPTER THREE

Civil War

ON January 14, 1918, in the evening, a meeting of the Helsinki Red Guard was held; for almost four hours disagreements with the executive committee of the Social Democratic Party were aired. The Red Guard decided that in the event of revolution it would take charge, and a party congress based on new elections would then be called to settle the controversy with the party executive committee.[1] Party leaders were helpless before the Red Guard.[2] Old party members no longer bothered to take part in guard meetings and activities.[3] One Socialist of long standing, Yrjö Mäkelin, told a prominent bourgeois figure that the Red Guard had no real leadership; hunger united its members.[4] The extremes on both the left and right began, more and more, to influence the course of events.[5] On January 19 the first serious clash between the Red Guard and the Civil Guard occurred.

The Red Guard in the city of Viipuri surrounded a factory which, it had been reported, was producing

[1] *Työmies*, January 15, 1918, p. 4; Karl H. Wiik, *Dagboksanteckningar från åren 1917 och 1918*, January 15, 1918.

[2] *Suomen vapaussota vuonna 1918*, Vol. VI (Helsinki: Otava, 1925), p. 466.

[3] *Työmies*, January 11, 1918, p. 4.

[4] K. G. Idman, *Maamme itsenäistymisen vuosilta* (Porvoo: WSOY, 1953), p. 241.

[5] K. W. [Karl Wiik], in *Suomen Sosialidemokraatti*, January 27, 1938, p. 7.

war materials.[6] Civil Guard members at work in the factory called for help. Aid was rushed into Viipuri from the countryside, and on January 22 the Civil Guard seized control of the railway station. Their strategy was based on the assumption that Russian troops in the city would remain neutral,[7] but the Russians considered it necessary, for their own security, to take certain measures designed to prevent acts of violence. Some members of the Red Guard were disarmed,[8] and the Soviet Commissar of War issued an order, shortly to be countermanded, which instructed Russian soldiers in Finland to disarm the Civil Guard.[9] The Civil Guard, for its part, proceeded to disarm Russian soldiers in Karelia;[10] then on January 24 Russian troops in Vaasa were stripped of their arms. The Vaasa incident was the first serious conflict between the Civil Guard and Russian soldiers,[11] and an explanation was demanded by the Russians in Helsinki. P. E. Svinhufvud, head of the Finnish Cabinet, was summoned on the afternoon of January 24 to the ship *Krechet* for an accounting before the central committee of the Baltic

[6] [Karl Wiik,] "Suomen työväenliikkeen kohtalokkailta hetkiltä," in *Suomen Sosialidemokraatti*, March 6, 1928, p. 7.

[7] J. O. Hannula, *Suomen vapaussodan historia* (Porvoo: WSOY, 1956), p. 55.

[8] Wiik, in *Suomen Sosialidemokraatti*, March 6, 1928, p. 7. At a meeting of the Social Democratic party executive committee on January 24, 1918, the Viipuri events were discussed. Finnish Social Democrats wanted the Russians in Helsinki and Petrograd to explain Russian participation in the Viipuri events. *Syyttäjistön arkisto*: Sos.-dem. järjestöt: Sosiaalidemokraattinen puoluetoimikunta, Esityslista (Valtionarkisto).

[9] Idman, *op.cit.*, p. 247; Carl Enckell, *Poliittiset muistelmani*, Vol. I (Porvoo: WSOY, 1956), pp. 225-226, 272b.

[10] Hannula, *op.cit.*, p. 47.

[11] G. Mannerheim, *Muistelmat*, Vol. I (Helsinki: Otava, 1952), p. 259; Hannula, *op.cit.*, p. 53.

Fleet.[12] In the evening, when Svinhufvud boarded the ship, negotiations lasting into the early hours of the morning were begun. The Finnish Whites in Viipuri were demanding that the Reds release their prisoners, and on the *Krechet* Svinhufvud noted that liberation of White prisoners in Viipuri would be a step in the direction of peace.[13] Svinhufvud was subsequently joined by two colleagues, and, after further discussion with the Russians, agreement was reached on three points. Hostilities were to be brought to an end, prisoners were to be released, and weapons which had been taken from Russian soldiers were to be returned.[14]

Two Social Democrats, Kullervo Manner and Eero Haapalainen, were also on board the *Krechet* and participated in part of the discussion. Manner assured

[12] Idman, *op.cit.*, p. 252; K. G. Idman, "öinen neuvottelu sotalaivalla," *Suomen vapaussota*, December 6, 1932, p. 78; Arthur Castrén, "Kun senaatti aiottiin vangita," *Itsenäinen Suomi*, December 6, 1927, p. 208. The central committee of the Baltic Fleet (*Tsentrobalt*) was formed early in May 1917. P. E. Dybenko, a member of the nine-man Bolshevik Executive Commission which was set up in Finland in the spring of 1917, was chairman of the *Tsentrobalt* until the July Days. While Dybenko was chairman, the *Tsentrobalt* included Bolsheviks, Mensheviks, and Social Revolutionaries. After the Bolshevik Revolution, N. F. Izmailov was elected chairman; A. A. Ruzhek was soon appointed military specialist. Both Izmailov and Ruzhek were present during the negotiations with Svinhufvud on board the *Krechet*. M. G. Roshal', *Na putiakh revoliutsii* (Moscow: Voennoe izdatel'stvo ministerstva oborony soiuza SSR, 1957), pp. 96, 103; P. E. Dybenko, *Miatezhniki* (Moscow: Izdatel'stvo Krasnaia nov', 1923), pp. 41, 51n; *Baltiiskie moriaki v podgotovke i provedenii velikoi oktiabr'skoi sotsialisticheskoi revoliutsii* (Moscow-Leningrad: Izdatel'stvo Akademii Nauk SSSR, 1957), pp. 334, 337; *Bol'shaia sovetskaia entsiklopediia*, Vol. IX (Moscow: Gosudarstvennoe slovarno-entsiklopedicheskoe izdatel'stvo "Sovetskaia entsiklopediia," 1934), p. 581; *Izvestiia gel'singforsskago soveta deputatov armii, flota i rabochikh*, December 12 (25), 1917, p. 4.

[13] Idman, *Maamme*, pp. 248, 253.

[14] *Ibid.*, p. 259; Idman, "öinen," p. 80.

Svinhufvud that Finnish Social Democrats did not want Russian aid in their struggle against the bourgeoisie,[15] and following the negotiations Svinhufvud was hopeful that he could prevent Russian troops in Finland from interfering in the country's internal affairs.[16] By the end of 1917 Russian troops in Finland numbered only about one half of the peak figure reached in August 1917,[17] but the speed with which the Russians were withdrawing failed to satisfy most of the Finnish bourgeoisie. It was feared that with Russian aid social revolution would spread to Finland,[18] and an awareness of this apprehension helps one to understand why the Finnish bourgeoisie was so adamant in its refusal to accept anything less than the immediate withdrawal of all Russian troops. Social Democrats expressed an understanding of Russia's desire to maintain military forces in Finland during wartime,[19] but bourgeois circles, particularly

[15] Wiik, *Dagboksanteckningar*, January 25, 1918; [Karl Wiik,] "Suomen työväenliikkeen kohtalokkailta hetkiltä," in *Suomen Sosialidemokraatti*, March 13, 1928, p. 6.

[16] Mannerheim, *op.cit.*, I, 261.

[17] U. V. Rauanheimo, "Venäläiset joukot Suomessa maailmansodan 1914-18 aikana," *Tiede ja Ase*, No. 8 (Helsinki: Otava, 1950), p. 167.

[18] Enckell, *op.cit.*, I, 258-259, 266, 307; Marvin Rintala, *Three Generations: The Extreme Right Wing in Finnish Politics* (Bloomington: Indiana University Press, 1962), p. 41.

[19] Socialist memorandum to Kerenskii, in *Syyttäjistön arkisto* F k 1: Y. Sirolan ja O. Tokoin papereita; paragraph one of the *valtalaki*, cited in Juhani Paasivirta, *Suomen itsenäisyyskysymys 1917*, Vol. I (Porvoo: WSOY, 1947), p. 211; "Sos.-dem. eduskuntaryhmän tiedonanto työväelle," in *Työmies*, November 8, 1917, p. 2; Otto Kuusinen and Edvard Gylling, cited in Wiik, *Dagboksanteckningar*, November 9, 1917; "Sos.-dem. Puolueneuvoston julistus venäläiselle sotaväelle," in *Työ*, January 23, 1918, p. 1. The proclamation printed in *Työ* was prepared by Edvard Gylling, Matti Turkia, and E. Härmä; it was approved unanimously by the executive council of the party. The above sources, with the exception

after the Bolshevik Revolution, would not acknowledge this strategic interest.[20]

In December 1917 Gustaf Mannerheim, soon to become commander in chief of the Finnish Civil Guard, returned to Finland after thirty years of service in the Russian Imperial Army.[21] In his eyes it was no longer a question of whether Finland would be drawn into the maelstrom of revolution—it was only a question of *when* it would happen. Mannerheim's struggle for freedom was a struggle against revolution, which, on the basis of Russia's experience, he felt would destroy Finland's culture and social structure.[22] On January 25, 1918, Mannerheim made a decision which he later viewed as having been instrumental in saving Europe from Bolshevism.[23] He had received a telegram from Svinhufvud stating that the Finnish Cabinet found it impossible to prevent a trainload of Russian soldiers from rein-

---

of the *valtalaki*, specifically stated that in *peacetime* Russian troops would not be permitted to remain in Finland.

[20] *Suomen vapaussota*, III, 139. This is the so-called Mannerheim version of the War of Independence. It is interesting to note that in directing Major General Hannes Ignatius to take charge of writing this history of the war, Mannerheim stated: "Then we shall get it as we ourselves have wanted it." Quoted in Rintala, *op.cit.*, p. 32. Some three decades after the conclusion of the war, the former Minister State Secretary and a Finnish military historian acknowledged, contrary to the official White history of Finland's war, that it was for strategic reasons that Russian troops were in their country throughout the First World War. Enckell, *op.cit.*, I, 64, 68, 117, 251; Rauanheimo, "Venäläiset," pp. 168-169.

[21] For details on Mannerheim's life, see Marvin Rintala, "The Politics of Gustaf Mannerheim," *Journal of Central European Affairs*, Vol. XXI, No. 1 (April 1961), pp. 67-83. On January 16, 1918, Mannerheim was orally empowered by Svinhufvud to form an army; on January 27 he received written authority to act as commander in chief of the White forces.

[22] Mannerheim, *op.cit.*, I, 247-248.

[23] *Ibid.*, II, 512.

forcing Russian garrisons in central western Finland (Etelä-Pohjanmaa); in a second telegram, Svinhufvud had reported a conversation with the chairman of the *Obkom* of the Army, Fleet, and Workers of Finland. The chairman had explained to Svinhufvud that the *Obkom* was of the opinion that revolution in Finland had begun and that it was Russia's duty to support the Finnish Reds with all the means at her disposal.[24] These two telegrams caused Mannerheim to call together, on January 25, his closest advisers;[25] in the evening he made the fateful decision to disarm during the night of January 27-28 the Russian garrisons in central western Finland.[26]

During the winter of 1917-1918 Finnish Social Democrats had expressed their desire to protect revolutionary Petrograd,[27] but the Finnish bourgeoisie was in error

[24] From September 1917 until April of the following year, I. T. Smilga was chairman of the *Obkom*. The *Obkoms* which were elected in May, June, and September 1917 included Bolsheviks, Mensheviks, and Social Revolutionaries. Mensheviks were not, however, represented in the *Obkom* elected by the *Oblast* Congress of Russian Soviets of Soldiers', Sailors', and Workers' Deputies of Finland early in December. V. Smirnov, *Iz revoliutsionnoi istorii Finliandii 1905, 1917, 1918 gg* (Leningrad: Leningradskoe oblastnoe izdatel'stvo, 1933), pp. 90, 102; *Baltiiskie*, pp. 340, 352; *Izvestiia gel'singforsskago soveta deputatov armii, flota i rabochikh*, November 30 (December 13), 1917, pp. 2-3. The main Russian organs in Finland during the period 1917-1918 were the *Obkom* of Finland, the *Tsentrobalt*, and the Helsinki Soviet of Soldiers', Sailors', and Workers' Deputies. The Helsinki Committee of the RSDLP (b), established in April 1917, was also an organ of considerable importance.

[25] *Suomen vapaussota*, II, 31-32.

[26] Mannerheim, *op.cit.*, I, 260.

[27] Yrjö Sirola, in *Työmies*, November 26, 1917, p. 3; Yrjö Sirola, in *Toiset valtiopäivät 1917 pöytäkirjat*, Vol. 1 (Helsinki: Valtioneuvoston kirjapaino, 1918), p. 413; "Sos.-dem. puolueneuvoston julistus venäläiselle sotaväelle," in *Työ*, January 23, 1918, p. 1.

when it read into this desire the design to imitate in Finland Russia's Bolshevik Revolution. Both the Tsarist and Provisional governments had reacted negatively to the question of Finnish independence, and Social Democrats feared that if the bourgeoisie should regain control of Petrograd, the heart of revolution in Russia, Finnish independence would at best be precarious.[28] For Finnish Social Democrats it was independence, not revolution, least of all revolution in imitation of the Bolsheviks, that was the vital issue of the time. Yrjö Sirola noted that the tactics used in one country could not be copied and transferred to another; Finland, moreover, did not yet have the economic base for a social revolution. Sirola added, however, that Social Democrats felt social revolution could occur in Finland without the economic prerequisites *if* revolution should first break out in those Western countries upon which Finland's economy was dependent.[29] Social Democrats were waiting for the great capitalist countries of the West to pave the way for social revolution in Finland,[30] although Otto Kuusinen, for one, was pessimistic about the chances of proletarian revolution succeeding in those countries.[31] Oskari Tokoi stated that if the workers should seize power in Finland irrespective of developments in the West, one could expect only reforms within the existing order of society.[32] Yrjö Sirola thought that democracy could be achieved,

[28] Yrjö Sirola and Otto Kuusinen, in *Toiset valtiopäivät*, 1, 58, 413.

[29] Yrjö Sirola, "Kehittyykö tilanne vallankumoukselliseksi?" in *Työmies*, January 12, 1918, p. 4.

[30] Yrjö Sirola, in *Sosialisti*, March 12, 1918, p. 7; Yrjö Sirola, in *Viesti*, February 22, 1919, p. 4.

[31] *Toiset valtiopäivät*, 1, 56.

[32] *Suomen Ammattijärjestön v. 1917 pidetyn edustajakokouksen pöytäkirjaluonnos*, November 12 [Työväen Arkisto 331.88 (471) (063) "1917"].

but the workers would be carrying through a bourgeois, not a social, revolution.[33]

Rejection by the Social Democrats of the bourgeois demand that Russian troops withdraw immediately from Finnish soil was considered a clear indication that the Social Democrats were planning to turn to Russian forces in Finland for support in a revolution based on the Bolshevik model.[34] Members of the Social Democratic Party executive committee openly warned, however, against seeking military aid from the Russians.[35] They thought it doubtful that the Bolsheviks would remain in power;[36] and for this reason they did not

[33] *Syyttäjistön arkisto*: Sos.-dem. järjestöt, marraskuun v. 1917 puoluekokous, p. 87; Sirola, in *Työmies*, January 12, 1918, p. 5.

[34] This view is still expressed by influential Finnish figures. See L. A. Puntila's article "Vapaussota-Kapina-Kansalaissota," in *Neljän vuosikymmenen takaa* (Porvoo: WSOY, 1958), p. 19. Referring to a declaration made by the executive council of the Social Democratic Party in January 1918, Puntila asserts that Social Democrats opposed the withdrawal of Russian troops. Puntila apparently attaches no significance to that part of the declaration which states: "Russian troops must be withdrawn from Finland as soon as possible, and under no circumstances should troops remain after the World War has come to an end." The declaration can be found in *Työ*, January 23, 1918, p. 1. Edvard Gylling was one of the three Social Democrats who drew up the declaration (see note 19 above); it is interesting to note that a man who was a key figure on the White side in the Finnish Civil War has written that Gylling as late as December 1917 sought the withdrawal of Russian troops and was a vigorous champion of Finnish independence. Herman Gummerus, *Jääkärit ja aktivistit* (Porvoo: WSOY, 1928), p. 470.

[35] Karl Wiik, cited in *Suomen sosialidemokraattisen puolueen kymmenennen edustajakokouksen pöytäkirjaselostus* (Turku: Sosialistin kirjapaino Osakeyhtiö, 1925), p. 26; Matti Turkia, cited in *Syyttäjistön arkisto*: Sos.-dem. järjestöt, marraskuun v. 1917 puoluekokous, p. 94; K. H. [Wiik], in *Työmies*, December 15, 1917, p. 3.

[36] Kullervo Manner and Oskari Tokoi, in *Suomen Ammattijärjestön v. 1917*, November 12; Otto Kuusinen, cited in Wiik, *Dagboksanteckningar*, November 17, 1917; Yrjö Sirola, in *Viesti*, Febru-

want to bind the fate of Finland to that of Bolshevik Russia.[37] A strong feeling of nationalism also prevented leading Social Democrats from turning to Russian soldiers for aid.[38] Yrjö Sirola pointed out, moreover, that if Finland claimed to be an independent republic but at the same time relied on Russian troops, other foreign powers might intervene in the country's internal affairs.[39] Both before and after the Bolshevik Revolution, Finnish Social Democrats considered international guarantees the best assurance that Finnish independence would be respected by the final victors in Russia's upheaval.[40] Even after Social Democrats had established a revolutionary government, they did not turn exclusively to Russia; they attempted to establish relations with the Western powers in the hope that Finland's revolution would be judged apart from the revolution in Russia.[41]

The fact that leading Social Democrats opposed military aid from Russia does not mean, however, that all Social Democrats were against seeking armed support

---

ary 22, 1919, p. 4; Kullervo Manner, in *Proletaari*, No. 1 (38), January 1928, p. 17; *Kommunisti*, No. 1 (37), January 15, 1928, p. 11; Sirola, in *Työmies*, January 12, 1918, p. 4.

[37] Edvard Gylling, cited in Wiik, *Dagboksanteckningar*, November 9, 1917.

[38] O. V. Kuusinen and Yrjö Sirola, *Suomen työväen tulikoe* (Superior, Wis.: Työmies Print, 1923), p. 121; O. V. Kuusinen, "Suomen ensimmäisen vallankumouksen viisitoistavuotismuisto," *Neuvosto-Karjala*, No. 1-2, 1933, p. 17; *Työmies* (SKP:n äänenkannattaja), No. 3 (5), 1934, p. 2.

[39] Yrjö Sirola, in *Suomen sosialidemokraattisen eduskuntaryhmän pöytäkirjat*, January 13, 1918, 12:00 noon.

[40] Karl Wiik, *Aktivismen och socialdemokratia*, pp. 13-14; Social Democratic Memorandum to Kerenskii: Työväen Arkisto 327 (47:471) "1917."

[41] Juhani Paasivirta, *Suomi vuonna 1918* (Porvoo: WSOY, 1957), p. 92.

from Russian troops in Finland. Driven by a sense of primitive internationalism, those workers who were not schooled in the principles of Social Democracy turned to Russian forces.[42] The Bolsheviks, moreover, maintained direct connections with the most radical elements in Finland.[43] Following the March Revolution in Russia, the Petrograd Committee of the Russian Social Democratic Labor Party (bolshevik) sent Adolf Taimi, a Petrograd Finn, to Helsinki to bolster the activities of the local party apparatus.[44] He soon became a member of the nine-man executive commission of the Helsinki committee of the RSDLP (b) and was given the task of maintaining contacts with the left wing of the Finnish Social Democratic Party as well as carrying on agitation among the workers in the harbor area.[45] Taimi urged Finnish Social Democrats to follow the tactics of the Bolsheviks and to make a social revolution.[46] Eero Haapalainen shared Taimi's opinion that Finland was ready for social revolution;[47] he too believed

[42] Wiik, *Aktivismen*, p. 7.

[43] Karl H. Wiik, "Mistä johtui vuoden 1918 Suomen sota," in *Kuoleman kentiltä* (Hämeenlinna: Osakeyhtiö Hämeen Kansan kirjapaino, 1924), p. 20.

[44] M. G. Roshal', "Bol'sheviki gel'singforsa v dni revoliutsii 1917 g. (mart-iiul')," *Istoricheskii arkhiv*, No. 5 (September-October), 1956, p. 150; A. Taimi, *Sivuja eletystä* (Petroskoi: Karjalais-Suomalaisen SNT:n Valtion kustannusliike, 1954), p. 191. In the 1920s Taimi was twice sent from Soviet Russia to Finland by the central committee of the Finnish Communist Party. In the spring of 1928 he was apprehended and sentenced to fifteen years in prison. Following Finland's defeat in the Winter War, Taimi was released to Soviet authorities.

[45] Roshal', *Na putiakh*, p. 103.

[46] Page 4 in the minutes of a meeting of members of the Red Guard and the executive committee of the Social Democratic Party held on January 11, 1918: *Vapaussodan arkisto* I B 29b "Yleisesikunta" (Valtionarkisto).

[47] *Suomen Ammattijärjestön v. 1917*, November 12.

that the Soviet government would give Social Democrats speedy and substantial aid.[48] Members of the executive committee of the party, however, questioned whether Russia would be so eager to aid Finnish Social Democracy in its domestic struggle. They were uncertain as to what the Russian attitude would be toward revolution in Finland;[49] and they did not exclude the possibility that Russia and Germany had reached an agreement leaving Finland in a German sphere of influence.[50] Events took a decisive turn when elements reflecting the views of Taimi and Haapalainen gained access to the party's most important organ at the January 19-22 meeting of the party executive council.

At the opening session, Otto Kuusinen reported on the political situation and suggested that it was fruitless to discuss whether the struggle with the bourgeoisie should be prevented or encouraged—it had already begun. In his view the party executive committee could no longer cope with the situation; a new organ, which would cooperate with the executive committee, the party secretary, and the Red Guard, should be formed and should include active revolutionaries. The establishment of this revolutionary organ would, according to Kuusinen, prevent the most radical elements in the party from acting on their own.[51] Yrjö Sirola shared the

[48] Oskari Tokoi, *Maanpakolaisen muistelmia* (Helsinki: Tammi, 1959), p. 212.

[49] Yrjö Sirola, *Tilanteen arvioiminen ja toiminnan määrittely (alustus)*: Työväen Arkisto 323.2 (471) "1918." This document is a report delivered on January 24, 1918, to a meeting of the executive committee of the party.

[50] Yrjö Sirola, cited in Wiik, *Dagboksanteckningar*, January 24, 1918; [Wiik,] in *Suomen Sosialidemokraatti*, March 6, 1928, p. 7.

[51] *Suomen sosialidemokraattisen puolueneuvoston pöytäkirjat*, January 19-22, 1918, pp. 3-5. A week before the meeting of the executive council, Kuusinen had advanced the idea of a small,

views expressed in Kuusinen's report, and he noted that the masses were driving the leaders forward.[52] He was not, however, so optimistic as Kuusinen regarding the revolutionary state of the party as a whole. Sirola doubted whether the majority of the party was revolutionary. The convocation of a conference of delegates representing municipal organizations throughout Finland was essential, so Sirola argued, in order to assess accurately the mood of the workers.[53]

The most important, and most controversial, question raised at the meeting of the executive council was the formation of the revolutionary committee. On January 20 the council voted 12 to 10 against a special organ which would deal with party matters. On the following day, however, the issue was brought up again in a set of proposals presented to the council by the committee on party tactics, a committee which was chaired by Yrjö Sirola and which also included Otto Kuusinen as one of

---

authoritative committee parallel to the executive committee of the party. Wiik, *Dagboksanteckningar*, January 13, 1918.

[52] *Suomen sosialidemokraattisen puolueneuvoston*, January 19-22, 1918, pp. 5, 44. On January 13 Sirola had stated at a meeting of the Social Democratic parliamentary group that if the workers should begin to act on their own, party leaders had three choices: they could join the masses with a conviction that they were with the majority; they could join the masses out of loyalty; or they could remain apart from the movement in order to preserve labor's strength for future battles. *Suomen sosialidemokraattisen eduskuntaryhmän*, January 13, 1918, 12:00 noon.

[53] *Suomen sosialidemokraattisen puolueneuvoston*, January 19-22, 1918, pp. 5, 18. For Sirola, the conference which he proposed should also discuss the relative strength of the bourgeoisie and the workers in various communities in order to determine whether the workers could hold power. Sirola, "Kehittyykö," p. 5. The executive council backed Sirola, and a conference of labor organizations was scheduled for February. *Suomen sosialidemokraattisen puolueneuvoston*, January 19-22, 1918, pp. 46, 55.

its seven members. The executive council was urged to elect a workers' executive committee (*työväen toimeenpaneva komitea*) to work closely with the party executive committee and to direct the activities of party organizations as well as the Red Guard.[54] In the discussion which followed, Kuusinen clarified a number of points. The new revolutionary organ would be on an equal footing with the executive committee; any disputes which might arise between the two bodies would be resolved at a meeting of the executive council.[55] Edvard Gylling, a self-styled right-wing Socialist, opposed the formation of an organ which would be the equal of the executive committee. His counterproposal was that representatives of the radical wing of the party be elected to an enlarged executive committee.[56] By a vote of 18 to 15 the formation of a workers' executive committee was rejected; the executive council backed Gylling. Sirola, Kuusinen, Manner, and Eloranta then announced their resignation from the executive committee. The party secretary stated that he, too, would resign if Manner and the others should withdraw from the executive committee.[57] This turn of events caused Gylling to urge the election of a bigger and entirely new executive committee; he proposed, and was supported by the executive council, that the matter be sent to a committee for mediation.[58] On January 22 the council unanimously accepted the committee's recommendation that

[54] *Ibid.*, pp. 34-35, 39.

[55] *Ibid.*, p. 47.

[56] *Ibid.*, pp. 47, 57. Kuusinen asserted that Gylling had not been in close enough contact with the revolutionary movement to be familiar with the situation then confronting the party.

[57] *Ibid.*, p. 52; Matti Turkia, in *ibid.*, p. 57.

[58] *Ibid.*, pp. 58, 60. The committee set up for the purpose of mediation included Gylling, Wiik, Harjula, Hurmevaara, and Lundberg.

a new executive committee be formed which would include the old executive committee *in toto* plus Adolf Taimi, Eero Haapalainen, A. Kiviranta, E. Elo, and L. Letonmäki.[59] The five new men represented the most radical elements in Finnish Social Democracy, and a sharp turn to the left in party policy was thus to be expected.[60]

The executive council had sanctioned the formation of sections (*jaostoja*) within the new executive committee at the latter's discretion,[61] and on January 23, at a meeting of the executive committee, Sirola proposed that two sections be formed.[62] One section, called an executive committee (*toimeenpaneva komitea*), would direct the activities of party organizations and the Red Guard; its tasks should, so Sirola argued, be entrusted to the five new men elected by the executive council the preceding day.[63] He stated that it might become neces-

[59] *Ibid.*, pp. 63-65. Members of the old executive committee were Manner, Sirola, Kuusinen, Eloranta, Turkia, Gylling, and Wiik. A noted White historian of the Finnish Civil War has written that of the twelve men elected to the new executive committee only Turkia, Wiik, Gylling, and Sirola (*sic*) were firm opponents of revolution. P. H. Norrmén, "Punaisten sotavalmistelut," in Kai Donner, Th. Svedlin, and Heikki Nurmio, eds., *Suomen vapaussota*, Vol. 1 (Jyväskylä: K. J. Gummerus Oy, 1921), p. 437.

[60] Kiviranta was assistant chairman of the staff of the Helsinki Red Guard; Elo in the fall of 1917 had been one of the most persistent proponents of a workers' dictatorship. *Suomen sosialidemokraattisen puolueneuvoston*, January 19-22, 1918, liite No. 2; statement by J. Pietikäinen, cited in Wiik, *Dagboksanteckningar*, November 18, 1917.

[61] *Suomen sosialidemokraattisen puolueneuvoston*, January 19-22, 1918, p. 63.

[62] *Syyttäjistön arkisto*: Sos.-dem. järjestöt, ehdotuksia puoluetoimikunnalle (No. 1); a copy of this document can also be found in Työväen Arkisto 323.2 (471) "1918." The proposals bear no signature, but from Karl Wiik's diary it is clear that Sirola prepared them. Wiik, *Dagboksanteckningar*, January 23, 1918.

[63] *Syyttäjistön arkisto*: Sos.-dem. järjestöt, ehdotuksia puoluetoimi-

sary for the workers to seize power, and he thus urged that reports concerning the political and practical questions involved in a seizure of power be prepared by two committees. The executive committee was exhorted to provide time in its meeting the following day, January 24, for a thorough discussion of revolution.[64]

In accordance with Sirola's proposal, the executive committee was split into two committees on January 23;[65] a discussion of the political situation, focusing

---

kunnalle (Nos. 1 and 2). The tasks which Sirola sought to assign to this committee, or section, were identical to those which the executive council's committee on tactics two days earlier had unsuccessfully attempted to put in the hands of a workers' executive committee. See notes 54 and 57 above. Defending the formation of a revolutionary committee, Sirola had stressed in the executive council the party's need for an organ which would be ready to meet any situation. *Suomen sosialidemokraattisen puolueneuvoston,* January 19-22, 1918, p. 49.

64 *Syyttäjistön arkisto*: Sos.-dem. järjestöt, ehdotuksia puoluetoimikunnalle (Nos. 15 and 16). It was implicit in Sirola's presentation that the reports which he considered so important should be prepared by the two sections of the executive committee called for in his first proposal.

65 I. I. Siukiiainen, *Revoliutsiia 1918 goda v Finliandii. Avtoreferat dissertatsii* (Petrozavodsk, 1958), p. 33, states that on January 23 a workers' executive committee was formed. An agenda sheet of the party executive committee makes it clear that on January 24 two committees existed; *an* executive committee (*toimeenpaneva komitea*) was given a task to perform before the January 24 meeting of *the* executive committee (*puoluetoimikunta*). *Syyttäjistön arkisto*: Sos.-dem. järjestöt, sosiaalidemokraattinen puoluetoimikunta, esityslista. On January 24 Karl Wiik and Yrjö Sirola referred to the existence of an executive committee (*toimeenpaneva komitea*). Wiik, *Dagboksanteckningar*, January 24, 1918; Yrjö Sirola, *Tilanteen*. The first public reference to the existence of two committees, a workers' executive committee and a general (political) committee, lists Haapalainen as chairman, Letonmäki secretary, of the executive committee; Manner is referred to as chairman, Sirola and Turkia secretaries, of the general committee. *Työmies*, January 26, 1918, p. 6. Wiik in a marginal notation to his

upon a written report delivered by Sirola, was put on the executive committee's agenda for the following day.[66] Sirola had stated on January 19 that the party must decide whether the workers should act offensively or defensively in the struggle against the bourgeoisie,[67] and by January 24 at least he had made up his mind—the Red Guard should be permitted to attack. Undoubtedly influenced by the clash in Viipuri between the Red Guard and the White Guard, Sirola felt that civil war in Finland had begun; the executive committee should develop a program of action in order to give unity to the movement and to prevent arbitrary action by the workers.[68] On three occasions, as long ago as 1906 and as recently as January 21, 1918, Sirola had stated that the masses should not be abandoned when they can no longer be restrained; Socialists should join the masses and try to salvage something from the situation.[69] In his report of January 24 Sirola presented a detailed program of socialization. He considered imperative,

book *Kovan kokemuksen opetuksia* (Helsinki: Työväen kirjapaino, 1918), p. 93, states that Taimi, Elo, and Kiviranta were also members of the workers' executive committee.

[66] *Syyttäjistön arkisto*: Sos.-dem. järjestöt, sosiaalidemokraattinen puoluetoimikunta, esityslista; a copy of this document can also be found in Työväen Arkisto 329 (471) 5 "1918."

[67] *Suomen sosialidemokraattisen puolueneuvoston*, January 19-22, 1918, p. 18.

[68] Sirola, *Tilanteen.* News of the Viipuri clash reached the executive council on January 20, and at a meeting of the executive committee on January 24 the incident was discussed at length. Wiik, *Dagbonsanteckningar*, January 20 and 24, 1918. Wiik states, in *Suomen Sosialidemokraatti*, March 16, 1928, p. 8, that the Viipuri events were interpreted by many Social Democrats as an attempt by the bourgeoisie to cut connections between Finland and Petrograd.

[69] Yrjö Sirola, "Järjestynyt työväki ja järjestymättömät," *Sosialistinen Aikakauslehti*, Näytenumero 4 (February), 1906, p. 56; *Syyttäjistön arkisto*: Sos.-dem. järjestöt, marraskuun v. 1917 puolue-

however, a thorough discussion by the Conference of Labor Organizations, which was to meet in February, of the points which he had raised. Without such a debate it would not be possible to set the revolutionary machine in motion.[70]

On January 25 the question of revolution was again brought up at a meeting of the full executive committee. Eero Haapalainen and E. Elo stated that in view of recent developments retreat was no longer possible; and for Kuusinen, taking power was now only a technical question.[71] Some members of the executive committee had not yet lost all hope in the preservation of peace, but they found themselves in the minority.[72] The ex-

kokous, p. 87; *Suomen sosialidemokraattisen puolueneuvoston*, January 19-22, 1918, p. 44.

[70] Sirola, *Tilanteen*. Sirola's program called for workers' control over production and distribution; the influence of Lenin's article "Uderzhat li bol'sheviki gosudarstvennuiu vlast'?" which Sirola read in late December 1917, is apparent. V. I. Lenin, *Sochineniia*, Vol. xxvi (Moscow: Gosudarstvennoe izdatel'stvo politicheskoi literatury, fourth edition, 1949), pp. 63-110; Yrjö Sirola, in *Työmies* (Sup.), November 17, 1928, p. 3. For further information on the Conference of Labor Organizations, see note 53 above.

[71] Wiik, *Dagboksanteckningar*, January 25, 1918; [Wiik,] in *Suomen Sosialidemokraatti*, March 16, 1928, p. 8; K. W. [Karl Wiik], in *ibid.*, January 27, 1938, p. 7. After civil war had begun, Kuusinen argued that further hesitation over seizing power would have had far more serious consequences; the masses were on the move and would not have listened to orders calling for restraint. *Suomen kansanvaltuuskunnan pöytäkirjat*, March 5, 1918, 8:00 P.M.

[72] [Wiik,] in *Suomen Sosialidemokraatti*, March 16, 1928, p. 8. In a marginal notation to his book *Kovan kokemuksen opetuksia*, p. 93, Wiik states that only he and Gylling sought to the very end a peaceful solution. On January 26, 1918, Wiik requested that he be relieved from membership in the executive committee since he was at odds with the policy which appeared to have achieved final victory in the committee; two days later his resignation was accepted. Letter dated January 26 to the executive committee of the Social Democratic Party; Wiik, *Dagboksanteckningar*, January 28,

ecutive committee decided to seize power.[73] On the same day, January 25, control of the Red Guard was placed by the workers' executive committee in the hands of E. Haapalainen, A. Taimi, and A. Vastén.[74] On Janu-

---

1918. Gylling's opposition to revolution has been recorded in *Viesti*, October 26, 1918, p. 2, and *Punainen Karjala*, November 30, 1931, p. 1. P. H. Norrmén, "Punaisten," p. 443, states that Wiik and Gylling doubted whether revolution could succeed and that they joined the revolutionary government for reasons of solidarity. Once civil war had begun, both Wiik and Gylling favored peace overtures. Wiik, *Dagboksanteckningar*, January 29 and February 7, 1918; *Suomen kansanvaltuuskunnan pöytäkirjat*, April 21, 1918, 10:15 A.M. It should be noted, however, that on at least one occasion—at the meeting of the executive committee on January 25, 1918—Gylling appears to have favored taking power. Wiik, *Dagboksanteckningar*, January 27, 1918.

[73] Edvard Gylling, in *Punainen Karjala*, January 31, 1928, p. 2; Yrjö Sirola, in *Karelo-Murmanskii krai*, No. 1 (January), 1928, p. 4. The author has not had at his disposal sources which state explicitly what Sirola's position was at the meeting of the executive committee held on January 25, but there can be little doubt as to what stand he probably took. Sirola later stated that the masses wanted to take power and that he felt one should not abandon them, although from the very beginning he thought the workers would be defeated. *Sosialistinen Aikakauslehti*, February 16, 1920, p. 52; Yrjö Sirola, "Ulkoasiain valtuutettuna vallankumoushallituksessa," in A. Halonen, ed., *Suomen luokkasota—Historiaa ja muistelmia* (Superior, Wis.: Työmies Society Print, 1928), p. 43. In 1906 Sirola had rejected the notion that one should fight only when victory was a certainty; a struggle should be undertaken, regardless of the consequences, when it can no longer be avoided. *Suomen sosialidemokraattisen puolueen viidennen edustajakokouksen pöytäkirja* (Helsinki: Sosialidemokraattinen Puoluetoimikunta, 1906), p. 222. Sirola, in *Työmies*, January 12, 1918, p. 5, opposed taking power by force, but he stated that events might make it necessary at least to attempt a seizure of power through revolution. One can assume that the passage by Parliament on January 12 of the law which gave Svinhufvud's Cabinet the power to establish a military force, and the clash in Viipuri between the Red Guard and White Guard, created the "necessity" of which Sirola spoke in his *Työmies* article.

[74] *Työmies*, January 29, 1918, p. 1.

ary 26 the workers' executive committee approved an order of the Red Guard concerning a seizure of power.[75] During the night of January 27-28 Finnish Reds seized control of Helsinki and set up a fourteen-member Revolutionary Government (*Kansanvaltuuskunta*) under the nominal leadership of Kullervo Manner. Simultaneously Finland's Peasant Army (*Suomen talonpoikaisarmeija*), under the command of Gustaf Mannerheim and acting on his decision of January 25, began to disarm, with little resistance, the Russian garrisons in Southern Ostrobothnia.[76] War had begun.

Finnish workers took arms in what to them was a civil war, whereas the Finnish peasantry went to battle in the belief that they were fighting a War of Independence against a foreign enemy.[77] The eventual triumph of the Finnish Whites was viewed by the bourgeoisie as a military victory against Russia, although scholarly study shows that in actual fact it was victory of White Finn over Red Finn.[78] Some forty thousand Russian troops

[75] V. M. Kholodkovskii, "Revoliutsiia v Finliandii v 1918 g. i interventsiia germanskogo imperialisma," *Novaia i noveishaia istoriia*, No. 4, 1957, p. 127.

[76] Hannula, *op.cit.*, pp. 58-61. In all, some 5,000 Russian troops were disarmed.

[77] During the Civil War, Sirola noted that the bourgeoisie had successfully played upon the national prejudice of the peasantry in northern Finland. *Sosialisti*, March 12, 1918, p. 7. Analyzing the reasons for proletarian defeat in the war, Kuusinen stated that the Finnish peasantry has always been blinded by two prejudices: nationalism and the right of ownership. O. V. Kuusinen, "Talonpoika ja työmies," *Kommunisti*, No. 1 (37), January 15, 1928, p. 23. In the 1920s Finnish Communists admitted that national prejudice was still strong among the peasantry; great difficulties would have to be overcome before the peasantry could be won over as an ally of the proletariat. "Kommunisti," in *Työväenjärjestöjen Tiedonantoja*, April 22, 1926, p. 4.

[78] Paasivirta, *Suomi vuonna 1918*; Rintala, *Three Generations*, pp. 49-53; Erik Allardt, "Patterns of Class Conflict and Working Class

71

still remained on Finnish soil late in January 1918,[79] but with the outbreak of war in Finland the speed with which Russian troops were being recalled by the Soviet government was increased rather than decreased.[80] The presence of Russian troops in Finland must not be neglected in an analysis of the Finnish Civil War, but, on the other hand, the war should not be seen as being nothing more than "a Russian wolf in Finnish sheep's clothing."[81]

The workers' feeling of strength (*voimantunto*) was increased by the presence of Russian troops,[82] but those members of the Finnish proletariat who counted on Russian aid were disappointed by the course of events.[83] In a memorandum dated January 30, the chief of the Red Guard's general staff reported that Russian troops

Consciousness in Finnish Politics," in Erik Allardt and Yrjö Littunen, eds., *Cleavages, Ideologies and Party Systems: Contributions to Comparative Political Sociology* (Turku: Transactions of the Westermarck Society, Vol. x, 1964), pp. 100-101. The assumption that Russia had been defeated by her neighbor was the foundation, as Rintala in *Three Generations* has meticulously documented, for dreams of a Greater Finland during the interwar years.

[79] Rauanheimo, "Venäläiset," p. 167; Hannula, *op.cit.*, p. 80; Mannerheim, *op.cit.*, I, 250; Paasivirta, *Suomi*, p. 123.

[80] Paasivirta, *Suomi*, p. 124.

[81] C. Jay Smith, Jr., "Russia and the Origins of the Finnish Civil War of 1918," *The American Slavic and East European Review*, December 1955, p. 501. This erroneous view is also a major theme of his book, *Finland and the Russian Revolution, 1917-1922* (Athens: University of Georgia Press, 1958). For L. A. Puntila, too, the domestic causes of the Finnish revolution are overshadowed by the Russian factor. He boldly asserts in *Neljän vuosikymmenen takaa*, p. 17, that the events of 1917-1918 would hardly have led to armed conflict if 40,000 Russian troops had not been on Finnish soil.

[82] Kuusinen and Sirola, *Suomen*, p. 121; Yrjö Sirola, in *Viesti*, August 3, 1918, p. 2.

[83] Sirola, in *Viesti*, August 3, 1918, p. 2; Sirola, in *ibid.*, February 24, 1920, p. 94.

on the eastern front had failed to carry out the plans which he had made with representatives of the *Obkom* of the Army, Fleet, and Workers of Finland. In order to avoid future disappointments based on illusions about Russian aid, he considered it imperative to ascertain just how far Russian troops in Finland would go in support of the Finnish Reds.[84] M. S. Svechnikov, commander of Russian forces in western Finland and later appointed commander of all Russian volunteers in Finland's Civil War by the military section of the *Obkom*, described the situation eloquently when he wrote of the attitude which prevailed among Russian forces under his command in Tampere:

> Voices were raised against interference in the Civil War. This was the attitude of the majority of those in the Tampere garrison. It was especially dangerous due to the fact that throughout their stay in Finland representatives of the Russian army had always emphasized in assemblies, meetings, manifestoes, etc., their solidarity with the Finnish workers and had promised to support them when the critical moment should come.[85]

In the fall of 1917 a member of the Finnish Social Democratic party executive committee had warned that it was one thing to deliver ceremonial speeches about international solidarity, but another to fight and suffer.[86]

[84] Ali Aaltonen, in *Vapaussodan arkisto* I A 1 a :-Sisäasiain osasto: "Yleinen tilanne." Aaltonen, a former lieutenant in the Tsarist army and a participant in the Russo-Japanese War, was one of the few Finnish Reds with military training.

[85] M. S. Svechnikov, *Revoliutsiia i grazhdanskaia voina v Finliandii 1917-1918 gody* (Moscow-Petrograd: Gosudarstvennoe izdatel'stvo, 1923), pp. 49, 61, 72.

[86] Karl Wiik, cited in *Suomen sosialidemokraattisen puolueen*

Svechnikov has written that Russian troops in Finland were close to a state of complete demoralization and that they had no desire to fight the White Guard.[87] Degeneration among Russian forces had reached such serious proportions that the Soviet government found it necessary to send to Finland a regiment of disciplined Lithuanians to control the anarchist elements in the Russian army.[88] White historians refer to the lack of discipline among Russian troops as complete, and they acknowledge that most of the soldiers adopted a totally indifferent attitude toward the war in Finland. These historians hasten to add, however, that the old demoralized Russian army was replaced by a volunteer force fighting for a revolutionary ideal. The bourgeois War of Independence thus becomes a war against Russian volunteer forces.[89] But this claim is weakened by Svechnikov, who as leader of the volunteers and assistant to the commander of the Finnish Red Guard was particularly well qualified on the subject. He has written that for

kymmenennen, p. 26. Wiik, in *Suomen Sosialidemokraatti*, February 19, 1928, p. 9, states that Stalin's speech to the November 1917 congress of the Finnish Social Democratic Party, as well as speeches by other Russians on different occasions, did not influence the real party leaders. The Finnish masses, however, were not immune. Russian promises of aid and declarations of solidarity undoubtedly influenced the course of events in 1917-1918, although the impact of this propaganda was perhaps strongest on bourgeois, rather than proletarian, circles. Carl Enckell, *op.cit.*, I, 266.

[87] Svechnikov, *op.cit.*, p. 44.

[88] *Suomen kansanvaltuuskunnan pöytäkirjat*, February 4, 1918, 9:30 P.M. The extent to which degeneration and indifference had penetrated the Russian army was brought out most vividly during the Civil War. It surprised both Finnish workers (Sirola, in *Viesti*, February 24, 1920, p. 94) and the bourgeoisie (Enckell, *op.cit.*, I, 266).

[89] Donner, Nurmio, Svedlin, eds., *op.cit.*, v, 23; *Suomen vapaussota*, III, 140, 144; *ibid.*, VI, 467.

purposes of defense he could use all the Russian soldiers under his command, but that in offensive operations he had at his disposal only Finnish Reds and the few Russians who stepped forward as volunteers. By the middle of March, Russian volunteers in all of Finland numbered no more than one thousand. Moreover, the order issued by the military section of the *Obkom* liquidating as of March 15 the old Russian army in Finland caused even volunteers to leave the country. The pull homeward, even among those devoted to revolution, was stronger than internationalism. The news that German troops were preparing to land in Finland and join the White forces, at the request of Finnish Activists and the White government, reduced even further the ranks of Russian volunteers.[90]

It is important to note also that the helping hand offered Finnish Reds by Russian soldiers was not always welcome. The Red Guard was badly in need of trained military leaders, but language difficulties,[91] as well as

[90] Svechnikov, *op.cit.*, pp. 71-73, 81, 91. The German Baltic Division on April 3-5 debarked in Hanko. A month earlier German troops had occupied the Åland Islands, but a disagreement between the German Foreign Office and the German military command had caused a postponement until April of the landing on the Finnish mainland. For further details on Germany's participation in the Finnish Civil War, see Yrjö Nurmio, *Suomen itsenäistyminen ja Saksa* (Porvoo: WSOY, 1957); Rintala, *Three Generations*, pp. 32-53; Paasivirta, *Suomi*, pp. 138-162. One should note that Mannerheim, in contrast to Svinhufvud's government and Finnish activists, vigorously opposed German aid.

[91] Yrjö Sirola, in *Työmies* (Sup.), August 31, 1928, p. 3; Kullervo Manner, "Suomen työväen vallankumous v. 1918," *Proletaari*, No. 1 (38), January 1928, p. 24; "Suomen työväen vallankumous v. 1918," *Kommunisti*, No. 1 (37), January 15, 1928, p. 16; "Rabochaia revoliutsiia v Finliandii v 1918 g.," *Proletarskaia revoliutsiia*, No. 8 (79), August 1928, p. 187; T. Lehen, "Suomen kansalaissodasta," *Proletaari*, No. 4 (25), April 25, 1925, p. 29; Paasivirta, *Suomi*, p. 127; Hannula, *op.cit.*, p. 105.

distrust of former Tsarist officers,[92] hindered the utilization of Russian personnel. It was, moreover, not only Russian officers who did not enjoy the confidence of Finnish workers.[93] National prejudice was strong; for many workers "a Russian was always a Russian."[94] Conflicts developed between the Finnish revolutionary government and the Russians which undoubtedly strengthened this prejudice. For example, when the Red Guard took control of the telegraph office in Helsinki, the chairman of the Helsinki Soviet of Soldiers', Sailors', and Workers' Deputies in an ultimatum to the Finnish revolutionary government demanded that Russian control over the communications center be restored. The alternative presented was a bombardment of the city by Russian ships in the harbor.[95]

Leaders of the Red Guard had counted on substantial support from Russian troops in Finland and were naturally disappointed when this aid failed to materialize. The political leaders of Finland's revolution, on the other hand, had no reason to be shaken by the indifference of Russian troops. Before the outbreak of civil war, the leaders of the Social Democratic Party had opposed

[92] Eino Rahja, "Suomen luokkasodan tappion syyt," *Kommunisti*, No. 5 (May 15), 1925, p. 224; Sirola, in *Työmies* (Sup.), August 31, 1928, p. 3; Lehen, in *Proletaari*, No. 4 (25), April 25, 1925, p. 29.

[93] Manner, in *Proletaari*, No. 1 (38), January 1928, p. 24; *Kommunisti*, No. 1 (37), January 15, 1928, p. 16; *Proletarskaia revoliutsiia*, No. 8 (79), August 1928, p. 187; Paasivirta, *Suomi*, p. 127; Hannula, *op.cit.*, p. 105.

[94] Lehen, in *Proletaari*, No. 4 (25), April 25, 1925, p. 29.

[95] *Suomen kansanvaltuuskunnan pöytäkirjat*, March 13, 1918, 8:50 P.M.; "Suomen työväen vallankumous v. 1918," *Kommunisti*, No. 1 (37), January 15, 1928, p. 14. In Russian circles the chairman of the Helsinki Soviet of Deputies, A. Sheinman, was considered a Finnophile. Idman, *Maamme*, p. 239. Sheinman was one of nine men elected in the spring of 1917 to an executive commission of the Helsinki Committee of the RSDLP (b). Roshal', *Na putiakh*, p. 103.

the use of Russian troops in Finland's internal affairs.[96] This stand was not altered even after the armed struggle had begun; the revolutionary government continued to negotiate the withdrawal of the forty thousand Russian soldiers still on Finnish soil. On January 29 Yrjö Sirola was sent to the *Obkom* with greetings from the revolutionary government, and in the discussion which followed it was brought out that the withdrawal of Russian troops would be advantageous to the new government. The Finnish peasantry would be favorably impressed and the number of mouths to be fed would be reduced.[97]

Russian troops were in Finland for the purpose of defending Petrograd against a possible German attack,[98] but in the interest of achieving an immediate peace with Germany, Lenin was willing by late February to withdraw all forces from Finland.[99] National interest dictated the policy of the Bolshevik government as well as the policy of Finland's revolutionary govern-

[96] The five radicals elected to the party executive committee on January 22—some of whom looked to Russia for aid—were leaders of the Red Guard rather than leaders of Finnish Social Democracy. Adolf Taimi, one of the five, has been described by Yrjö Sirola as a minor figure in the Finnish party. Y. S., "Kun se selkeni. Muistelma SKP:n perustamisajoilta," *Proletaari*, No. 6 (69), October 1933, p. 7.

[97] *Suomen kansanvaltuuskunnan pöytäkirjat*, January 29, 1918, midnight.

[98] Rauanheimo, "Venäläiset," pp. 168-169; Enckell, *op.cit.*, I, 64, 68, 117, 251. It is asserted in the Mannerheim version of Finland's war that since Germany had recognized Finnish independence on January 4, 1918, there was no longer any threat of a German attack on Petrograd through Finland and consequently no strategic justification for Russian forces on Finnish soil. *Suomen vapaussota*, III, 139. In view of Belgium's fate, this picture seems unrealistic; it is even rejected by the former Minister State Secretary. Enckell, *op.cit.*, I, 144.

[99] Rintala, *Three Generations*, p. 52.

ment. On March 1 a treaty between the Finnish Republic
and Soviet Russia was signed; in paragraph fourteen the
revolutionary government of Finland pledged its support for the speedy evacuation of all Russian troops.[100]
On March 3 Germany and Russia concluded the Treaty
of Brest-Litovsk, which, in article six, stipulated that
Russian troops should be withdrawn from Finland.[101]
On March 6 the revolutionary government issued an
order forbidding Finnish authorities and the Red Guard
from preventing in any way the evacuation of Russian
troops and materiel.[102] On March 11 the government
notified the city of Helsinki that the latter's financial
responsibility for the billeting of Russian troops had
ended with the signing of the Finnish-Soviet treaty.[103]
By the middle of March, several weeks before the first
decisive battles in the Finnish Civil War, the evacuation
of Russian troops was completed.[104] Only a small number

[100] Paragraph fourteen is quoted in *Kommunisti*, No. 3 (128),
March 25, 1934, p. 140, and Smirnov, *op.cit.*, p. 225. At Lenin's
insistence, the final draft of the treaty was an agreement with the
"Finnish Socialist Workers' Republic" and not, as the Finns had
wanted, with the "Finnish Republic." Edvard Gylling, "Ensimäinen
Sosialististen tasavaltain välinen sopimus," *Kommunisti*, No. 1
(37), January 15, 1928, p. 27. Gylling and Oskari Tokoi were
signatories for the Finnish government.

[101] Defending the Treaty of Brest-Litovsk against attacks from the
left opposition, Lenin is said to have argued that withdrawal of
Russian forces would aid, rather than hinder, the Finnish revolution; in battle Russian soldiers retreated in panic and even drew
with them troops of the Red Guard. T. L. [Tuure Lehén], "Suomen
luokkasodan kokemuksista," *Kommunisti*, No. 5 (130), May 23,
1934, p. 246. Article six is quoted in Rintala, *Three Generations*,
p. 52.

[102] *Suomen kansanvaltuuskunnan pöytäkirjat*, March 6, 1918,
8:00 P.M.

[103] *Vapaussodan arkisto* 166 b:-Helsingin punaiset viranomaiset—
Rahaasiain toimikunta, tulleita kirjeitä.

[104] Rintala, *Three Generations*, p. 52; Hannula, *op.cit.*, p. 106; T.

of volunteers, led by Svechnikov, remained to lend assistance to the Finnish Reds.

It is difficult to avoid the conclusion that Russia's role in the Finnish Civil War was negligible. The hands of the Bolshevik government were tied by the struggle for national survival;[105] Russian help, such as it was, came mainly in the form of arms given to the Finnish Reds.[106] Significant military aid in Finland's war came from another direction. On February 25 the main force of the German-trained Finnish Jägers returned to Finland and became indispensable leaders of the White army. A week before their arrival the Whites had received a valuable shipment of German arms, and early in April some twelve thousand German troops landed on Finnish soil. On April 13 the German Baltic Division captured Helsinki; on the following day the Whites

L., in *Kommunisti*, No. 5 (130), May 23, 1934, p. 246. The Russian fleet in Helsinki was icebound and consequently could not leave until early April. Hannula, *op.cit.*, p. 106. Article six of the Treaty of Brest-Litovsk recognized that ice might prevent an immediate evacuation of the fleet.

105 M. Maizel', *Stranitsy revoliutsionnoi istorii finliandskogo proletariata* (Leningrad: "Priboi," 1928), pp. 108-109; Svechnikov, *op.cit.*, p. 44; Juhani Paasivirta, "Sosialidemokraattinen puolue ja Suomen itsenäistyminen," in *Suomen sosialidemokraattinen työväenliike 1899-1949* (Helsinki: KK:n kirjapaino, 1949), p. 147.

106 Sirola, in *Viesti*, February 24, 1920, p. 94; Paasivirta, *Suomi*, p. 127; Enckell, *op.cit.*, I, 266. Before the outbreak of civil war in Finland, attempts by the Red Guard to obtain arms from Russian troops met with little success; even during the war Russian troops were not enthusiastic about giving weapons to the Finnish Reds. Rintala, *Three Generations*, pp. 50-51. Eino Rahja, a key figure in the Red Guard, is said to have accused Lenin of dooming the Finnish Revolution to destruction in advance. Bitterness over the failure of the Russian proletariat to aid the Finnish Reds was, moreover, fairly widespread. *Vapaus*, February 3, 1935, p. 4; Kullervo Manner, "Klassovaia voina v Finliandii," in *Finliandskaia revoliutsiia* (Moscow: Gosudarstvennoe izdatel'stvo, 1920), p. 47.

in Helsinki expressed their gratitude to General von der Goltz and his troops. One White historian has written: "All of Helsinki rejoiced and in many different ways showed boundless gratitude to her liberators."[107] One cannot say with any certainty that German aid was the decisive factor in the defeat of the Finnish Reds, but without this aid the struggle would have been longer and much more difficult.[108] With the capitulation of Helsinki, it was a short road to total defeat for the Finnish Reds. Finland's revolutionary government had moved from Helsinki east to Viipuri, but by April 25 White forces had advanced to the outskirts of that city. All hope was lost. On April 26 leaders of the Red Guard and members of the revolutionary government fled to Soviet Russia,[109] where, disheartened by military defeat and under the spell of Lenin's dynamic personality, many Finnish Social Democrats became Communists.

[107] Hannula, *op.cit.*, pp. 156-157, 247, 263. Many in England came to the conclusion that the Finnish Whites were allies of Germany. Finnish Reds, on the other hand, were viewed by some as Western oriented because of their anti-German sentiments. Paasivirta, *Suomi*, p. 164. German influence in Finland caused London to offer military assistance to the Finnish Reds. The latter, in fact, appear to have dispatched a telegram requesting aid. But the revolutionary government soon repudiated the telegram in question and categorically rejected all English assistance. *Suomen kansanvaltuuskunnan pöytäkirjat*, April 4, 1918, 6:20 P.M.; *ibid.*, April 17, 1918, 6:00 P.M.

[108] Yrjö Sirola, in *Proletarskaia revoliutsiia*, No. 8 (79), August 1928, p. 170; "Tezisy TsK KPF," *Proletarskaia revoliutsiia*, No. 8 (79), August 1928, pp. 187-188. This is, of course, an unusual admission for the party to make. Communist sources almost invariably insist that it was German aid which decided the outcome of the Finnish Civil War.

[109] *Suomen työväen vallankumous 1918: Arviota ja itsekritiikkiä* (Leningrad: Kirja, 1928), p. 193. One member of the revolutionary government, Edvard Gylling, remained behind. He had hopes, which were quickly dashed, of reaching a compromise with the bourgeois parties on the question of Finland's future. Väinö Tanner, *Kuinka se oikein tapahtui* (Helsinki: Tammi, 1957), p. 218.

CHAPTER FOUR

Formation of the Finnish Communist Party: "Left-Wing" Communism, An Infantile Disorder

FINNISH emigrants who found their way to Moscow established a club in which they began to discuss Lenin's doctrine of revolution. Organization on a broader scale was proposed by Yrjö Sirola, whose familiarity with Lenin's writings predated the outbreak of the Finnish Civil War by a month or two,[1] and in the summer of 1918 the Foreign Organization of Finnish Social Democrats (*Suomalaisten sosialidemokraattien ulkomainen järjestö*) was formed. This new organization was to further the cause of revolution (*vallankumousperujen hoito*) and direct troops of the Finnish Red Guard in Karelia. Another important task was to care for the thousands of Finnish Reds who now found themselves immigrants in the new Russia.[2] A central com-

[1] Y. S. [Yrjö Sirola], "Kun se selkeni. Muistelma SKP:n perustamisajoilta," *Proletaari*, No. 6 (69), October 1933, p. 8; *Työmies* (Sup.), November 17, 1928, p. 3.

[2] Sirola, "Kun se selkeni," pp. 8-9; L. Letonmäki, in *Punainen Karjala*, May 27, 1933, p. 3. It is difficult to determine how many Finnish Reds sought refuge in Soviet Russia. Estimates run from 4,000 [Oskari Tokoi, *Maanpakolaisen muistelmia* (Helsinki: Tammi, 1959), p. 250] to 10,000 [M. S. Svechnikov, *Revoliutsiia i grazhdanskaia voina v Finliandii 1917-1918 gody* (Moscow-Petrograd: Gosudarstvennoe izdatel'stvo, 1923), p. 104]. In "Mitä tahtoo Suomalainen Kommunistinen Puolue?" *Suomalaisten kommunistien sarja-*

81

mittee, under the chairmanship of Kullervo Manner, was set up in Moscow with a section in Petrograd.[3] For Otto Kuusinen the formation of the Foreign Organization of Finnish Social Democrats was not, however, enough. Kuusinen, whose introduction to Leninism came in April 1918 when he read *State and Revolution*,[4] urged the formation of a Communist party.[5]

On August 25, 1918, a convention of some 100 to 150 *(toista sataa)* Finnish Socialists, called together by the central committee of the Foreign Organization of Finnish Social Democrats,[6] opened in Moscow. Debate centered around platforms submitted to the convention by groups in Moscow and Petrograd. The position of the Moscow group was succinctly expressed in two sentences of the draft proposal, in essence Kuusinen's proposal, put forth by the program committee of the Moscow section of the Foreign Organization central committee: *"The workers can conquer the bourgeoisie only by using violence*. Victory cannot be achieved through a struggle in parliament or the labor unions, nor through activity within the cooperative movement." The Petrograd group supported proletarian revolution,

julkaisu, No. 5 (Pietari: 1918), p. 68, the number of Finnish refugees in Petrograd, some of whom later returned to Finland, is put at 6,000 in the spring of 1918.

[3] "Mitä tahtoo," p. 60; Letonmäki, in *Punainen Karjala*, May 27, 1933, p. 3; Y. S., in *Proletaari*, No. 3-4 (49-50), October-November 1930, p. 42. Tokoi, *op.cit.*, p. 223, states that the central committee of the Foreign Organization of Finnish Social Democrats included, in addition to Manner, only four men: Otto Kuusinen, L. Letonmäki, Oskari Tokoi, and Matti Turkia. According to Letonmäki, in *Punainen Karjala*, May 27, 1933, p. 4, Sirola was also a member of the central committee.

[4] "Mitä tahtoo," p. 5.

[5] Y. S., in *Proletaari*, No. 6 (69), October 1933, p. 9.

[6] *Kumous*, No. 7 (September 7, 1918), p. 69.

but at the same time explained that "it is necessary at present for the laborers to engage in parliamentary, trade union, cooperative, municipal, and other activities."[7] The Petrograd Finns approved of the points in the Moscow draft calling for armed revolution and a dictatorship of the proletariat, but since it was uncertain as to when revolution would come—it might take many years—they considered practical work a necessity.[8] On August 29, after five days of debate, ballots were cast. Seventy-four delegates voted for the Moscow theses; sixteen voted in favor of sending them to committee; four abstained.[9] The majority of those who voted against the theses were trade union men, the most notable of whom was J. Lumivuokko.[10] Some of the

[7] "Mitä tahtoo," pp. 3-4, 13, 42; Juhani Paasivirta, *Suomi vuonna 1918* (Porvoo: WSOY, 1957), pp. 313-314. The most notable of the Petrograd group was Edvard Valpas. For some reason he was not present at the convention. Anton Huotari, in *Syyttäjistön arkisto*: Sosialidemokraattiseen puolueeseen kuuluvia, vangittuja kansanedustajia koskevia kuulustelu pöytäkirjoja (Valtionarkisto); Rudolf Lahti's unpublished manuscript on the founding congress of the Finnish Communist Party. Both Huotari and Lahti were present at the convention.

[8] *Viesti*, October 19, 1918, p. 5.

[9] "Mitä tahtoo," p. 22.

[10] Toivo Antikainen, in T. Antikainen, ed., *SKP:n taistelun tieltä: Muistelmia, kuvauksia ja aineistoa SKP:n 15-vuotistaipaleelta* (Leningrad: Kirja, 1934), p. 10; *Punainen Karjala*, March 29, 1934, p. 4; *Vapaus*, April 1, 1934, p. 4; J. K. Lehtinen, "Toveri J. Lumivuokko 50-vuotias," *Kommunisti*, April 23, 1934, No. 4 (129), p. 198; Huotari, *op.cit.*; E. K. Louhikko, *Teimme vallankumousta* (Helsinki: OY Suomen Kirja, 1943), p. 190. Lauri Sulander, who accompanied Toivo Antikainen to the Moscow convention from Petrograd, has stated that a number of trade union men were excluded from the convention even before the vote was taken. Lauri Sulander to author, January 11, 1963. This is substantiated by Huotari, *op.cit.*, and the manuscript written by Rudolf Lahti. Lahti, one of those who was prevented from reentering the meeting room, told Finnish police that he was present at the conven-

sixteen, such as Lumivuokko, later became Communists, although most remained "enemies of Communism."[11] The conference expelled those who had voted against the Moscow theses,[12] and on August 29 it was announced that a Finnish Communist Party had been formed.[13]

The convention of Finnish Socialists continued as a congress of Finnish Communists. The congress, whose co-chairmen were Yrjö Sirola and Kullervo Manner, met for eight days and elected the first central committee of the Finnish Communist Party: Yrjö Sirola (chairman),[14] Otto Kuusinen, Lauri Letonmäki, K. M. Evä, and Jukka Rahja.[15] Soon added to the central committee through

---

tion for four and one-half days (Valtionarkisto: KKO 455 SD 1920, p. 3 of Lahti's account), and so it is evident that the group was excluded on the day of the crucial vote. According to Lahti and Huotari, there were between ten and fifteen (*toista kymmentä*) people in the group.

[11] Iurii Sirola, *Kommunisticheskaia partiia Finliandii* (Moscow-Leningrad: Moskovskii Rabochii, 1929), p. 34. Lumivuokko's conversion came quickly; at the Second Congress of the Finnish Communist Party he was elected to the central committee. E. K. Louhikko, on the other hand, traveled in the opposite direction. He became an important figure in the Social Democratic wing of the Finnish trade union movement. In his memoirs Louhikko states that he was one of the sixteen who voted against Kuusinen's theses. Louhikko, *op.cit.*, pp. 187-188.

[12] Huotari, *op.cit.*; *Bol'shaia sovetskaia entsiklopediia*, Vol. LVII (Moscow: Ogiz, 1936), p. 602.

[13] "Suomen Kommunistinen Puolue 15 vuotta," *Kommunisti*, No. 13 (121), August 25, 1933, p. 579.

[14] Elli Stenberg, "Yrjö Sirola," in *Suomalaisia sosialisteja*, Vol. III (Helsinki: Työväen Sivistysliitto, 1947), p. 138; Valtionarkisto: KKO 455 SD 1920, p. 17 of J. A. Lehtosaari's interrogation papers. Lehtosaari later denied (pp. 131-132) saying that Sirola had been elected chairman.

[15] "Mitä tahtoo," pp. 23, 27; T. Lehén, in *Kipinästä tuli syttyi* (Helsinki: Yhteistyön kirjapaino, 1958), p. 11. Lehén was present at the founding congress of the Finnish Communist Party. Lehén to author, January 11, 1963.

cooption were Kullervo Manner and Eino Rahja.[16] Petrograd was designated the center of operations,[17] and within half a year the party had established about twenty-five Communist organizations (clubs) among Finnish workers and peasants in Soviet Russia.[18] As is evident from the first and third of the five theses adopted on August 29, the new party advocated revolution and a dictatorship of the proletariat:

1. The workers must energetically prepare for armed revolution and not try to return to the pre-revolutionary stand of Finnish labor organizations, namely, the old parliamentary, trade union, and co-operative struggle. . . .

3. The working class must take all power into its hands by revolution and must establish an iron dictatorship of the proletariat. . . .[19]

An editorial which appeared shortly after the party congress in a newspaper published by the central committee stated that the workers in Finland were full of bitterness, hate, and a desire for revenge. They were only

[16] Louhikko, *op.cit.*, p. 190. This is substantiated by J. A. Lehtosaari's interrogation papers, *op.cit.*, p. 18.

[17] Yrjö Sirola, in *Työmies* (Sup.), September 1, 1928, p. 3; Sirola, in *Pervyi kongress kommunisticheskogo internatsionala. Protokoly zasedanii v Moskve so 2 po 19 marta 1919 goda* (Petrograd: Izdatel'stvo Kommunisticheskogo internatsionala, 1921), p. 31; O. W. Kuusinen, *Suuri vuosisatamme* (Helsinki: Yhteistyön kirjapaino, 1961), p. 77.

[18] Sirola, in *Pervyi kongress*, p. 31. In the summer of 1919 many of the organizations ended their activities as clubs and became Finnish-language collectives. They were registered in the Russian Communist Party and enjoyed a status identical to that of the Russian-language collectives. *Vapaus*, January 19, 1921, p. 2. By early 1923 there were 1067 Finnish-language party members, from 93 collectives, in the Russian Communist Party. *Vapaus*, April 24, 1923, p. 4.

[19] "Mitä tahtoo," p. 21.

85

waiting for a new armed struggle and a new, shining hour of revolution.[20] Kuusinen wrote that in preparation for the imminent revolution the party's task was to establish in Finland, with haste, secret revolutionary organizations.[21] A trained officer corps, noticeably absent among Red forces during the Finnish Civil War, was now under rapid development. In the summer of 1918 university students proficient in Russian were put through courses for Russian officers, and by the end of the year Finnish-language courses, first under the direction of Eino Rahja and then his brother Jukka, were begun. A high point was reached in the fall of 1920 with the formation of the Finnish Section of the Petrograd Infantry School.[22]

It was not difficult to anticipate the position which the Finnish Communist Party would take with respect to the March 1919 parliamentary election in Finland. As if to clear up any misunderstanding that might exist, the

[20] *Vapaus*, October 15, 1918, p. 1.

[21] O. V. Kuusinen, "Kuntoon salaiset järjestöt Suomessa!," *Kumous*, No. 21-24 (January 18, 1919), pp. 79, 84.

[22] In May 1921 the Petrograd Infantry School was split into a Petrograd Infantry School and an International Military School. The latter had many national sections, one of the most notable being the Finnish section. In August 1926 the International Military School ended operations; most of its students and staff transferred to the Leningrad Infantry School. From 1920 until 1926 Kustaa Rovio was in charge of all Finns who received military training in Leningrad. It is interesting to note that these Finns helped to put down the Kronstadt Rebellion; they also played an important role in the 1922 struggle in Soviet Karelia against Finnish White forces. *Vapaus*, December 13, 1919, p. 1; *ibid.*, December 13, 1923, p. 4; *ibid.*, December 8, 1923, pp. 1-3; *ibid.*, December 22, 1920, p. 2; Toivo Antikainen, "Suomalaiset vallankumoukselliset Venäjän kansalaissodassa," *Kommunisti*, No. 9-10 (33-34), September-October 1927, pp. 434-435; *Vapaus*, December 11, 1928, p. 3; *Punainen Karjala*, July 6, 1933, p. 2; *Kymmenen vuotta Neuvosto-Karjalaa 1920-1930* (Petroskoi: AKSNT:n Toimeenpaneva Keskuskomitea, 1933), p. 146.

chairman of the party wrote in January 1919: "Finally —firstly and lastly—one must remember that elections only dupe the workers, causing them to expect something which will not come: causing them to expect from parliamentarism, which *is not able* to solve the questions of the time, at least relief."[23] At the First Conference of the Finnish Communist Party, held in February, 1919, a declaration prepared by Kuusinen and called the "Communist Ballot" (*Kommunistinen vaalilippu*) was approved. The desired response to the election was spelled out in detail for all Finnish workers. Parliamentary elections were of some value when capitalism was so very strong, but now the situation is different: "*The international revolution of the proletariat has begun*—this is a fact already recognized by everyone."[24] Accepting the validity of this assumption, Finnish emigrants supported with enthusiasm the establishment of a Communist International. Yrjö Sirola had been present at a select gathering in the Kremlin early in January 1919 where the decision was made to urge the formation of a Third International. On behalf of the Finnish Communist Party central committee, Sirola signed the invitation which was broadcast to the world late in January; and at the First Congress of the Comintern he became a member of the executive committee.[25]

[23] Yrjö Sirola, in *Vapaus*, January 18, 1919, p. 2.

[24] *Suomen kommunistinen puolue. Puoluekokousten, konferenssien ja keskuskomitean plenumien päätöksiä*, Vol. 1 (Leningrad: Kirja, 1935), pp. 20, 497; Yrjö Sirola, in *Viesti*, No. 6 (June 24), 1920, p. 271; "Kommunistinen vaalilippu," in *Vapaus*, February 20, 1919, p. 2.

[25] Edward Hallett Carr, *The Bolshevik Revolution 1917-1923*, Vol. III (New York: The Macmillan Company, 1953), pp. 118-119; Jane Degras, ed., *The Communist International, 1919-1943. Documents*, Vol. 1 (London: Oxford University Press, 1956), pp. 5, 453;

The erroneous conviction that world revolution was imminent had captivated the imagination of Finnish emigrants. Workers in Finland, however, were not under the same spell. They turned a deaf ear to the advice that they boycott the parliamentary election. Communists had overestimated the strength of revolutionary forces in Finland.[26]

In September 1919 delegates to the Second Congress of the Finnish Communist Party gathered in Petrograd.[27] At this congress it was decided to turn over to Russian authorities all establishments (factories, plants, etc.) hitherto managed by the central committee of the Finnish Communist Party, in order to enable the central committee to give its undivided attention to activity in Finland.[28] Finnish emigrants continued to believe that Finland was ripe for revolution. The legacy of the Civil War did, in fact, seem to support this conclusion. Reds and Whites alike had suffered during the war, but for the former the worst came later. Between seventy thousand and eighty thousand Reds had been imprisoned,[29] and of that number some ten thousand

Työmies (Sup.), April 5, 1936, p. 1; *Vapaus*, March 20, 1936, p. 2. The quota set for delegates attending the First Congress of the Comintern from a large country was five. It would, therefore, appear that Finland was in a special category. Her five representatives, full delegates with voting rights, were Yrjö Sirola, Otto Kuusinen, Kullervo Manner, Eino Rahja, and Jukka Rahja. A. Tivel' and M. Kheimo, eds., *10 let Kominterna v resheniiakh i tsifrakh* (Moscow-Leningrad: Gosudarstvennoe izdatel'stvo, 1929), p. 26; *Pervyi kongress*, p. 5.

[26] Introduction by Yrjö Sirola to M. Maizel', *Stranitsy revoliutsionnoi istorii finliandskogo proletariata* (Leningrad: Priboi, 1928), pp. 144-145; *SKP taistelujen tiellä*, Vol. IV (Helsinki: Yhteistyön kirjapaino, 1948), p. 33.

[27] *Vapaus*, September 22, 1919, p. 2; Louhikko, *op.cit.*, p. 209.

[28] *Vapaus*, September 1, 1925, p. 3.

[29] Maizel', *op.cit.*, p. 128; R. H. Oittinen *Työväenkysymys ja*

died. Red casualties in prison were roughly triple what they were in battle.[30] The ground had thus been cultivated for political radicalism in Finland during the 1920s. In the words of a former Finnish Communist, "The Civil War of 1918 and the subsequent reign of terror did more to open the way to Communism in Finland than all other factors put together."[31] Moreover, Finnish emigrants who led the Finnish Communist Party—Kuusinen, Sirola, and Manner—enjoyed a reputation which still carried weight with workers in Finland,[32] and hopes of the Finnish Communists were un-

---

työväenliike Suomessa (Helsinki: Tammi, 1954), p. 158; Paasivirta, *Suomi*, p. 291; Marvin Rintala, *Three Generations: The Extreme Right Wing in Finnish Politics* (Bloomington: Indiana University Press, 1962), p. 26.

[30] *Suomen vapaussota vuonna 1918*, Vol. vi (Helsinki: Otava, 1925), p. 475n; J. O. Hannula, *Suomen vapaussodan historia* (Porvoo: WSOY, 1956), p. 304; Rintala, *op.cit.*, p. 26. Maizel', *op.cit.*, p. 128, states that 15,000 Reds died as a result of prison conditions. Paasivirta, *Suomi*, p. 228, states that about 20,000 Reds died after the war. Official Social Democratic sources estimate that the figure is between 8,370 and 15,000. Cited by Väinö Tanner, *Kuinka se oikein tapahtui* (Helsinki: Tammi, 1957), p. 357. According to the statistics compiled by the Social Democratic Party, the Reds lost 3,580 men in battle.

[31] Arvo Tuominen, "The Northern Countries and Communism," *The Norseman*, Vol. xii, No. 4 (July-August 1954), p. 219. The strength of Finnish Communism today is partially explained by the legacy of civil war. For a discussion of this point, see Marvin Rintala, "The Problem of Generations in Finnish Communism," *The American Slavic and East European Review*, Vol. xvii, No. 2 (April 1958), pp. 190-202; Hannu Soikkanen, "Sosiaalidemokraatti vai kommunisti?" *Suomalainen Suomi*, March 1961, pp. 147-152; Hannu Soikkanen, "Työväenliikkeen jakautumisonglema itsenäisyyden alkuvuosina," *Turun Historiallisen Yhdistyksen julkaisu*, Vol. xv, pp. 261-289; Jaakko Nousiainen, *Kommunismi Kuopion läänissä* (Joensuu: Pohjois-Karjalan kirjapaino OY, 1956). A leading Finnish sociologist disagrees with those who assume that the Civil War still has a great influence on voting behavior. Erik Allardt, "Traditional and Emerging Radicalism," draft, p. 30.

[32] Oittinen, *op.cit.*, p. 179.

doubtedly high. At the second party congress a new central committee was elected to advance the cause of proletarian revolution: Sirola and V. Jokinen (chairmen), K. M. Evä (secretary), Kuusinen, Manner, L. Letonmäki, J. Lumivuokko, Eino Rahja, and J. Kohonen.[33]

The Communist bid for control over labor in Finland did not go unchallenged. Right-wing, revisionist Socialists undertook immediately following the Civil War the resurrection of the once powerful but now humbled Finnish Social Democratic Party.[34] At this time Väinö Tanner became a political figure of national importance,[35] focusing the attention of Finnish Social Democracy on everyday, practical matters.[36] For Tanner,

[33] *Vapaus*, September 13, 1919, p. 1.

[34] Soikkanen, "Työväenliikkeen," p. 268. Before the Civil War the Social Democratic Party had been the largest group in Parliament, but on May 15, 1918, when Parliament again met, only one delegate (Matti Paasivuori) was there to represent the large Socialist group. Tanner, in *Suomen sosialidemokraattinen työväenliike 1899-1949* (Helsinki: KK:n kirjapaino, 1949), p. 151.

[35] Väinö Leskinen has noted that his mentor, Tanner, received his initial schooling in Social Democracy from the revisionist wing of the Finnish Social Democratic Party. Leskinen, in Olli Laitinen and Matti Nieminen, eds., *Kuin kallioon hakattu* (Helsinki: KK:n kirjapaino, 1956), p. 94.

[36] Marvin Rintala, "Väinö Tanner in Finnish Politics," *The American Slavic and East European Review*, Vol. xx, No. 1 (February 1961), p. 88; R. H. Oittinen, in *K.-A. Fagerholm, mies ja työkenttä—mannen och verket* (Helsinki: Oy Tilgmann, 1961), p. 8. This emphasis on practical matters was not merely a transitory phase in Tanner's political development. In 1929, for example, he could see the existence of only two tactics for European Social Democracy: a radical tactic leading to civil war, or a tactic which emphasized practical work. Väinö Tanner, "Onko puolueessamme eri suuntia?" in *Suomen Sosialidemokraatti*, November 7, 1929, p. 5; Tanner, in *ibid.*, November 21, 1929, pp. 4-5. Väinö Hupli, an important figure in the 1918-1920 reconstruction of the Social Democratic Party, later criticized the party for going too far in the field of practical endeavor. He added that the party had a good organization (the "how") but lacked spirit (the "why"). He

elected chairman of the Social Democratic Party executive committee in December 1918, the real task of Finnish Social Democracy was to split the bourgeoisie and further the development of a radical bourgeois group.[37]

The rebirth of the Finnish Social Democratic Party, and particularly the support which it received in the 1919 parliamentary election, did not go unnoticed in Petrograd. Early in May 1919 it was proposed at a meeting of the Finnish Communist central committee that members of the committee be placed permanently in Finland in order to direct the organization's underground work. Right-wing Social Democrats in Finland represented a danger to the Communist Party, and it was imperative that men be sent to Helsinki to strengthen the weak local leadership.[38] The decision was to send Otto Kuusinen, at that time vice-commissar of the Red officer school for Finnish emigrants, and on May 27, 1919, he departed from Petrograd[39] to cut the

---

advocated more theory and a turn to the left in party policy. Väinö Hupli, "Mitä meiltä puuttuu," in *ibid.*, March 24, 1926, p. 2.

[37] Tanner, in *Suomen sosialidemokraattisen puolueen kahdennentoista edustajakokouksen pöytäkirja* (Helsinki: Sosialidemokraattinen puoluetoimikunta, 1920), pp. 94-95. Tanner never really abandoned this task, a fact which, in 1929, brought him into conflict with an opposition group led by the party secretary, Karl Wiik. In Wiik's view Tanner still appeared to pin his hopes on bourgeois liberalism, which, for the most part, no longer existed. Karl Wiik, in *Suomen Sosialidemokraatti*, November 21, 1929, p. 5; Wiik, in *ibid.*, November 10, 1929, p. 6.

[38] Kuusinen, *Suuri*, pp. 77-79; J. Lehtosaari, in Antikainen, ed., *op.cit.*, p. 45.

[39] Kuusinen, *Suuri*, pp. 79, 81; Antikainen, ed., *op.cit.*, p. 45; *Vapaus*, February 21, 1920, p. 2; *Suomen kommunistinen puolue*, p. 497; Yrjö Sirola, in *Työmies* (Sup.), September 1, 1928, p. 3; Kuusinen, in *Viesti*, No. 3 (March 24), 1920, pp. 136-137. According to Kuusinen, he was accompanied to Finland by J. Lehtosaari. In late 1919 or early 1920 two members of the central committee, L. Letonmäki and J. Lumivuokko, joined Kuusinen. While in Fin-

91

ground out from under Tanner's policy of class conciliation and to prepare a revolution of the proletariat.[40]

Due to Kuusinen's efforts *Sosialistinen Aikakauslehti*, a journal containing articles written by Communists and left-wing Socialists, began to appear soon after his arrival in Finland.[41] In the first issue, writing under a pseudonym, Kuusinen set forth the party line: "There was a time when the Finnish proletariat had to seek the ABC's of political freedom through a constitution and the vote. Such methods of action are, however, no longer of any use. The working class will no longer move forward by voting."[42] In the fall Kuusinen attacked left Socialists in Finland for not demanding that the parliamentary system be abolished; their tolerance smacked of support for bourgeois democracy. Kuusinen was only

---

land illegally, Letonmäki wrote under the initials "L. M." and Lumivuokko under the pseudonym "P. Hauli." Kuusinen wrote under various names: Usko Sotamies, Sukulainen, Ilmari V., and others. Antikainen, ed., *op.cit.*, pp. 80, 110, 114, 226.

[40] K. M. [Kullervo Manner], in *Vapaus*, February 21, 1920, p. 2. Kuusinen made it clear to Finnish workers what he meant by proletarian revolution: "A revolution of the proletariat means, of course, that the proletariat—disregarding existing law—rises to the revolutionary struggle, overthrows the bourgeoisie, abolishes the legal system of the bourgeoisie, and takes power into its own hands." O. W. Kuusinen, "Suomen Sosialidemokratian johtajille," *Sosialistinen Aikakauslehti*, April 16, 1920, p. 98. Lehtosaari, in Antikainen, ed., *op.cit.*, p. 45, states that military action in Soviet Karelia by Finnish Whites was also a factor which caused the central committee to send Kuusinen to Finland.

[41] Arvo Tuominen, *Sirpin ja vasaran tie* (Helsinki: Tammi, 1957), pp. 117, 130; *SKP taistelujen tiellä*, Vol. vii (Helsinki: Yhteistyön kirjapaino, 1951), p. 63; Jaakko Kivi to author, April 26, 1962. Kivi was an important figure in the Communist movement during the 1920s.

[42] Usko Sotamies, "Valkoinen hallitusmuoto," *Sosialistinen Aikakauslehti*, No. 1 (August 1), 1919, p. 4.

repeating the view expressed by the Finnish Communist Party second congress: "If the workers send representatives to Parliament, they must devote all their energy to bringing about its complete destruction."[43]

After half a year in Finland Kuusinen began to see that the workers would not follow the party line. If he continued to support the policies advocated in Petrograd, he would remain a general without troops. In December 1919 a significant turn of events occurred, in the form of a letter to the journal *Sosialistinen Aikakauslehti*: "*O. W. Kuusinen* at one time was badly poisoned by parliamentarism; then after he went to Russia following the 1918 revolution he became a left Communist; but now he has achieved an intellectual balance. This intellectual balance makes him most thorough, the most clearheaded, and the most versatile scientific interpreter of the Finnish labor movement."[44] The issues of immediate interest to Finnish workers concerned party and trade union activity. Kuusinen now urged workers to join the Social Democratic Party and the Trade Union Organization in order to wrest them from the

[43] Usko Sotamies, "Kirje vasemmistososialismista ja kommunismista," *Sosialistinen Aikakauslehti*, No. 6 (October 16), 1919, pp. 83-84; *Viesti*, November 22, 1919, p. 1.

[44] *Sosialistinen Aikakauslehti*, December 16, 1919, p. 152. The letter is dated November 30 and is signed by "——nen." This shift in tactics was to cause a serious breach within the central committee of the party. Arvo Tuominen in *Sirpin*, p. 121, states that a "civil war" in the party began as early as the summer of 1919. There is no evidence, however, to support such an assertion. An open break between the Kuusinen and Manner groups does not appear to have occurred until the following spring; an unbiased account of the nature of the struggle differs considerably from the picture presented by Tuominen in his memoirs. Although an important source of information, Tuominen's memoirs are such a mixture of fiction and fact that one must avoid accepting at face value the material which he presents.

control of Tanner and his supporters.[45] A test of forces between right- and left-wing Socialists, the latter being supported by the Finnish underground apparatus of the Finnish Communist Party,[46] occurred at the December 1919 congress of the Finnish Social Democratic Party.

Debate at the Social Democratic congress was dominated by sharp exchanges between the right and left, little significance being attached by either extreme to the views of a small center group. The left wing thought that world revolution was just around the corner and was in favor of joining the Comintern. Eino Pekkala summed up the position of this group when he stated: "In other words, we are living in a revolutionary period, at a time when the realization of Socialism is no longer a theoretical question, as it has been up to now, but rather a stern reality." In the eyes of Sulo Vuolijoki, revolution in England was the key to world revolution; some sort of revolution would occur there within a year.[47]

Right-wing Social Democrats interpreted the congress solely in terms of a struggle between the forces of Communism and the forces of Social Democracy.[48] Im-

[45] Tuominen, *Sirpin*, pp. 119, 129.

[46] *Ibid.*, pp. 130, 132.

[47] *Suomen sosialidemokraattisen puolueen kahdennentoista*, pp. 20, 128, 135-136, 236-237.

[48] This was made particularly clear in a speech delivered by Väinö Hupli on the question of whether the Finnish Social Democratic Party should remain in the Second International or join the Comintern. Hupli supported membership in the Second International, stating that the congress should make clear on this issue whether the party was behind Communism or Social Democracy. *Ibid.*, p. 163. K. H. Wiik, on the other hand, noted that the International question was not a black and white issue of Communism or Social Democracy. Due to the shortcomings of the Second International, a Social Democrat could be opposed to membership in that organization. *Ibid.*, p. 167.

mediately after the left had succeeded in electing Kaarlo Luoto as third chairman of the congress, Taavi Tainio, party secretary, announced that he would propose Luoto's expulsion from the Social Democratic Party as soon as Luoto stepped to the rostrum to assume his duties as third chairman. The congress noted Luoto's criminal past and record of moral turpitude, but for Tainio this was not the main issue. His attention was focused upon attacks against the Social Democratic Party made in articles which had been appearing in Kuopio, "Finland's Moscow,"[49] in a newspaper edited by Luoto. The left saw in Tainio's proposal to expel Luoto from the Social Democratic Party an attempt to purge the party of left elements in general. There were, moreover, indications that this idea was not entirely foreign to the right wing at the congress. J. F. Aalto, a leading figure in the center group, announced to the congress that he had heard many say that by expelling Luoto from the party they hoped to cause members of the extreme left to leave the congress.[50]

The actions of the center group at the congress were based on the assumption that far from all workers who supported Communism and "leftism" were Communists; many were considered honest Social Democrats who should not be driven into the arms of Communism.[51]

[49] Nousiainen, *op.cit.*, p. 63; Tuominen, *Sirpin*, p. 215.

[50] *Suomen sosialidemokraattisen puolueen kahdennentoista*, pp. 24, 58, 70, 78, 80, 176, 240-241. Tainio proposed that the congress also expel Ivar Lassy from party membership because of the radical nature of the journal *Sosialistinen Aikakauslehti*.

[51] Ernst Lähde, in *Suomen Sosialidemokraatti*, November 14, 1929, p. 6. Lähde was the most outspoken member of the center group at the 1919 Social Democratic Party congress, although by 1926 he had become a vigorous proponent of right-wing Socialism in both party and trade union affairs.

The antiparliamentarism of the left was attacked, but it was considered in part a product of the soft, right-wing stand of the party's major newspaper.[52] Those at the congress who took a middle of the road position found it necessary to warn against turning the Social Democratic Party into what the left charged it already was, a bourgeois reform party.[53] Members of the center group did not want to see included in the resolutions of the congress points which could be used as weapons against the party. They opposed, in particular, any decision by the congress which would enable Social Democrats to enter a coalition government.[54] In view of the recent Civil War it was self-evident that a coalition government including Social Democrats and members of the bourgeoisie would not materialize for years.[55] The center

[52] J. F. Aalto, in *Suomen sosialidemokraattisen puolueen kahdennentoista*, p. 184. The attitude of the left toward parliamentarism was summed up by Sulo Vuolijoki a month before the Social Democratic congress. He stated that the left was not against parliamentary means, but that Parliament should be used only when times are difficult. "We never consider Parliament an aim in itself; it is only one means of achieving our objective." S. W., in *Sosialistinen Aikakauslehti*, November 1, 1919, p. 100.

[53] J. F. Aalto, in *Suomen sosialidemokraattisen puolueen kahdennentoista*, p. 140; Eino Pekkala, in *ibid.*, p. 128. When Social Democrats entered a cabinet for the first time in the post-Civil War period, in December 1926, Väinö Tanner described the program of his minority government as "a radical bourgeois program." *Valtiopäivät 1926 pöytäkirjat*, Vol. II (Helsinki: Valtioneuvooston kirjapaino, 1927), p. 2083. J. H. Vennola and K. H. Wiik noted that Tanner's government had presented to Parliament a reform program, not a Socialist program. *Ibid.*, pp. 2034, 2040.

[54] Lähde, in *Suomen Sosialidemokraatti*, November 14, 1929, p. 6; *Suomen sosialidemokraattisen puolueen kahdennentoista*, pp. 140-141, 217-218, 226. For thirteen years, from 1906 to 1919, Social Democrats were prohibited from entering a Cabinet unless specifically authorized to do so by a party congress.

[55] When Väinö Tanner formed a minority Social Democratic government in 1926, a leading bourgeois member of Parliament

group could see only two immediate results, both negative, from a decision by the congress to sanction the participation of Social Democrats in a coalition government: a split within the Social Democratic Party would occur,[56] and Communists would be given an opportunity to accuse the party of supporting, at least in principle, ministerial socialism.[57]

The outcome of the Social Democratic Party congress was a victory for the right wing. The congress voted to expel Kaarlo Luoto from the party,[58] to remain a member of the Second International,[59] and to permit Social Democrats under certain conditions to enter a coalition government.[60] The triumphant climax came

---

stated that Parliament's tolerance of this government meant that the Civil War wounds had at least to a degree healed. J. H. Vennola, in *Valtiopäivät 1926*, II, 2034. It was not until 1937, however, that Social Democrats and members of the bourgeoisie joined together in a coalition government.

[56] Ernst Lähde and Otto Toivonen, in *Suomen sosialidemokraattisen puolueen kahdennentoista*, pp. 217-218. K. H. Wiik agreed with Lähde that a split within the party might develop; Wiik expressed regret that the executive committee of the party had decided to raise the government question at the party congress. *Ibid.*, p. 228.

[57] Lähde, in *Suomen Sosialidemokraatti*, November 14, 1929, p. 6. The question of ministerial socialism was one issue involved in a split within the Social Democratic Party in the late 1920s. *Suomen Sosialidemokraatti*, February 27, 1928, p. 2.

[58] *Suomen sosialidemokraattisen puolueen kahdennentoista*, pp. 254-256. The congress decided that Ivar Lassy, on the other hand, should not be expelled. Since Lassy's transgressions were purely political, unlike those of Luoto, enough support could not be mustered to revoke his membership.

[59] *Ibid.*, pp. 236-237. The congress empowered the party executive council to review this decision after the Second International had been able to meet. The executive council was also authorized to determine what steps should be taken if a new, unifying International should be founded.

[60] *Ibid.*, pp. 215, 217, 231. One of the conditions stipulated

when Väinö Tanner was reelected chairman, and Taavi Tainio secretary, of the party executive committee. What followed was not unexpected. One third of those who were present at the congress resigned from the party.[61] Moreover, entire election district organizations left the party: Western Kuopio, Kajaani, Northern and Southern Oulu, and Southern Vaasa.[62] Eino Pekkala and Sulo Vuolijoki proceeded to form a Provisional Socialist Party Executive Committee (*Väliaikainen Sosialistinen Puoluetoimikunta*), and the party split which had been alluded to at the congress now became a reality.[63] In Tanner's view no power on earth could have prevented the split. Tainio went even further: not even God could have influenced the course of developments.[64]

---

that both the executive council of the party and the Social Democratic parliamentary group would have to support participation in such a government by a two-thirds majority. Furthermore, the bourgeoisie would first have to release all political prisoners.

[61] Karl Wiik, in *Suomen sosialidemokraattisen puoluetoimikunnan pöytäkirjat*, February 19, 1936. Väinö Tanner asserted in 1936 that all who had resigned were Communists, whereas Wiik pointed out that some had returned to the Social Democratic Party because their opinions differed from those of the Communists.

[62] Soikkanen, "Työväenliikkeen," p. 284.

[63] According to Ernst Lähde, both the right and left at the party congress were determined to split the party no matter what the cost. *Suomen Sosialidemokraatti*, November 14, 1929, p. 6. Statements by the Provisional Socialist Party Executive Committee were published in *Savon Kansa*. In March 1920 the executive council of the Social Democratic Party voted to expel from the party, in so far as they still belonged to it, members of the Provisional Committee: Sulo Vuolijoki, Eino Pekkala, Ida Kantanen, A. Raatikainen (chairman), and Tuomas Heinonen. *Suomen sosialidemokraattisen puolueneuvoston pöytäkirjat*, March 17-18, 1920, p. 12; Ilkka Hakalehto, *Suomen kommunistinen puolue ja sen vaikutus poliittiseen ja ammatilliseen työväenliikkeeseen 1918-1928* (Porvoo: WSOY, 1966), p. 155.

[64] *Suomen sosialidemokraattisen puolueneuvoston*, November 1-3, 1920, pp. 28, 40.

The Provisional Socialist Party Executive Committee called for the formation of a new radical party. At a meeting held on May 13-14, 1920, the Socialist Workers' Party of Finland (*Suomen Sosialistinen Työväenpuolue*) came into existence. A draft program prepared by the Provisional Socialist Executive Committee and Otto Kuusinen was examined and approved. The founding congress went on record as favoring membership in the Third International.[65] Intervention by Finnish authorities followed, and on May 14 police dispersed the Congress. Among those arrested were Eino Pekkala and Sulo Vuolijoki.[66] This action delayed, but did not prevent, the new party from establishing roots in Finnish society. On June 19 the Socialist Municipal Organization of Helsinki (*Helsingin Sosialistinen Kunnallisjärjestö*) decided to join the Socialist Workers' Party. Since no other organizations had joined the party, this decision meant that the Socialist Municipal Organization of Helsinki had transformed itself into the Socialist Workers' Party.[67] At the June meeting a party program was approved; all other decisions which had been made or outlined at the May congress were ratified; and an executive committee was elected. In contrast to the program adopted in May, and over the objections of Kuusinen, the new program did not commit the party to member-

---

65 *Suomen Työmies*, January 9, 1921, p. 1; *ibid.*, March 12, 1921, p. 1. Authorship of the draft program is attributed solely to Kuusinen in *Suomen kommunistinen puolue*, p. 499, and Tuominen, *Sirpin*, p. 133. Tuominen has noted elsewhere, however, that Kuusinen's draft was watered down and not accepted in its original form. Antikainen, ed., *op.cit.*, p. 79.

66 Tuominen, *Sirpin*, p. 134; *Suomen kommunistinen puolue*, p. 499; *Suomen Työmies*, January 9, 1921, p. 1; *Kipinästä*, p. 61.

67 *Suomen Työmies*, January 9, 1921, p. 1. It was the Socialist Municipal Organization of Helsinki which had set up the Provisional Socialist Party Executive Committee.

ship in the Comintern.[68] The police consequently refrained from active intervention, and the party was permitted to vie with the Social Democratic Party for the loyalty of Finnish Workers. Arvo Tuominen, soon to be elected secretary of the Socialist Workers' Party, states that within only a few months party membership soared to about 25,000.[69]

As membership in the Socialist Workers' Party rose impressively, membership in the Social Democratic Party plummeted. It is, however, incorrect to assume, as does Arvo Tuominen, that the total membership of the Socialist Workers' Party came from the ranks of the Social Democratic Party.[70] The decline in the Social Democratic Party, from 67,022 to 51,376 members,[71]

[68] Tuominen, *Sirpin,* pp. 134-135.

[69] *Ibid.*, p. 134. At the first meeting of the executive council of the Socialist Workers' Party, December 27-28, 1920, Tuominen was elected secretary. He remained in that post until January 1922, when he was arrested.

[70] *Ibid.*, pp. 134, 136.

[71] *Statistical Picture of the Finnish Social Democratic Party and the Various Fields of Activity of the Workers' Movement* (Helsinki: Työväen kirjapaino, 1950), p. 4. The weakness of the Social Democratic Party in the 1920s is missed in one of the few works in English dealing with Communism in Finland. The reader is told that Väinö Tanner "excluded Finnish Communists from positions of executive leadership in the Social Democratic Party and steadily increased its electoral strength throughout the 1920's." James H. Billington, "Finland," in Cyril E. Black and Thomas P. Thornton, eds., *Communism and Revolution: The Strategic Uses of Political Violence* (Princeton: Princeton University Press, 1964), p. 121. A more accurate picture, supplementing the one implicit in the decline of party membership, is presented when one examines the number of seats occupied by the Social Democratic Party in Parliament and its percentage of the popular vote in the elections of 1919 (80, 38%), 1922 (53, 25.1%), 1924 (60, 29%), 1927 (60, 28.3%), and 1929 (59, 27.4%). Göran von Bonsdorff, *Suomen poliittiset puolueet* (Helsinki: Tammi, 1957), pp. 28, 37.

would account for barely more than one half of the figure cited by Tuominen for the Socialist Workers' Party membership. Moreover, it is not certain that all who resigned from the Social Democratic Party subsequently joined the Socialist Workers' Party. The number of resignations was, nonetheless, alarming and gave rise to the formation of a formal opposition group, the so-called Center Group (*Keskustaryhmä*), within the Social Democratic Party. J. F. Aalto, described by Väinö Tanner as the leader of the Center Group,[72] wrote in late May 1920 that many of those who were leaving the party to join the Socialist Workers' Party were not Communists, even though there were Communists behind the formation of the new party. In the opinion of Aalto, workers were being driven to the left by the aftermath of civil war, by the right-wing tone of the major newspaper of the Social Democratic Party, and by the leadership of the Social Democratic Party.[73] He did not agree with Tanner that the wisest tactic for the party was to concentrate on preventing the more liberal bourgeoisie from being pushed into the arms of reaction. A policy of compromise with the bourgeoisie would not

[72] Tanner, in *Suomen sosialidemokraattinen*, p. 185. Aalto later became "a fanatic Tannerite." Väinö Tanner to author, January 17, 1963.

[73] A—— to [J. F. Aalto], in *Kansan Työ*, May 21, 1920, p. 1; *Kansan Työ*, May 29, 1920, p. 1. According to Antti Ojala, a district secretary for the Socialist Workers' Party, between five and ten percent of those who belonged to the Socialist Workers' Party were also members of the Finnish Communist Party. From the early 1920s until the mid-1930s Ojala was a member of the Communist Party. Antti Ojala to author, September 20, 1962. Hertta Kuusinen has stated that the Socialist Workers' Party was founded by Communists, Socialists, and nonparty workers. *Pravda*, August 30, 1958, p. 3. The variegated composition of the Socialist Workers' Party is confirmed by two Finnish scholars: Soikkanen, "Työväenliikkeen," p. 285; Paasivirta, *Suomen poliittisen*, p. 76.

lead to great reforms; it would only drive workers to the extreme of *making* revolution.[74]

Early in June 1920 fifty-one Socialists, including eighteen members of Parliament, issued a Declaration to the Finnish Working Class. Those factors were presented which in the view of the Center Group had caused members of the Social Democratic Party to resign.[75] The newspaper *Suomen Sosialidemokraatti* and the leaders of the Social Democratic Party again came under fire. The fifty-one signatories were convinced that if the state of affairs within the Social Democratic Party continued unchanged, the party would be rent asunder completely.[76] In an attempt to avoid disaster, they urged:

1. That an extraordinary party congress be called for the fall, or a regular party congress for January;

2. That those organizations and individuals who had resigned from the party await the party congress, which would correct the ills which had led to resignation from the party;

3. That those who had not resigned remain in the party.[77]

[74] *Kansan Työ*, June 3, 1920, p. 1; *ibid.*, June 7, 1920, p. 1. The view that compromise would not lead to major reforms was, in fact, shared by right-wing Socialists. Taavi Tainio, in *Suomen sosialidemokraattisen puoluetoimikunnan*, June 8, 1920.

[75] J. F. Aalto, in *Suomen sosialidemokraattisen puolueneuvoston*, November 1-3, 1920, p. 23.

[76] Johan Helo, in *ibid.*, November 1-3, 1920, p. 38.

[77] The complete text of the Declaration can be found in *Kansan Työ*, June 8, 1920, p. 1. According to one prominent member of the Center Group, the Declaration was drawn up by Johan Helo and Rh. Svento. Mikko Ampuja, *Pajasta parlamenttiin* (Helsinki: Tammi, 1947), p. 174. The text, in any case, merely repeats the points made by J. F. Aalto in the articles which he wrote in May–June 1920 for the newspaper *Kansan Työ*.

As a result of the Declaration heated discussions took place in the top organs of the Social Democratic Party. Within the confines of the executive committee, even Taavi Tainio noted that charges made by the Center Group against the newspaper *Suomen Sosialidemokraatti* were in part justified. He stated that if the tone of the newspaper did not become more radical, it was possible that before long the Communist Party (the Socialist Workers' Party) would become the largest party in Finland.[78] The Center Group had two representatives on the Social Democratic executive committee, but it was not until a fall meeting of the executive council that the Center Group gave a thorough presentation of its views before a leading party organ. One delegate charged that the executive committee had taken no special steps to prevent the split in the party; all that the committee had done was to send speakers to those districts which had already resigned from the party.[79] The Center Group demanded an emphasis on class struggle and a sharp turn to the left in party policy. Its adherents were not, however, willing to turn as far left as had the Norwegian Labor Party, even though one Finn who signed the Declaration of the Center Group wrote with hindsight that the radical tactics of the Norwegian Labor Party in the early 1920s, which led to Comintern membership for four years, had met the demands of the situation and had, in contrast to the tactics of the Finnish Social Democratic Party, contributed significantly to the weakening of Communism.[80]

[78] *Suomen sosialidemokraattisen puoluetoimikunnan*, October 16, 1920.

[79] K. Nordlund, in *Suomen sosialidemokraattisen puolueneuvoston*, November 1-3, 1920, p. 20.

[80] *Ibid.*, November 1-3, 1920, pp. 21-22; *Kansan Työ*, June 8, 1920, p. 1; *ibid.*, May 29, 1920, p. 1; Ernst Lähde, in *Suomen Sosia-*

J. F. Aalto, looking at the Finnish situation, came to the heart of the matter in a perceptive speech to the executive council:

Communists have belonged to the Social Democratic Party and, quite naturally, have resigned. They would struggle against the party regardless of how "left" it was. It should be noted, however, that the Social Democratic Party also includes a large group non-Communist in nature but which can be influenced by Communist agitation, especially if there is weakness in party activity and if party tactics do not satisfy the group's class instinct.[81]

One opponent of the Center Group expressed in equally clear language the viewpoint of his faction: We must go in either one direction or the other—it is either Bolshevism or right-wing Socialism.[82] The executive council gave a vote of confidence to the executive committee, and party policy remained essentially unchanged in spite of exhortations as well as warnings by the Center Group.[83]

---

lidemokraatti, November 14, 1929, p. 6. When the Norwegian Labor Party voted in 1923 to withdraw from the Comintern, the minority proceeded to declare the foundation of the Communist Party of Norway. Arvo Tuominen, "Kommunismi Pohjolassa," *Sosialistinen Aikakauslehti*, No. 8, 1954, pp. 9, 19; *Työväenjärjestöjen Tiedonantaja*, November 7 and 9, 1923, p. 1.

[81] *Suomen sosialidemokraattisen puolueneuvoston*, November 1-3, 1920, p. 41.

[82] Kotonen, in *ibid.*, November 1-3, 1920, p. 34.

[83] *Ibid.*, November 1-3, 1920, p. 47. The fears of the Center Group appear to have been well founded, as the continuous drop in party membership indicates. There is disagreement in official Social Democratic circles about the precise figures for party membership during the period 1921-1924, but a sharp downward trend is noted by all. *Uusi Aika*, April 3, 1925, p. 1; *Suomen Sosialidemokraatti*, April 8, 1925, p. 7; *ibid.*, April 20, 1925, p. 7; *Statistical*, p.

While Social Democrats were struggling among themselves over the question of how to prevent the growth of Communism in Finland, steps were being taken by leading Communist figures to make of the somewhat loose and ill-defined Socialist Workers' Party, soon to be described as a recruit school for the Communist Party,[84] an effective political force. The Socialist Workers' Party found itself lacking experienced political leaders as a result of the Civil War; this problem was heightened by the fact that the party included many youthful newcomers.[85] Late in June 1920 Otto Kuusinen had gone to

---

4. In 1925 this uninterrupted decline in party membership became a subject of debate in the Social Democratic press, and some leading figures who had opposed the Center Group in 1920 now joined forces with the opposition in an attempt (which was successful at the Social Democratic Party congress of 1926) to wrest control of the top party apparatus from the right-wing Socialists. The most important sources on the 1925-1926 split within the Social Democratic Party are: Väinö Hupli, in *Uusi Aika*, April 3, 1925, p. 1; editorial, in *ibid.*, April 6, 1925, p. 1; "Vasemmistolainen," in *Työväenjärjestöjen Tiedonantaja*, April 9, 1925, p. 2; Taavi Tainio, in *Suomen Sosialidemokraatti*, April 8, 1925, p. 7; Hupli, in *ibid.*, April 20, 1925, p. 7; Tainio, in *ibid.*, April 27, 1925, p. 5; Hupli and Tainio, in *ibid.*, January 25, 1926, pp. 4-5; Rieti Itkonen and Tainio, in *ibid.*, January 28, 1926, p. 5.

84 Proceedings of the 1921 Communist Party congress, cited in *Suomen kommunistinen puolue*, p. 50.

85 S. H. [Seth Heikkilä], in *Suomen Työmies*, January 9, 1921, p. 1. Heikkilä preceded Arvo Tuominen as secretary of the Socialist Workers' Party. Tuominen, *Sirpin*, p. 136. Although not so hard pressed as the Socialist Workers' Party, the Social Democratic Party also found the lack of trained cadres a serious problem. Taavi Tainio, in *Suomen Sosialidemokraatti*, April 27, 1925, p. 5. Attention has been called to the youthful composition of the Socialist Workers' Party by Hannu Soikkanen, "Sosiaalidemokraatti," p. 149; Väinö Hupli, in *Suomen Sosialidemokraatti*, September 15, 1929, p. 5; Taavi Tainio, in *Suomen sosialidemokraattisen puolueen kahdennentoista*, p. 58; *Suomen Sosialidemokraatti*, April 23, 1925, p. 5. Marvin Rintala, in his scholarly study *Three Generations*, p. 21, notes that the failure to appeal to older Social Democrats after

Sweden,[86] and in discussions which took place there the following month it was decided to hold courses in Stockholm in order to create a cadre of trained political leaders for the Socialist Workers' Party.[87] Early in September 1920 some twenty influential figures in the Socialist Workers' Party, coming from many areas of Finland, reached Stockholm secretly in small groups.[88]

1918 was a serious weakness of Finnish Communism. One should perhaps also note the reverse side of the coin. A chief weakness of the Social Democratic Party was its inability to attract Finnish youth, many of whom subsequently joined the Socialist Workers' Party and the Communist Party. It is significant that the Youth League was one of the first organizations wrested from the hands of the Social Democratic Party in the years immediately following the Civil War. During the period 1919-1921 the Social Democratic Party also lost control of the Finnish Trade Union Organization, the Social Democratic League of Women, the Workers' Temperance League, and the Workers' Athletic Union. Tuominen, *Sirpin*, pp. 127, 146-149; Soikkanen, "Työväenliikkeen," p. 284.

[86] Tuominen, *Sirpin*, p. 169; T. Lehen, in *Kipinästä*, p. 47.

[87] Jaakko Kivi to author, April 26, 1962. According to another source, the purpose of the courses was to develop a cadre of full-fledged Communists in Finland. Jalmari Kuusela to author, March 31, 1962. It is apparent that the courses were designed both to set the Socialist Workers' Party on its feet and to ensure that control of the party would be in Communist hands. Although it is impossible to know how many leaders of the Socialist Workers' Party actually belonged to the Communist Party, it is difficult to avoid the conclusion that in proportion to their total membership in the Socialist Workers' Party, estimated at between five and ten percent, Communists were overrepresented in the party's top organs.

[88] Tuominen, *Sirpin*, pp. 173, 178. Only Arvo Tuominen and Emil Tuomi, as guests of the Swedish Trade Union Organization, traveled openly to Stockholm. Of those who attended the courses, the author has interviewed Arvo Tuominen, Emil Tuomi, Jalmari Kuusela, and Jaakko Kivi. At least three other participants are alive and in Finland today, but they deny any knowledge of the Stockholm courses. The courses were attended by some twenty Finns from Finland and by perhaps fifteen Finns who had been living in Sweden since their defeat in the Finnish Civil War. Jaakko Kivi to author, April 26, 1962.

106

For three weeks Kuusinen, Sirola, and J. Lumivuokko—all members of the central committee of the Finnish Communist Party[89]—gave intensive instruction in economics, trade union matters, international affairs, and the history of the Finnish labor movement.[90] The importance of the courses for the future development of the Socialist Workers' Party was later noted in veiled fashion by one of the participants. He wrote that it was not until the first meeting of the Socialist Workers' Party executive council, held just three months after the conclusion of the Stockholm courses, that that organization was formed which was the backbone of the party.[91]

Those members of the Finnish Communist central committee who were still in Soviet Russia wrongly charged that the Stockholm courses were designed to subvert, rather than support, the party.[92] At the heart of

[89] See chapter four, page 90, and notes 104 and 119 below. A fourth member of the central committee, Lauri Letonmäki, was also in Stockholm. Jalmari Kuusela to author, March 31, 1962; Jaakko Kivi to author, April 26, 1962; Iu. Iuvenalii, *Bor'ba klassov v Finliandii* (Moscow-Leningrad: Gosudarstvennoe Sotsial'no-Ekonomicheskoe izdatel'stvo, 1931), p. 163.

[90] Arvo Tuominen to author, October 2, 1962; Tuominen, *Sirpin*, pp. 189, 194-195. Kuusinen's lectures on economics were gathered together and printed in book form. Tuominen, *Sirpin*, p. 189; Jaakko Kivi to author, April 26, 1962; Jalmari Kuusela to author, March 31, 1962.

[91] E. T—mi [Emil Tuomi], in *Suomen Työmies*, January 4, 1922, p. 2. Tuomi has stated that his own political activity did not really begin until after the Stockholm courses. Emil Tuomi to author, April 10, 1962. According to Tuominen, *Sirpin*, pp. 195-196, the courses ended late in September.

[92] Jaakko Kivi to author, April 26, 1962. Arvo Tuominen has written that the Stockholm group sought to repudiate the Comintern as well as the Finnish Communist Party and to make of the Socialist Workers' Party an independent revolutionary organ. Tuominen also claims that the Stockholm group disclaimed all

107

the crisis in the Communist leadership—the roots of which go back to late 1919 when Otto Kuusinen achieved his "intellectual balance"—was a difference of opinion about party activity in Finland.[93] The Stockholm group did not find erroneous the concept that force would be needed to overthrow the bourgeoisie, and the Stockholm members of the central committee did not dispute the view held by Kullervo Manner, leader of the central committee in Soviet Russia, that world revolution was coming.[94] The Stockholm group did take issue, however, with the ultraleftism of the Manner group.[95] The ultraleftists in the party completely re-

secret activity. Tuominen, *Sirpin,* pp. 197, 202, 245. These assertions are vigorously rejected by three other men who attended the courses. Emil Tuomi to author, April 10, 1962; Jalmari Kuusela to author, March 31, 1962; Jaakko Kivi to author, April 26, 1962. The Stockholm group unquestionably saw the necessity of both the Socialist Workers' Party and the Communist Party; open and secret activity were to be combined.

93 Yrjö Sirola, "Suomen kommunistinen puolue," *Kommunisti,* No. 7 (43), July 1928, p. 299. Sirola was later severely criticized for his account of the crisis within the leadership of the Finnish Communist Party. *Kommunisti,* No. 13 (121), August 25, 1933, p. 580; Yrjö Sirola, "Puolueemme itsekritiikkiä," *Proletaari,* No. 5 (55), May 1931, p. 20. Sirola's account of the crisis can also be found in *Työmies* (Sup.), September 1, 1928, p. 3; Sirola, *Kommunisticheskaia,* pp. 39-41.

94 O. W. Kuusinen, "Suomen Sosialidemokratian johtajille," *Sosialistinen Aikakauslehti,* April 16, 1920, p. 98; P. Hauli [J. Lumivuokko], "Sosialisoimisen edellytyksistä," *Sosialistinen Aikakauslehti,* March 16, 1920, p. 70; P. Hauli, "Työväen taloudelliset järjestöt luokkataisteluvälineinä," *Sosialistinen Aikakauslehti,* May 1, 1920, p. 122; Kullervo Manner, in *Vapaus,* January 11, 1921, p. 1.

95 Sirola, "Puolueemme," p. 19; Y. S. [Yrjö Sirola], "Toveri Manner 50 vuotias," *Proletaari,* No. 3-4 (49-50), October-November 1930, p. 43. According to Tuominen, *Sirpin,* p. 190, Kuusinen completed a translation into Finnish of *"Left Wing" Communism, An Infantile Disorder* while in Stockholm. The Finnish text was printed in the summer of 1920. *Vapaus,* December 10, 1932, p. 3.

jected parliamentary and even trade union activity, preparing solely for an imminent armed revolt.[96] Manner saw impending revolution and the existence of civil war in Finland, whereas Kuusinen would say only that the Finnish proletariat no longer lacked a desire for revolution.[97] The Stockholm group accepted the thesis that the Socialist demands of the working class could not be realized through parliamentary activity, but the group felt that certain ulcerous wounds in capitalist society could be treated and bandaged in Parliament.[98] The Stockholm position with respect to the trade union movement was made clear by J. Lumivuokko when he rejected the notion that one should oppose trade-union organizations due to their capitalist leanings. Trade union organizations could be influenced, he said; they should be organized, under the leadership of Socialists convinced of the approaching world revolution, in such a way as to achieve a broad base.[99]

[96] SKP:n KK, "Kommunismin lipun alla: SKP:n taistelukutsu Suomen työtätekeville puolueen 15-vuotispäivänä," *Vapaus*, August 30, 1933, p. 2.

[97] Kullervo Manner, in *Vapaus*, June 2, 1920, p. 2; Kullervo Manner, in *The Communist International*, No. 11-12 (June-July), 1920, p. 2416; O. W. Kuusinen, in *Viesti*, March 24, 1920, p. 140.

[98] A report delivered by Arvo Tuominen in December 1920 to a meeting of the executive council of the Socialist Workers' Party. *Suomen sosialistisen työväenpuolueen puolueneuvoston kokouksen pöytäkirja*: Työväen Arkisto 329.6 (471) "1920."

[99] Hauli [Lumivuokko], "Työväen taloudelliset," pp. 121-122. Elsewhere Lumivuokko argued against those who charged that the achievements of the trade union movement were without meaning. He felt that the achievements *were* significant, although he denied that they could improve the lot of the workers to such a degree that a sharp, revolutionary clash would no longer be necessary. J. Lumivuokko, *Kommunisti ammatillisessa liikkeessä* (Kuopio: Savon Kansan kirjapaino, 1921), p. 53. It is interesting to note that the general position of the Stockholm group was similar to that which was

Organizational matters were also a cause of the split within the central committee of the Finnish Communist Party.[100] In the spring of 1920, several months before the Stockholm courses were held, those members of the central committee who were outside Soviet Russia sent a communication to the Comintern containing proposals for the reorganization of party activity.[101] The demand was voiced that the center of party work and of party leadership should be moved to Finland.[102] The party was criticized for its excessive centralization, and more representative elections to the higher party organs were called for.[103] But from Moscow came charges that there was opposition to the concept of a dictatorship of the proletariat.[104] The split within the leadership of

---

expressed at the founding congress of the Finnish Communist Party by those in opposition to the theses proposed by Kuusinen. It is significant that two of the sixteen who voted against the theses, J. Lumivuokko and E. K. Louhikko, contributed to the success of the Stockholm courses. Louhikko, although not one of those who attended the courses, had arranged to have the Swedish Trade Union Organization invite Arvo Tuominen and Emil Tuomi to Sweden. Tuominen, *Sirpin*, p. 173; Jaakko Kivi to author, April 26, 1962. Louhikko was also the contact who in July 1920 carried the necessary funds from Stockholm to Finland. Jaakko Kivi to author, April 26, 1962.

100 Iuvenalii, *op.cit.*, p. 163.

101 *Suomen kommunistinen puolue*, p. 498.

102 Antikainen, ed., *op.cit.*, p. 13; Emil Tuomi to author, April 10, 1962; Jalmari Kuusela to author, March 30, 1962. In 1921 a congress designed to heal the breach within the party was held in Petrograd; Arvo Tuominen proposed that the central committee be moved to Finland. Hugo M. Ahokanta to author, November 17, 1962. Ahokanta was one of three men who examined the credentials of the delegates to the party congress.

103 Sirola, "Suomen kommunistinen puolue," p. 299; Iuvenalii, *op.cit.*, p. 163; Jalmari Kuusela to author, March 30, 1962.

104 *Vapaus*, May 14, 1920, p. 2. Because of this opposition the executive committee of the Comintern appointed a temporary central committee of the Finnish Communist Party to conduct the

the Finnish Communist Party became more formalized in the fall of 1920 when the political courses were held in Stockholm. In actual fact the party had divided into two factions, each with its own leadership and own meetings.[105] The Stockholm group had an organizational committee and is described in an official publication as having been outside the Finnish Communist Party.[106] The leaders of the group refused to obey an order from the Manner faction, which represented a majority in the central committee, to return to Soviet Russia, and so to their sins was added the crime of violating party discipline.[107]

Those members of the central committee who were in Soviet Russia discovered that in addition to having to deal with the Stockholm Opposition, they also had to cope with opposition elements in Petrograd. Many Finnish emigrants who were receiving military instruction in Petrograd clashed with the leadership of the Communist Party in what proved to be a life and death struggle.[108] The Petrograd opposition charged that lead-

---

affairs of the party until its next congress. The central committee included Kullervo Manner, Otto Kuusinen, K. M. Evä, and Eino Rahja. The author has found no sources indicating that the Stockholm group recognized this temporary committee, and since a congress called together by Manner in July 1920 still referred to certain men in the Stockholm group as members of the central committee (*Suomen kommunistinen puolue*, p. 498), one must conclude that the temporary central committee did not really replace the central committee which had been elected in September 1919.

[105] Sirola, "Suomen kommunistinen puolue," p. 299.

[106] *Suomen kommunistinen puolue*, p. 63.

[107] *Kommunisti*, No. 13 (121), August 25, 1933, p. 580; "Suomen kommunistinen puolue 15-vuotias," *Neuvosto-Karjala*, No. 8-9, 1933, p. 19; *Suomen Sosialidemokraatti*, October 4, 1951, p. 4; Sirola, "Suomen kommunistinen puolue," p. 299; Antikainen, ed., *op.cit.*, p. 13.

[108] The fact that the Petrograd opposition was centered in the

ers of the party had been partially responsible for the defeat of the Finnish Reds in 1918.[109] Members of the Finnish party were accused of having fled from Finland during the Civil War and of having left the rank and file to its own fate.[110] Attention was called to the poor handling of emigrant problems following the Red evacuation to Soviet Russia. The Petrograd opposition asserted that party leaders were negligent also in their preparations for a new revolution.[111] They were attacked for their bourgeois origins; only sons and daughters of the working class could lead a new revolution to victory in Finland and the world.[112] The high living of the

---

military school is noted in *Suomen kommunistinen puolue*, pp. 32-33; Tuominen, *Sirpin*, p. 180; Antti J. Luostarinen, "Murhenäytelmä Leningradissa," *Kevättervehdys* (Helsinki: Sosialidemokraattinen puoluetoimikunta, 1941), p. 16; Jalmari Kuusela to author, March 30, 1962. The Petrograd opposition also included some Finnish members of the *Cheka*. Lauri Sulander to author, January 11, 1963. Sulander belonged to the Petrograd opposition and was a member of the *Cheka*.

[109] Lauri Sulander to author, January 11, 1963; Hugo M. Ahokanta to author, November 17, 1962. Ahokanta lived in Petrograd for an extended period of time and knew most of the Petrograd opposition leaders personally.

[110] Zinoviev, in *Kommunaardien muistojulkaisu: kommunismin puolesta kaatuneille elokuun 31 p:nä 1920 veriteon uhrien muistolle* (Leningrad: SKP:n KK, 1926), p. 12. This allegation troubled at least one member of the central committee. At the political courses held in Stockholm in 1920, Yrjö Sirola wanted to know if he had done right in fleeing from Finland at the end of the Civil War; he wanted to know whether the workers who remained behind could understand correctly his motives. N. K. [Niilo Kavenius], in *Vapaa Sana*, August 2, 1945, p. 5. In the eyes of one prominent member of the Petrograd opposition, it was Kullervo Manner who stood out for his cowardliness in the closing days of the Civil War. Lauri Sulander to author, January 11, 1963.

[111] Lauri Sulander to author, January 11, 1963; Hugo M. Ahokanta to author, November 17, 1962.

[112] *Vapaus*, March 21, 1920, p. 2; *ibid.*, March 27, 1920, pp. 3-4;

Rahja brothers, leading figures in the party who were closely associated with Zinoviev, added to the unrest in Petrograd circles.[113]

A clash between the central committee and the Petrograd opposition came at the March 18-20, 1920, party conference. In spite of last-minute intimidation by members of the central committee, opposition forces dominated the conference.[114] The Petrograd opposition was accused of having gained control of the conference through underhanded means,[115] and the central committee, led by Manner, walked out.[116] On the following day Rahja and Evä announced that in the eyes of the central committee the conference had ended.[117] At this point the executive committee of the Comintern inter-

---

Punainen Karjala, September 16, 1931, p. 4; Lauri Sulander to author, January 19, 1963.

113 Hugo M. Ahokanta to author, November 17, 1962; Luostarinen, "Murhenäytelmä," p. 17; Tuominen, *Sirpin*, p. 180. Eino and Jukka Rahja had at one time both been members of the central committee of the Finnish Communist Party; together they were instrumental in setting up the Petrograd military courses for Finnish emigrants. A third brother, Jaakko Rahja, figured less prominently in party activity. See note 121 below for information on the bonds between the Rahja brothers and Zinoviev.

114 On the eve of the conference some twenty members of the Petrograd opposition, including Lauri Sulander, were arrested but then released in time to attend. Sulander asserts that 92% of the delegates shared the views of the Petrograd opposition, 4% supported the central committee, and 4% were neutral. Lauri Sulander to author, January 11 and 19, 1963.

115 *Vapaus*, April 21, 1920, pp. 2-3; *ibid.*, April 23, 1920, pp. 2-3; *ibid.*, April 24, 1920, pp. 2-3.

116 *Ibid.*, April 24, 1920, p. 2; Lauri Sulander to author, January 19, 1963.

117 Lauri Sulander to author, January 11, 1963. *Vapaus*, April 24, 1920, p. 2, alludes to this step in the conflict. Sulander has stated that the chief spokesmen for the central committee at the conference were K. Manner, E. Rahja, and K. M. Evä. Lauri Sulander to author, January 19, 1963.

vened. Zinoviev promised members of the Petrograd opposition that a congress would soon be called to resolve the party crisis.[118] Months passed, however, with no party congress.[119] Late in August 1920 the Petrograd opposition, threatened with imprisonment and death,[120] sent to the Comintern and to the Russian Communist Party the last in a long series of letters calling for a party congress. The letter was in the form of an ultimatum, but it remained unanswered.[121] This silence was

[118] Lauri Sulander to author, January 11 and 19, 1963. Zinoviev's pledge was made in the presence of Sulander.

[119] According to *Suomen työväen vallankumous 1918. Arviota ja itsekritiikkiä* (Leningrad: Kirja, 1928), p. 195, the Third Congress of the Finnish Communist Party was held sometime in July 1920. It must be noted, however, that neither the Stockholm opposition nor the Petrograd opposition were represented at the congress. Tuominen, *Sirpin*, p. 172; Lauri Sulander to author, January 11, 1963. In June 1920 the central committee of the Finnish Communist Party had expelled seven members of the Petrograd opposition from the party. *Vapaus*, June 9, 1920, p. 3. The Third Congress recommended that the Russian Communist Party take away their party cards; it also attacked the Stockholm opposition. *Suomen kommunistinen puolue*, pp. 32, 498. In view of these facts, it would be more accurate to describe the Third Congress of the Finnish Communist Party as a factional meeting called by Kullervo Manner. This is suggested by Yrjö Sirola when he states that both the Stockholm and Manner groups held factional meetings (*fraktiakokouksensa*). Sirola, "Suomen kommunistinen puolue," p. 299. If the Third Congress was held after July 9—the author has not been able to establish the exact date of the congress—the first Chief Prosecutor in the Soviet State did not consider it a genuine party congress. N. V. Krylenko, in *Suomen Työmies*, April 7, 1922, p. 4.

[120] Lauri Sulander to author, January 11 and 19, 1963; Luostarinen, "Murhenäytelmä," p. 18.

[121] The letter demanded by August 30, 1920, an explanation for the delay in summoning a party congress. In the absence of a reply, it was stated that responsibility for what might happen after August 30 would have to be borne by others. Lauri Sulander to author, January 11 and 19, 1963. All the letters written by the Petrograd opposition went first to Petrograd authorities, where,

followed by violence. On August 31, 1920, six members of the Petrograd opposition opened fire at a meeting of Finnish emigrants;[122] seven people, including Jukka Rahja and Väinö Jokinen, lay dead when the shooting ceased.[123]

News of the bloodshed soon reached Stockholm, and its impact was like that of a bomb.[124] It reinforced the conviction of the Stockholm group that party headquarters should be moved from Soviet Russia to Finland.[125] If the central committee could not even control a small group of Finnish emigrants located in the same country, how could it expect to lead an entire revolutionary

due to the intimate relationship between the Rahja brothers and Zinoviev, they were pigeonholed. The existence of the letters was later brought to light when a logbook containing data on incoming correspondence was examined by investigators. Lauri Sulander to author, January 11, 1963. The close relationship between the Rahja brothers and Zinoviev is confirmed in Tuominen, *Sirpin*, p. 200. During the July Days, moreover, Zinoviev and Eino Rahja helped Lenin escape to Finland. G. Zinov'ev, "Lenin i iiul'skie dni," *Proletarskaia revoliutsiia*, No. 8-9 (67-68), August-September 1927, p. 71. In *Kommunaardien*, pp. 11-16, Zinoviev shows particular attachment to Jukka Rahja.

122 The six were Sulander, Höglund, Joronen, Krogfors, Paasi, and Halonen. Krylenko, in *Suomen Työmies*, April 11, 1922, p. 5. Paasi and Halonen were Red officers; the others were *Cheka* members. Lauri Sulander to author, January 19, 1963. Luostarinen, "Murhenäytelmä," is an eyewitness account written soon after the shooting. Antti Luostarinen to author, November 30, 1962.

123 *Kommunaardien*, p. 27. Among the many wounded were Jaakko Rahja and K. M. Evä. *Ibid.*, p. 28; *Izvestiia*, September 7, 1920, p. 1. One of the wounded soon died, bringing the total number of dead to eight. *Ibid.*, September 10, 1920, p. 1. Short biographies of the eight can be found in *Kommunaardien*, pp. 66-75. The Petrograd opposition focused its discontent on four figures: Jukka Rahja, Eino Rahja, Kullervo Manner, and K. M. Evä. Lauri Sulander to author, January 19, 1963. Since E. Rahja and Manner did not attend the meeting, two of the prime targets were missing.

124 Tuominen, *Sirpin*, p. 179.

125 Jalmari Kuusela to author, March 31, 1962.

movement outside the confines of Russia?[126] The Stockholm members of the central committee condemned the murders but at the same time expressed an understanding of what had happened.[127] The Stockholm leaders were in agreement with the Petrograd opposition on at least one point: the central committee had made mistakes in its handling of emigrant problems.[128] The chasm between the factions led by Kuusinen and Manner grew wider. It took the personal intervention of Lenin to restore unity to the Finnish Communist Party.

Lenin urged Kuusinen to return to Soviet Russia, and in February 1921 Kuusinen traveled from Stockholm to Moscow.[129] In the spring of 1921 a provisional

[126] Tuominen, *Sirpin*, p. 182.

[127] *Ibid.*, pp. 180-181; Emil Paajanen to author, June 1, 1962. Paajanen read a mimeographed copy of a letter sent by the Stockholm members of the central committee to Finland and to Soviet Russia soon after the murders. Lauri Sulander also gives evidence supporting the thesis that while rejecting force as a means to settle intraparty disputes, the Stockholm group nonetheless understood the Petrograd opposition. In 1921 the fate of those involved in the crime was debated by the Central Control Commission of the Russian Communist Party. A. A. Soltz talked with three members of the central committee of the Finnish Communist Party— Sulander and others in the Petrograd opposition were brought from prison to attend the meeting as observers—and leniency for the accused was recommended by Otto Kuusinen. Eino Rahja, on the other hand, demanded, and was supported by Kullervo Manner, the death penalty. Lauri Sulander to author, January 11, 1963. At the congress of the Finnish Communist Party held in 1921, the Manner-Rahja group accused the Kuusinen-Sirola group of not having acted firmly enough against the so-called revolver men. Hugo M. Ahokanta to author, November 17, 1962.

[128] Sirola, "Suomen kommunistinen puolue," pp. 298-299. Kullervo Manner, Eino Rahja, and K. M. Evä refused to admit that the central committee had made any mistakes. Jalmari Kuusela to author, March 30, 1962.

[129] Poika Tuominen, "Vastaus Tuure Lehenille," *Sosialistinen Aikakauslehti*, No. 12, 1954, p. 26; Tuominen, *Sirpin*, pp. 241-242.

116

(*pariteettinen*) central committee as well as a special committee designed to prepare for a party congress were set up under Comintern leadership.[130] In July Finnish Communists gathered in Petrograd to resolve the differences which had arisen within the party leadership over the independence of the Kuusinen-Sirola group in Sweden. The Russians had urged that this unity congress be as large as possible,[131] and approximately fifty delegates, most of whom had no prior knowledge of the split within the central committee,[132] came from Finland.[133] Although members of the Manner-Rahja group considered cooperation with the Kuusinen-Sirola group impossible,[134] a common, Bolshevik basis for ending the party crisis was found:

> The party congress gave credit to the central committee for having remained on the spot and for having steadfastly defended the prerequisites of a Communist party: the necessity of party unity and party discipline, and the necessity of fulfilling one's duty. The party congress reprimanded the opposition members of the central committee for breaking discipline and

Kuusinen went to Moscow by way of Soviet Karelia. Edvard Gylling, in *Punainen Karjala,* October 4, 1931, p. 4; *Suomen Työmies,* March 16, 1921, p. 6.

[130] Sirola, "Suomen kommunistinen puolue," p. 299.

[131] Hugo M. Ahokanta to author, November 17, 1962.

[132] Hugo M. Ahokanta to author, November 17, 1962.

[133] Antikainen, ed., *op.cit.,* p. 13; Tuominen, *Sirpin,* p. 292. In addition to the delegates from Finland, about twenty emigrants attended the party congress. Of those present the author has talked with Emil Paajanen, Jalmari Kuusela, Arvo Tuominen, Emil Tuomi, Betty Peltonen, and Hugo M. Ahokanta.

[134] Eino Rahja was particularly adamant on this point, and, no doubt at his instigation, a tract charging that Kuusinen was an informant for the Finnish police was circulated shortly before the party congress got under way. Hugo M. Ahokanta to author, November 17, 1962.

for weakening the central committee at a time when they should have rallied closely around it. At the same time the party congress criticized the weaknesses and errors ["ultra-Bolshevism"] which had appeared in party work, and the congress pointed the way to their liquidation.[135]

The party congress was an overwhelming triumph for those members of the central committee who had been in Stockholm,[136] and the relative ease with which victory was achieved can no doubt be attributed to decisions made earlier at the Third Congress of the Comintern. At this Comintern congress, in contrast to the Second Congress, the major question was not how to take advantage of an already existing revolutionary situation but how to *create* one. Comintern leaders had discovered that revolution was not so obedient, so tame, that it could be led on a leash. For Trotsky, revolution was now a question of perhaps years, not months.[137] The views expressed by Lenin in his pamphlet *"Left-Wing" Communism, An Infantile Disorder* became the dominant chord at the Third Congress. No longer was left extremism "a thousand times less dangerous and less significant than the mistake of right doctrinairism."[138] The cure for the disease had become much more diffi-

[135] Sirola, "Suomen kommunistinen puolue," p. 299. At least one member of the central committee, Eino Rahja, refused to abandon his ultraleftism. See chapter five, notes 90 and 101.

[136] Betty Peltonen to author, February 10, 1963. Hugo M. Ahokanta has stated that if one discounts the comments made by Eino Rahja, the party congress was a rather united gathering; Kuusinen even praised Manner for the progress which he had made. Hugo M. Ahokanta to author, November 17, 1962.

[137] Degras, ed., *op.cit.*, I, 230; Carr, *op.cit.*, III, 385.

[138] V. I. Lenin, *"Left-Wing" Communism, An Infantile Disorder* (New York: International Publishers, 1940), p. 83.

cult. The slogan advanced at the Third Congress was: *To the masses.* A policy of "united front" with non-Communist workers' organizations was recommended. Communists were called upon to join reactionary trade unions and to participate in bourgeois parliaments. Organization and agitation, not direct preparations for civil war, were the order of the day.[139] Given the context of the Third Congress of the Comintern, it is easy to see why Lenin intervened personally in the affairs of the Finnish Communist Party. Otto Kuusinen, with his practical experience in directing a united front policy, had become invaluable. At Lenin's request, Kuusinen prepared for the Third Congress the important organizational theses;[140] the necessity of both a legal and illegal apparatus, always in the hands of "the same single central party committee," was skillfully expounded.[141] As an indication of work well done, Kuusinen became a member of the Comintern's three-man secretariat. Sirola, the second most important figure in the Stockholm opposition, regained his position on the executive committee of the Comintern by replacing Kullervo Manner.[142] There was, therefore, really little doubt as to which faction within the Finnish party would emerge

[139] Degras, ed., *op.cit.*, I, 241-256; Hugh Seton-Watson, *From Lenin to Malenkov* (New York: Frederick A. Praeger, Inc., 1956), p. 100.

[140] Y. S. [Yrjö Sirola], in *Vapaus*, October 3, 1931, p. 1; *International Press Correspondence*, Vol. XI, No. 52 (October 8, 1931), p. 949; Hugo M. Ahokanta to author, November 17, 1962. The theses were presented to the congress by a German delegate.

[141] "Extracts from the Theses on the Structure of Communist Parties and on the Methods and Content of Their Work, Adopted by the Third Comintern Congress," in Degras, ed., *op.cit.*, I, 256-271.

[142] Degras, ed., *op.cit.*, I, 453-455.

triumphant in the battle which immediately followed the Comintern congress.[143]

Imbued with the Comintern resolutions and the decisions of the party congress, Finnish Communists returned to Finland. Their task, as defined by the Comintern, was to create an experienced, large, revolutionary, mass Communist Party. For all Communist parties the trade union movement was now of decisive importance.[144] The Finnish Trade Union Organization, moreover, was already controlled by Communists and left-wing Socialists, although it was this organization, above all, which would soon become the *enfant terrible* for Moscow. Matti Väisänen, elected chairman of the Trade Union Organization in May 1920, had given notice that directives from Moscow would not be followed blindly. He had stated that there were different forms and methods by which Socialism could be achieved. Finnish workers should listen to advice from both the East and West, then decide what is best and most useful for the working class.[145]

[143] Arvo Tuominen contests the view that Kuusinen and his supporters achieved victory easily. Tuominen, *Sirpin*, pp. 290-306.

[144] Degras, ed., *op.cit.*, I, 243, 245-246. On the return trip to Finland many of those who attended the party congress remained in Lempaala, a village just inside the Soviet border, for extensive political indoctrination. Betty Peltonen to author, February 10, 1963. Similar courses had been conducted there just before the party congress. Emil Paajanen to author, June 1, 1962.

[145] *Suomen Ammattijärjestön viidennen Helsingissä toukokuun 25-29 p:nä pidetyn edustajakokouksen pöytäkirja* (Kotka: Kyminlaakson Työväen kirjapaino, 1920), p. 36.

CHAPTER FIVE

Right Deviation and Left Deviation

IN January 1922 the executive committee of the Socialist Workers' Party was arrested,[1] and during the summer of the following year Finnish authorities proceeded
to ban the entire party on the grounds that it was fo-
menting revolution.[2] Among the some three hundred
party functionaries imprisoned in August 1923 was
Niilo Wälläri, a former chairman of the Socialist
Workers' Party; a man who, like Matti Väisänen, felt
that Finnish workers should consider all good advice—
regardless of its point of origin—but that decision-
making should be a prerogative of those actually in
Finland.[3] Wälläri had occasion to stress this view in
1924 when emigrant Communists, preparing for the
presidential election which was to be held early the
next year, issued instructions to the workers in Finland.

[1] Arvo Tuominen, *Sirpin ja vasaran tie* (Helsinki: Tammi, 1957),
p. 244; Niilo Wälläri, in *Suomen Sosialidemokraatti*, October 17,
1954, p. 3.

[2] Göran von Bonsdorff, *Suomen poliittiset puolueet* (Helsinki:
Tammi, 1957), p. 16; Arvo Tuominen, *Maan alla ja päällä* (Hel-
sinki: Tammi, 1958), p. 161. In May 1923 the Socialist Workers'
Party of Finland had become the Finnish Workers' Party (*Suomen
Työväenpuolue*). *Suomen Työmies*, May 17, 1923, p. 3; Ilkka
Hakalehto, *Suomen kommunistinen puolue ja sen vaikutus poliit-
tiseen ja ammatilliseen työväenliikkeeseen 1918-1928* (Porvoo:
WSOY, 1966), p. 185.

[3] Wälläri had begun to advance this view before the Socialist
Workers' Party was outlawed. N. Wälläri, in *Suomen Työmies*,
March 27, 1930, p. 2; Emil Paajanen to author, June 1, 1962.

Moscow called upon Finnish Communists and left-wing Socialists to select Otto Kuusinen as their candidate for the highest political office in Finland;[4] emphasis was to be put on a union of workers and small farmers.[5] Wälläri, on the other hand, considered the small farmers innately hostile to the class struggle of the workers. He proposed that Matti Väisänen, not Kuusinen, be nominated for the Presidency.[6] Opposition to Moscow's orders was widespread,[7] and in December 1924 Väisänen, then in a prison cell, became the presidential candidate of Communists and left-wing Socialists in Finland.[8]

In April 1925 a program, in the form of a letter drawn up by N. Wälläri, M. Väisänen, and K. Kulo, was sent to workers outside the prison.[9] The central

[4] *Suomen kommunistinen puolue. Puoluekokousten, konferenssien ja keskuskomitean plenumien päätöksiä*, Vol. I (Leningrad: Kirja, 1935), p. x; T. Antikainen, ed., *SKP:n taistelun tielta: Muistelmia, kuvauksia ja aineistoa SKP:n 15-vuotistaipaleelta* (Leningrad: Kirja, 1934), p. 250.

[5] *Suomen kommunistinen puolue*, p. 92; *Proletaari*, No. 5 (45), August 1929, p. 7.

[6] Kalle Lepola, in *Vapaus*, February 23, 1930, p. 3; Lepola, in Antikainen, ed., *op.cit.*, pp. 283-284; *SKP taistelujen tiellä*, Vol. x (Helsinki: Yhteistyön kirjapaino, 1954), p. 105. At the time of the presidential election, Lepola was in prison with Wälläri. In June 1926 Lepola was released in a prisoner exchange with the Soviet Union and became a member of the central committee of the Finnish Communist Party. Hugo M. Ahokanta to author, November 21, 1962; *Työväenjärjestöjen Tiedonantaja*, June 29, 1926, p. 1.

[7] Arvo Tuominen, in *Bol'shaia sovetskaia entsiklopediia*, Vol. LVII (Moscow: Ogiz, 1936), p. 602; *Suomen kommunistinen puolue*, pp. 86, 92; *Proletaari*, No. 5 (45), August 1929, p. 7.

[8] Paavo Hirvikallio, *Tasavallan presidentin vaalit Suomessa 1919-1950* (Porvoo: WSOY, 1958), pp. 27-28, 42; *Työväenjärjestöjen Tiedonantaja*, November 10, 1924, p. 1; *ibid.*, December 20, 1924, p. 1; Kullervo Manner, "Luokkatietoisten työläisten taistelutahdon peittämispyrintö presidentti ehdokaskysymyksessä," *Proletaari*, No. 4 (25), April 25, 1925, pp. 12-13.

[9] Lepola, in Antikainen, ed., *op.cit.*, pp. 265-266, 278; Lepola, in

theme was forcefully stated in the final paragraph: *"Emigrants must not be given any authority with regard to Finnish affairs. That is our main hope."*[10] This point was reiterated in the fall of the same year when Wälläri and his supporters, known in prison circles as the Break Away from the Emigrants (*irti-emigranteista*) group,[11] issued a written reply to remonstrations from the central committee of the Finnish Communist Party.[12] Independence from Finnish emigrants also figured prominently in the discussions which began in 1924-1925 among trade union men concerning the feasibility of founding a new, legal party. Wälläri became the leader of this group,[13] and, although he acknowledged the usefulness of a secret Communist Party, he did not want the latter to interfere with the activities of the former. Only a legal party could become a mass party.[14] In 1927, shortly after his release from prison, Wälläri continued to urge the formation of a class-oriented mass party. It would act independently of Moscow: *"Our activity is, and must be, free from foreign factors and circles."*[15]

Vapaus, February 23, 1930, p. 3. K. Kulo had been a secretary of the Socialist Workers' Party. *Suomen Työmies*, April 4, 1922, p. 4.

[10] The complete text of the letter can be found in Antikainen, ed., *op.cit.*, pp. 265-266.

[11] *Ibid.*, p. 265; *Vapaus*, February 23, 1930, p. 3; Hugo M. Ahokanta to author, November 21, 1962. The most active opponents of the April letter were known as the "Ten Carpenters"; both Ahokanta and Lepola belonged to this group.

[12] Antikainen, ed., *op.cit.*, p. 274.

[13] *Ibid.*, pp. 253, 290-292.

[14] Wälläri, referred to by Kalle Lepola in *Proletaari*, No. 7 (32), December 1926, pp. 3, 6. Lepola does not mention Wälläri by name, although Lepola has noted elsewhere that the article in *Proletaari* was an official response by the Communist Party leadership to Wälläri. Antikainen, ed., *op.cit.*, pp. 292-293.

[15] Quoted in *Suomen Sosialidemokraatti*, July 5, 1929, p. 6, from

In the letter sent from prison in April 1925 Wälläri and his supporters had urged that a tone of moderation be adopted toward the Center Group in the Social Democratic Party; they also supported more restrained and cautious tactics in the trade union movement. These two points struck a responsive chord with members of the trade union organizations. Disregarding the Comintern view that trade unions could not be "apolitical" or neutral,[16] some left-wing trade unionists in Finland proposed that the unions become neutral and refrain from all political activity.[17] These men attacked right-wing Socialists but felt that cooperation could be achieved with the Center Group in the Social Democratic Party.[18] Finnish emigrants charged that the tactic of a united front from below had been turned into some sort of a means for achieving an alliance with Social Democracy.[19] Further indication of Moscow's loose control over the trade union movement in Finland came when the Communist faction at the Finnish Trade Union Organization Congress held in May 1926 refused to follow instructions concerning the election of a new

---

an article written by Wälläri in 1927; see also *ibid.*, July 9, 1927, p. 7, and *Proletaari*, No. 2 (34), September 1927, p. 8.

[16] Theses of the Third Comintern Congress, cited in Jane Degras, ed., *The Communist International 1919-1943*, Vol. 1 (London: Oxford University Press, 1956), p. 275.

[17] *Työväenjärjestöjen Tiedonantaja*, April 7, 1925, p. 2; *ibid.*, April 8, 1925, p. 2; *ibid.*, May 23, 1925, p. 2; *ibid.*, June 27, 1925, p. 2; *Suomen Sosialidemokraatti*, July 9, 1927, p. 7.

[18] *Työväenjärjestöjen Tiedonantaja*, June 27, 1925, p. 2. Lepola states that Wälläri's group, in prison, considered cooperation possible with J. F. Aalto, J. Helo, M. Ampuja, K. H. Wiik, and M. Paasivuori. Antikainen, ed., *op.cit.*, p. 267. Out of prison, it would appear that Edvard Valpas was at this time the chief advocate of cooperation with the Center Group in the Social Democratic Party.

[19] Statement made in August 1925 at a congress of the Finnish Communist Party. *Suomen kommunistinen puolue*, p. 92.

chairman.[20] It was not until 1929, however, that Moscow realized Communists and left-wing Socialists in the Finnish trade union movement were not puppets on a string.

At the Eighth Congress of the Finnish Trade Union Organization, held in May 1929, even the most trusted Communists failed to obey orders from the Politburo of the Finnish Communist Party.[21] The central issue at the Trade Union congress was the so-called Copenhagen Agreement. In February 1928 the Soviet Union, Norway, and Finland had sent representatives to Copenhagen to negotiate an agreement which would further cooperation between the trade union organizations of the three countries and which would be an initial step toward unifying the trade union organizations of the East and West.[22] In April 1929 the central committee of the Finnish Communist Party instructed Communists and left-wing Socialists, who controlled the Finnish trade union movement, to ratify the Copenhagen Agreement at the Eighth Trade Union Congress.[23] Since February of the preceding year much had happened, however, to cause Finnish trade unionists to look upon the agreement in a new light.

In accordance with the principles expressed in the Copenhagen Agreement, the Finnish and Norwegian

[20] *Ibid.*, p. 504. Contrary to the wishes of Moscow, Matti Paasivuori was elected chairman of the Trade Union Organization. It is curious that Moscow supported a candidate, E. K. Louhikko, who had already flexed muscles of independence. Late in 1925 Louhikko had asserted that he "danced neither to Moscow's tune nor to that of Finnish Social Democrats." His actions, instead, were dictated by the interests of the trade union movement. *Suomen Sosialidemokraatti*, January 2, 1926, p. 5.

[21] *Suomen kommunistinen puolue*, pp. 236, 289-290.

[22] *Suomen Työmies*, February 5, 1930, p. 2.

[23] O. Piatnitskii, in *Pravda*, August 29, 1929, p. 2.

trade union organizations had invited the Amsterdam and Red trade union Internationals to hold a unity congress.[24] The Red International had accepted the invitation, but the sincerity of the Russians became suspect when A. Lozovskii, head of the Red International, stated in March 1928 that it would be as impossible to unite the Amsterdam and Red Internationals as it would be to join fire and water.[25] M. P. Tomskii, chairman of the Central Council of Russian Trade Unions, announced in December 1928 that it was utopian even to think of unity.[26] These public declarations, coupled with a negative response by the Danish and Swedish trade union organizations to a Norwegian proposal that they join the Copenhagen Agreement, caused the Norwegian organization to postpone ratification of the Copenhagen Agreement.[27] At the Eighth Congress of the Finnish Trade Union

[24] M. Tranmael, in *Suomen Ammattijärjestön kahdeksannen Helsingissä toukokuun 10-16 p:nä 1929 pidetyn edustajakokouksen pöytäkirja* (Helsinki: Oy Työn kirjapaino, 1929), p. 171; *Suomen Työmies*, February 5, 1930, p. 2. In 1922 Finnish trade unionists voted to join the Red International, but formal adherence was postponed by the leaders of the Finnish Trade Union Organization. In 1926 the Seventh Congress of the Finnish Trade Union Organization repealed its decision of 1922 and resolved to remain independent until the formation of a unified trade union international. The Norwegian Trade Union Organization withdrew from the Amsterdam International in 1922, although in a vote taken the following year Norwegian trade unionists rejected membership in the Red International. They, like the Finns, belonged to neither the Amsterdam nor the Red International when the Copenhagen Agreement was negotiated.

[25] M. Tranmael, in *Suomen Ammattijärjestön kahdeksannen*, p. 171. The Amsterdam International had from the very beginning rejected the proposal calling for a joint conference with the Red International.

[26] *Ibid.*, p. 171; *Suomen Työmies*, February 5, 1930, p. 2.

[27] M. Tranmael, in *Suomen Ammattijärjestön kahdekannen*, p. 171.

Organization it was clear that under the prevailing circumstances ratification of the Copenhagen Agreement would in all probability cause the withdrawal of the Social Democrats;[28] the congress voted, as had Norwegian trade unionists, to delay ratification.[29]

Another major issue under discussion at the Eighth Congress of the Finnish Trade Union Organization was the question of participation in the activities of the Geneva International Labor Office. At the Seventh Trade Union Congress, held in 1926, the slogan emanating from Moscow had been "unity in the trade union movement,"[30] and in order to avoid a split within the Finnish Trade Union Organization, the Communists and left-wing Socialists had voted to rescind a previous decision forbidding the dispatch of a delegate to Geneva,[31] which

[28] Matti Paasivuori, in *ibid.*, p. 6.

[29] *Ibid.*, pp. 215-216; editorial, in *Suomen Työmies*, May 8, 1930, p. 2. The following sources indicate conclusively that it was a desire for unity within the Finnish Trade Union Organization which led Communists and left-wing Socialists to postpone ratification of the Copenhagen Agreement: *Suomen Ammattijärjestön kahdeksannen*, p. 215; "K:i," in *Työväenjärjestöjen Tiedonantaja*, May 22, 1929, p. 3; Matti Väisänen, in *ibid.*, May 29, 1929, p. 4; N. Wälläri, "Trade Union Movement in Finland Threatened," *International Press Correspondence*, Vol. IX, No. 26 (May 31, 1929), p. 573; O. Piatnitskii, in *Pravda*, August 29, 1929, p. 2; editorial, in *Suomen Työmies*, May 8, 1930, p. 2. Confirmation of this point comes also from two men who were both members of the Finnish Communist Party but who reacted differently to orders from Moscow concerning ratification: Hj. Långström to author, September 13, 1962; Hugo M. Ahokanta to author, April 27, 1962.

[30] Secretary of the Russian Trade Unions, in *Suomen Ammattijärjestön seitsemännen Helsingissä toukokuun 3-8 p:nä 1926 pidetyn edustajakokouksen pöytäkirja* (Helsinki: Oy Työn kirjapaino, 1926), p. 9; Tuominen, *Maan*, p. 206; Jaakko Kivi to author, April 26, 1962.

[31] *Suomen Ammattijärjestön seitsemännen*, pp. 174, 177, 179. In 1923, 1924, and 1925 the leaders of the Finnish Trade Union

permitted the executive committee to send a representative to the International Labor Office. At the Eighth Trade Union Congress extreme leftists wanted to abrogate the decision made in 1926, but they were isolated.[32] Uno Nurminen, a member of the executive committee, expressed the opinion of the majority when he stated that the factors which had led to the 1926 decision were still valid, that the situation had not changed in three years.[33] Nurminen had come to grips with the central question, that of continuity or change; for in August 1928 the Sixth Comintern Congress had heralded a new era, one of revolutionary growth: the proletariat was ready for self-sacrifice and heroism.[34] Kullervo Manner, who, as chairman of the central committee, was second to none in the Finnish Communist Party,[35] labeled Nurminen's statement an example of "the stabilization psychology of right opportunists."[36] Matti Väisänen, elected secretary of the Trade Union Organization in

---

Organization, disregarding the will of the Sixth Trade Union Congress, had sent representatives to Geneva. See E. Huttunen, in *ibid.*, pp. 67-69.

[32] *Suomen Ammattijärjestön kahdeksannen*, p. 218. There appears, however, to have been more support for the party line on this issue than on ratification of the Copenhagen Agreement.

[33] Nurminen, in *ibid.*, p. 189.

[34] Draft theses submitted to the Comintern congress, in *Kommunisti*, No. 5 (41), May 1928, p. 220.

[35] Tuominen, *Maan*, p. 22, states that when Otto Kuusinen became a leading figure in the Comintern, practical leadership of the Finnish Communist Party was put in the hands of Kullervo Manner. Yrjö Sirola has written that Manner was chairman of the party most of the time during the period 1918-1930. Y. S., "Toveri Manner 50 vuotias," *Proletaari*, No. 3-4 (49-50), October-November 1930, p. 43. Manner is referred to in one authoritative source as dictator of the Finnish Communist Party. *Suomen Työmies*, May 20, 1930, p. 3; *ibid.*, May 27, 1930, p. 4.

[36] Manner, in *Punainen Karjala*, January 30, 1930, p. 2.

1929,[37] may have been expressing the view of the majority at the congress when he wrote in a letter to the local Communist press: "My opinions may be opportunism and a right deviation. It is all the same to me. Above all, I am a trade unionist; the preservation of unity in the Trade Union Organization is to me more important than 'isms' and 'lisms.' "[38]

By the late summer of 1929 the situation within the left labor movement in Finland was explosive. Finnish trade union leaders were described by Moscow as never having really been in sympathy with Communism.[39] The attacks on Niilo Wälläri, who did not figure prominently in the events which took place at the Eighth Trade Union Congress but who for many years had been at odds with Moscow, were intensified.[40] The forces opposing Moscow lacked formal organization, but an important change occurred when Eino Pekkala, vice-chairman of the Communist and left-Socialist bloc in Parliament,[41] and Hugo M. Ahokanta, a trusted member

---

[37] *Suomen Ammattijärjestön kahdeksannen*, p. 220. Social Democrats refused to stand for any office filled at the Eighth Trade Union Congress. *Ibid.*, pp. 216, 220; N. Wälläri, *Myrskyssä ja myötätuulessa* (Helsinki: Oy Kodaprint Ab, 1951), p. 32.

[38] *Työväenjärjestöjen Tiedonantaja*, May 29, 1929, p. 4. A similar attitude prevailed in Germany. Edward Hallett Carr, *The Bolshevik Revolution 1917-1923*, Vol. III (New York: The Macmillan Company, 1953), p. 218, states that "the trade unions had a stronger hold on the loyalty of the German worker than any political party."

[39] *International Press Correspondence*, Vol. IX, No. 62 (November 1, 1929), p. 1342.

[40] *Proletaari*, No. 3-4 (43-44), June-July 1929, p. 22. Wälläri had previously been attacked at the conferences of the Finnish Communist Party held in 1926 and 1927, and at the April 1929 plenum of the central committee. *Suomen kommunistinen puolue*, pp. 140, 173, 210; *Kommunisti*, No. 1-2 (61-62), January-February 1930, p. 15.

[41] Jalmari Kuusela, secretary for the parliamentary bloc, to author, March 31, 1962. The parliamentary group is described in one Communist publication as "under the influence of the illegal

of the Finnish Communist Party until 1929, broke with the past.[42] In September 1929 Ahokanta sent to a newspaper published in Kuopio an article which represented the first public expression of group opposition to Moscow.[43] The article, signed by "A Group of Left Workers" (*Joukko vasemmistotyöläisiä*), attacked extremists in the left who had begun to work against the decisions of the Eighth Trade Union Congress. The group declared that "until such time as we decide otherwise, on the basis of experience and in an order determined by proper regulations, each and every one of us must obey those decisions which were arrived at jointly." Anarchy would be the alternative in an organization such as the Finnish Trade Union Organization.[44]

It was not long before the "opportunists," generally known as the *hoipertelijat* ("those who totter"), took

---

Communist Party"; elsewhere it is noted that members of the Communist Party formed a majority in the group. *International Press Correspondence*, Vol. IX, No. 34 (July 19, 1929), p. 726; *Suomen kommunistinen puolue*, p. 297.

[42] Hugo M. Ahokanta to author, November 17, 1962. Ahokanta, seriously wounded in the Finnish Civil War, joined the party in its infancy. He enjoyed many positions of trust and spent a number of years in Finnish prisons. As an old and trusted Communist, Ahokanta in 1929 first tried to resolve his differences with Moscow by writing to the central committee of the Finnish Communist Party. He hoped to settle the issues without a great clash between opposing forces; this was impossible. Ahokanta brought to the opposition the pen of an experienced journalist.

[43] Hugo M. Ahokanta to author, April 27, 1962.

[44] *Savon Työ*, September 14, 1929, p. 3. A week after the Trade Union congress some members of the left who had voted to postpone ratification of the Copenhagen Agreement did a *volte-face*. "They [Rosenberg, Yrjö Lehtinen, Kuusela, Longström, and others] openly declared their intention to break decisions which had been unanimously reached by the workers." A two-page mimeographed letter circulated in December 1929 by "Suomen Työväen Vasemmistoryhmä" to "Hyvä Toveri."

steps to give more cohesion to their group. On December 7, 1929, seventeen men met and formed the Left Group of Finnish Workers (*Suomen työväen vasemmistoryhmä*). At this meeting Emil Tuomi reported on the split within the left labor movement. He noted that the division was due to an incorrect appraisal of the Finnish situation: the extreme left (*huitojat*) judged the situation more revolutionary, the masses more active, and the disruptive work of Social Democrats in the trade union movement less significant than was actually the case. Tuomi proposed that a special organizational machine, headed by a central committee (*Keskustoimikunta*), be formed to cope with the problems which confronted the left labor movement. Approval followed, and a six-man central committee was elected: E. Pekkala (chairman), U. Nurminen (vice-chairman), H. M. Ahokanta (secretary), E. Tuomi, K. Kulo, and A. Raatikainen.[45]

A mimeographed letter, expanding on the factors dealt with by Tuomi in his report to the first meeting of the Left Group of Finnish Workers, was drawn up and circulated by the central committee.[46] This letter took particular exception to the line adopted at the Sixth Comintern Congress: "It is alleged that in Finland today there is an especially tense and revolutionary situation: the broad masses of workers are supposedly ready for revolution, which, it is said, would occur if

[45] *Suomen työväen vasemmistoryhmän Helsingin työväentalolla joulukuun 7 p:nä 1929 pidetyn kokouksen pöytäkirja.* The second most important organ formed was a trade union committee; among its members were Matti Väisänen (chairman), N. Wälläri, and U. Nurminen.

[46] *Suomen työväen vasemmistoryhmän keskustoimikunnan pöytäkirjat*, December 13 and 17, 1929.

one could only get rid of certain leaders who retard the course of developments."[47] But local Communists who supported Moscow took issue with the opposition's interpretation of the new Moscow line: "It is clear to everyone that at the moment there is no revolutionary, still less an 'especially' revolutionary, situation in Finland." Adherents to the Moscow line claimed, however, that a significant change had recently occurred. The chief features of Finnish life were now an intensification of the class struggle, a capitalist crisis, and a general turn to the left by the workers.[48] A member of the Finnish Communist central committee urged members of the opposition to familiarize themselves with this third stage of the capitalist crisis, a period "when serious international conflicts and tremendous internal class struggles shake the very roots of capitalism, when the colonies of the capitalist powers begin to stir, the workers everywhere turn to the left, and the revolutionary movement advances triumphantly in spite of furious oppression."[49] Those tactics which were applicable in the trade union movement in 1926—tactics of unity involving a *modus vivendi* with Social Democratic leaders —must give way to the demands of the new world situation.[50] Charges by the opposition that left-wing Communism (*kommunistinen äkkijyrkkyys*) would drive many trade unionists into the arms of Social Democratic leaders were dismissed by the central committee of the Finnish Communist Party as irrelevant: those who

[47] A three-page mimeographed letter from "Suomen Työväen Vasemmistoryhmä" to "Hyvä Toveri."

[48] *Työväenjärjestöjen Tiedonantaja*, December 20, 1929, p. 4.

[49] Letter from "Vesa" [Kalle Lepola] to Hugo M. Ahokanta, dated December 1929.

[50] *Työväenjärjestöjen Tiedonantaja*, December 14, 1929, p. 5.

would abandon the left labor movement belonged in the camp of the Social Fascists.[51]

At a meeting of the Left Group of Finnish Workers central committee on December 26, 1929, there was unanimous agreement—reached after much discussion —that publication of a newspaper was essential.[52] On January 11, 1930, an editorial board was elected: E. Pekkala, E. Tuomi, U. Nurminen, O. Jalava, and D. Karvonen. Hugo M. Ahokanta was named assistant to the managing editor (*toimitussihteeri*), as well as political editor.[53] A week later the first issue of *Suomen Työmies* appeared. The articles in this and later issues developed three major themes:

1. The split within the left labor movement is a direct result of the revolutionary line announced by the Sixth Comintern Congress.[54]

2. Finnish workers must be masters in their own house because only they know what the real situation is in Finland.[55]

3. Trade union unity must be preserved; the views of all trade unionists (Left Socialists, Communists,

---

[51] Letter from Kalle Lepola to Hugo M. Ahokanta.

[52] *Suomen työväen vasemmistoryhmän keskustoimikunnan pöytä-kirjat*, December 26, 1929.

[53] *Ibid.*, January 11, 1930.

[54] Editorial, in *Suomen Työmies*, January 18, 1930, p. 2; editorial, in *ibid.*, February 27, 1930, p. 2; N. Wälläri, in *ibid.*, March 27, 1930, p. 2.

[55] Editorial, in *ibid.*, January 18, 1930, p. 1; N. Wälläri, in *ibid.*, March 27, 1930, p. 2; *ibid.*, April 25, 1930, p. 3; *ibid.*, May 8, 1930, p. 1; editorial, in *ibid.*, May 15, 1930, p. 2. According to a Russian writer, it was the newspaper *Suomen Työmies* which "began the struggle against 'interference from Moscow' in the affairs of the workers' movement in Finland." I. Iuvenalii, *Bor'ba klassov v Finliandii* (Moscow-Leningrad: Gosudarstvennoe Sotsial'no-Ekonomicheskoe izdatel'stvo, 1931), p. 164.

Social Democrats, and those who are "apolitical") must be respected. For this reason, the Trade Union Organization cannot be a political party or assume those tasks which belong to political parties.[56]

In the spring of 1930 Niilo Wälläri, a member of three subcommittees of the Left Group central committee and a newly appointed editor for *Suomen Työmies*,[57] assumed a more prominent role in the opposition.[58] It is, therefore, not surprising that the question of forming a new party, a task which Wälläri for years had been striving to accomplish, should be raised at this time. On May 4, 1930, the Helsinki and Sörnäinen Socialist worker associations held a joint meeting which elected a central committee for a new party.[59] The nine permanent members of this committee were N. Wälläri, K. Kulo, M. Väisänen, H. M. Ahokanta, U. Nurminen, E. Härmä, L. Härmä, O. Jalava, and F. Pietikäinen.[60] One principle endorsed at the meeting had, by now, a long history:

[56] *Suomen Työmies*, January 18, 1930, p. 1; Erkki Härmä, in *ibid.*, January 18, 1930, p. 3; editorial, in *ibid.*, February 6, 1930, p. 2; K. Kulo, in *ibid.*, February 11, 1930, p. 3; M. Väisänen, in *ibid.*, February 14, 1930, p. 3. Hugo M. Ahokanta, in a letter to Kalle Lepola, accused the central committee of the Finnish Communist Party of having adopted an attitude which dictated that Finnish trade union organizations observe nothing but Communist Party politics. Hugo M. Ahokanta to author, April 27, 1962.

[57] Wälläri, *Myrskyssä*, p. 218. The three subcommittees to which Wälläri belonged were trade union, finance, and foreign affairs.

[58] Hugo M. Ahokanta to author, November 17, 1962.

[59] *Suomen Työmies*, May 6, 1930, p. 1; editorial, in *ibid.*, May 27, 1930, p. 2. As early as March 1930 Wälläri had gained ground for the formation of a new party. *Työväenjärjestöjen Tiedonantaja*, March 11, 1930, p. 2.

[60] *Suomen Työmies*, May 6, 1930, p. 1. The absence of two names, E. Pekkala and E. Tuomi, is significant. They opposed the formation of a new party. Niilo Wälläri to author, March 27, 1962; Emil

For these reasons—while fighting the Social Democratic Party, which has sunk into class conciliation, and all bourgeois parties—we also strongly oppose the efforts of emigrant leaders of the Finnish Communist Party to become the masters of Finland's labor movement and to issue orders concerning its internal affairs. We fight the bureaucratic policies of the Finnish Communist Party because the workers themselves must have the power of decision in their own mass organizations.[61]

The leaders of the new party hoped that it would gain the support of all who did not adhere to the extreme wing of either the Social Democratic Party or the left labor movement,[62] a very unrealistic aim,[63] as the *Suomen Työmies* group had many big names, but lacked mass support.[64]

The birth at this time of a semi-Fascist movement provided the finishing touch to the demise of what Moscow called "leader opportunism." In response to the increased militancy of Finnish Communists, and in admiration of Benito Mussolini, there arose in Finland an extreme right-wing movement known as the Lapua

---

Tuomi to author, April 10, 1962; *Työväenjärjestöjen Tiedonantaja*, May 9, 1930, p. 6. Pekkala and Tuomi felt that the time was not yet ripe for a new party; they adopted a "wait and see" attitude. Uno Nurminen to author, April 18, 1962.

[61] *Suomen Työmies*, May 8, 1930, p. 1.

[62] Niilo Wälläri to author, March 27, 1962; Uno Nurminen to author, April 18, 1962.

[63] Niilo Wälläri to author, March 27, 1962.

[64] K. L. Kulo to author, June 18, 1962. It would appear that the masses were indifferent not only to the *Suomen Työmies* group, but to all workers' parties. Moscow was more disturbed by this indifference than by the activities of the opposition group. *Työväenjärjestöjen Tiedonantaja*, March 10, 1930, p. 2.

movement.[65] In November 1929 several thousand residents of the village of Lapua broke up a series of Communist youth meetings and stripped the participants of their red shirts. The impact of this incident was far-reaching: "Farmers, clergymen, academicians, industrialists, military leaders, and territorial expansionists of all occupations united in a movement which formally announced its goal to be the extinction of Communism in Finland." Followers of the Lapua movement assumed the existence of a law higher than written statutes, the law of Lapua (*Lapuan laki*).[66] One prominent figure in the movement stated that it was the spirit rather than the letter of law which was supreme.[67] This view led to acts of violence which "initiated a chain reaction of political murders, beatings, and kidnappings intended to carry out the law of Lapua."[68]

In actuality the Finnish Communist Party represented no immediate threat to Finnish society.[69] In 1925 the

[65] Väinö Tanner to author, January 17, 1963.

[66] Marvin Rintala, *Three Generations: The Extreme Right Wing in Finnish Politics* (Bloomington: Indiana University Press, 1962), pp. 164-165. This is the most authoritative source in any language on the Lapua movement.

[67] A. W. [Artturi Vuorimaa], in *Rintamamies*, August 8, 1930, p. 5.

[68] Rintala, *op.cit.*, p. 170. The first President of Finland, K. J. Ståhlberg, was one of the many Finnish citizens kidnapped. The crime was planned by Major General K. M. Wallenius, chief of the General Staff of the Finnish Army.

[69] *Ibid.*, p. 180; K. A. Lohi, in *Valtiopäivät 1930 pöytäkirjat* (Helsinki: Valtioneuvoston kirjapaino, 1930), p. 945; Minister of the Interior (Linturi), in *ibid.*, p. 959; Rh. Sventorzetski, in *ibid.*, p. 1027; Väinö Tanner to author, January 17, 1963; Yrjö Sirola, in *Työmies* (Sup.), September 5, 1928, p. 3. This evidence makes unreasonable the assertion of an American scholar that Finnish Communists in 1929 were plotting with organized leadership one of four bids for power staggered at ten-year intervals (1918, 1929, 1939,

party had set its sights on doubling the number of its members and party cells. By 1927, however, the number of cells had increased by 4 per cent only, active members by 8 per cent. It soon became clear that the ultimate goal of the Lapua movement was not the crushing of Communism but rather the destruction of all parties and of parliamentary government.[70] The Lapua movement seems, moreover, to have halted a downward trend in Communist Party membership, and Lapua action appears to have increased, rather then decreased, the danger of Communism. At a meeting of the Finnish Communist Party central committee in the summer of 1932, it was announced that 80 per cent of the party's members had joined "after the Fascist upheaval."[71]

In June 1930 Niilo Wälläri and the *Suomen Työmies* group proposed that all workers—Social Democrats, left-wing Socialists, and Communists—join together in a common front against the Fascist danger.[72] Wälläri noted that in Germany, in 1920, Communists, Socialists, and even democratic members of the bourgeoisie had united to defeat the right-wing elements involved in the Kapp *putsch*. Precedent, however, carried no weight with Finnish Communists. The only common front possible was a united front *from below*, which must be formed "over the heads of the Social Fascist and opportunist

---

and 1948). James H. Billington, "Finland," in Cyril E. Black and Thomas P. Thornton, eds., *Communism and Revolution: The Strategic Uses of Political Violence* (Princeton: Princeton University Press, 1964), p. 130.

[70] Rintala, *op.cit.*, p. 183.

[71] *Kommunisti*, No. 19 (103), October 15, 1932, p. 885; *Suomen kommunistinen puolue*, p. 386.

[72] N. Wälläri, in *Suomen Työmies*, June 7, 1930, p. 2; editorial, in *ibid.*, June 12, 1930, p. 2; *ibid.*, June 17, 1930, p. 2.

leaders."[73] Attention was called in a *Suomen Työmies* editorial to the futility of this approach:

A united front over the heads of leaders is a phrase which in a real united-front situation has never yet been realized. Its application in practice would mean that the leading organs of those central organizations whose masses one is trying to get into a united front would have to be ignored and that unity would have to be achieved behind their backs. Theoretically, this should work splendidly. But what large, functioning organization has such an undisciplined membership that it would ignore those leading organs which it has elected and join the masses of other organizations in united action?[74]

The *Suomen Työmies* group sought negotiations with all leading organs, regardless of their place in the political spectrum, but Communists refused to embrace such a proposal.[75] Social Democrats were also hesitant, as they considered the *Suomen Työmies* group "full-blooded Communists."[76] Since the *Suomen Työmies* group did not disagree with the Moscovites on principles, a united front between them—but not with Social Democracy—

[73] Editorial, in *Työväenjärjestöjen Tiedonantaja*, June 10, 1930, p. 2. "Social Fascists" were the leaders of the Social Democratic Party; "opportunists" were the *Suomen Työmies* group.

[74] Editorial, in *Suomen Työmies*, June 12, 1930, p. 2.

[75] *Ibid.*, June 17, 1930, pp. 2-3; *Työväenjärjestöjen Tiedonantaja*, June 10, 1930, p. 2; *Suomen kommunistinen puolue*, pp. 305-306.

[76] Editorial, in *Suomen Sosialidemokraatti*, February 12, 1930, p. 3. A more restrained position was taken by the left wing in the Social Democratic Party. Its adherents felt that there should be some contact with the *Suomen Työmies* group, although they feared that members of this opposition were still Communists. Johan Helo to author, June 8, 1962. *Kansan Työ*, a Social Democratic newspaper controlled by the left wing in the party, often referred to members of the *Suomen Työmies* group as "moderate Communists."

138

was possible.[77] At best the Social Democratic Party was willing to endorse its own united front from below.[78]

The Finnish Communist Party declared that right opportunism, with its supporters of a united front from above, constituted the main danger in the party, but that left-wing extremism was also a factor with which to contend.[79] As the Fascist persecutions gained momentum, some Finnish Communists began to feel that the party should turn solely to secret activity and prepare for a decisive battle.[80] They were convinced that nothing could be done without weapons.[81] In September 1930 it

[77] *Suomen Sosialidemokraatti*, June 13, 1930, p. 4.

[78] At the Social Democratic congress held in 1926, the party defined its attitude toward Communism: "in taking a stand on the so-called 'Finnish Socialist Party' we must draw a distinction between Communist leaders and the workers under their influence, in order to make the latter's return to the Social Democratic Party a natural and easy process." *Suomen sosialidemokraattisen puolueen neljännentoista edustajakokouksen pöytäkirja* (Helsinki: Sosdem puoluetoimikunta, 1926), p. 110. At the next congress of the Social Democratic Party, convened early in 1930, right-wing Social Democrats regained control (which they had lost in 1926) of the leading party organs. Judging from earlier events, it is likely that the new leadership considered even a united front from below too daring for the Social Democratic Party. In any case, one can be certain that right-wing Social Democrats were not willing to steer the party along a course more radical than that which had been adopted at the 1926 party congress.

[79] *Suomen kommunistinen puolue*, pp. 268, 308.

[80] Statement made at the April 1930 plenum of the central committee of the Finnish Communist Party, referred to in *ibid.*, p. 268. On December 5, 1929, Parliament passed a bill abolishing the right of Communists to free association. The Lapua movement was also demanding that legislation be passed which would abolish freedom of the press and which would remove Communists from Parliament as well as from organs of local government. On March 28, 1930, Communist printing presses in the city of Vaasa were smashed by members of the Lapua movement. Rintala, *op.cit.*, pp. 166-167.

[81] *SKP:n Tiedonantaja*, No. 10, 1930, p. 8.

was noted at a Conference of the Finnish Communist Party that a number of party members favored arming the workers and engaging in guerrilla warfare, a view prevalent in the Finnish Communist Youth League. Members wanted direct armed action against the Fascists—the Communist youth had a tendency to view themselves as the vanguard of the class struggle. Some Finnish workers, moreover, were under the impression that the Red Army would cross the border to free them from bourgeois rule.[82] In the eyes of the *Suomen Työmies* group, these sentiments were a logical outgrowth of the decisions announced at the Sixth Comintern Congress.[83]

Left extremism in Finland took on an organized form in the fall of 1930 with the formation in Helsinki of the Finnish League of Red Soldiers (*Suomen Punaisten Rintamamiesten Liitto*).[84] Members of the league issued a program, called "Activity or Passiveness?" in which they condemned participation in elections, opposed trade union activity, rejected all open work, and even went so far as to thank the Fascists for rendering legal activity impossible.[85] The slogan of the league was that death in

[82] *Suomen kommunistinen puolue*, pp. 268, 306, 335-336, 394.

[83] An editorial in *Suomen Työmies*, February 27, 1930, p. 2, stated that only Finnish youth and unorganized labor would carry out the Comintern's revolutionary line.

[84] Antikainen, ed., *op.cit.*, p. 477.

[85] *Suomen kommunistinen puolue*, p. 351; Antikainen, ed., *op.cit.*, p. 29; *SKP:n Tiedonantaja*, No. 3 (March), 1931, p. 4. By November 1930 all legal activity by the Communists was impossible: On June 14, 1930, Communist publications had been banned by an executive order; on July 5 the Ministry of the Interior, after discussions in the Council of State (*Valtioneuvosto*), had ordered the arrest of all Communist and left-wing Socialist members of Parliament; on July 14 bills barring Communists from organs of local government had been approved; in the fall of 1930 Parliament proceeded to pass other major anti-Communist bills. Rintala, *op.cit.*, pp. 175, 177, 181, 184.

battle is preferable to life in a capitalist society.[86] In their publication *Toveri*, members of the league stated that they were living on the threshold of a bloody civil war.[87] The official line of the Finnish Communist Party, on the other hand, was that Finland was not yet ripe for armed revolt; the situation was only moving *toward* civil war.[88] Left extremism in Finland was condemned at the conference of the Finnish Communist Party which took place in 1931,[89] although there were some emigrants who supported—at least in principle—the Finnish League of Red Soldiers.[90] The existence of the league was a challenge to the authority of the Finnish Communist Party, but this threat was soon removed as a result of quick action by Finnish police.[91]

[86] Kullervo Manner, in *Proletaari*, No. 6 (56), June 1931, p. 29.

[87] *Toveri*, No. 4, 1930, p. 1. Only four issues of *Toveri* were printed. Antikainen, ed., *op.cit.*, p. 477.

[88] *SKP:n Tiedonantaja*, No. 10, 1930, p. 8; *ibid.*, No. 3 (March), 1931, p. 4.

[89] *Suomen kommunistinen puolue*, p. 351.

[90] At the Communist Party congress held in 1925, Eino Rahja had led an opposition group of left extremists. Although he had been removed from the central committee of the party in 1927, an intensive campaign against him continued as late as 1933. Members of the Finnish League of Red Soldiers boasted, moreover, that they were in contact with Leningrad, where opposition elements led by Rahja were centered. *SKP taistelujen tiellä*, Vol. II (Helsinki: Kansankulttuuri, 1946), p. 62; *Suomen kommunistinen puolue*, pp. 92, 351; Antikainen, ed., *op.cit.*, pp. 14-15, 260; Mika Waltari, *Neuvostovakoilun varjossa* (Helsinki: Otava, 1942), pp. 32, 55-56; *Vapaus*, January 25, 1933, p. 4; *ibid.*, January 28, 1933, p. 4; *ibid.*, September 10, 1933, p. 2; *ibid.*, September 14, 1933, p. 4.

[91] The league claimed that it was supporting the Finnish Communist Party and following Comintern decisions and theses. *Toveri*, No. 4, 1930, p. 3. These assertions were strongly rejected by the central committee of the Finnish Communist Party. *SKP:n Tiedonantaja*, No. 1, 1931, p. 7. Some feel that had the league not been suppressed by Finnish authorities, the Communist Party would have been rent asunder from within. Niilo Wälläri to author,

In 1932 left extremism in the Finnish Communist Party assumed another form when it overestimated the importance of instinct *(vaistovaraisuuden yliarvioiminen)*.[92] In April 1932 Hanna Malm, wife of Kullervo Manner, wrote that even without a Communist Party the Finnish workers would always struggle due to their instinct for self-preservation.[93] A month later she stated that the role of the Communist Party in the class struggle was to make of this instinctive stirring a conscious movement, it was the task of the party to raise the workers to a *higher* political level.[94] In the summer of 1932 the Communist Party central committee charged Hanna Malm with underestimating the importance of the party in the class struggle, and she was sharply reprimanded, but not silenced.[95]

At a Soviet celebration in Uhtua (Ukhta) commemorating the fifteenth anniversary of the Finnish Revolution, Hanna Malm criticized members of the left wing in the prerevolutionary Finnish Social Democratic Party *(siltasaarelaiset)* for their role in the events of 1918. She reopened a question already settled in the summer of 1932 by a plenum of the central committee.

March 27, 1962. Since membership in the league was very small and, in the words of one informant, had at its disposal scarcely anything more lethal than pocketknives, one must conclude that Wälläri's observation is a gross exaggeration. One cannot, however, dismiss the Finnish League of Red Soldiers as an insignificant organization. This is evident from the fact that the two leading organs of the Finnish Communist Party, *Proletaari* and *SKP:n Tiedonantaja*, devoted considerable space to attacks on the league.

[92] *Suomen kommunistinen puolue*, p. 384.

[93] Hanna Malm, in *Vapaus*, April 23, 1932, p. 1.

[94] Hanna Malm, in *ibid.*, May 24, 1932, p. 2.

[95] Toivo Antikainen, in *Punainen Karjala*, June 1, 1933, p. 3; *Kommunisti*, No. 4 (112), February 28, 1933, p. 182.

She was, in other words, breaking party discipline.[96] In March 1933 Malm acknowledged that her deviation from the party line lay not only in oral and written statements made in Uhtua, but in also sending two letters, voicing differences of opinion with the leadership of the Finnish Communist Party, to party officials in Soviet Karelia; she had thus made herself "guilty of gross defamation of the leadership of the Finnish Communist Party and of certain of its members."[97] These defamatory remarks were scored at a plenum of the central committee in the summer of 1933; the plenum also firmly rejected the notion that the Finnish Communist Party should sit back and await mass movements which would give birth to themselves.[98] Hanna Malm was expelled from the party for one year, and within a few months her husband, Kullervo Manner, was included in this "right opportunism masked in 'left' phrases."[99] The "antiparty group" was condemned by the Comintern's Political Secretariat, to which Otto Kuusinen had been reelected in 1928 for the eighth consecutive year, for having spearheaded "a struggle against the central committee of the Finnish Communist Party and against its leaders."[100] This ultraleftism was, however, limited

[96] *Punainen Karjala*, June 1, 1933, p. 3.

[97] Hanna Malm, quoted in *ibid.*, June 1, 1933, p. 3.

[98] *Ibid.*, June 1, 1933, p. 3; *Kommunisti*, No. 2 (127), February 25, 1934, p. 91; *ibid.*, No. 14 (122), September 25, 1933, p. 635. Arvo Tuominen, *Kremlin kellot* (Helsinki: Tammi, 1957), pp. 264-265, claims that Hanna Malm, referring back to the Stockholm Opposition of 1920, was particularly hostile at this plenum to Otto Kuusinen. This assertion is made credible by statements in *Kommunisti*, No. 13 (121), August 25, 1933, p. 580.

[99] *Punainen Karjala*, June 1, 1933, p. 3; *Kommunisti*, No. 2 (127), February 25, 1934, p. 91.

[100] *Kommunisticheskii internatsional pered VII vsemirnym kongressom* (Moscow: Partizdat TsK VKP (b), 1935), p. 307. In 1935, when the Great Purges were getting under way, Kullervo Manner

to a small group;[101] it caused no change in the party line which pointed to right opportunism—not left extremism—as the main danger.[102]

The 1933 plenum of the central committee did, nonetheless, make a decision which initiated a new line in the Finnish trade union movement. In 1930 the Finnish Trade Union Organization had been proscribed, and a new trade union organization—the Finnish Confederation of Trade Unions (*Suomen Ammattiyhdistysten Keskusliitto*)—had been set up in its stead by Social Democrats. Communists, unlike the *Suomen Työmies* group,[103] had refused to join the new trade union organization.[104] In 1933, however, the central committee

---

and Hanna Malm were arrested and sentenced to death. Their sentences were subsequently reduced to ten years at forced labor through the intervention of leading Comintern figures. Tuominen, *Kremlin*, pp. 313, 315. Tuominen, who had taken up residence in the Soviet Union in 1933, was elected a member of IKKI and a candidate member of its Presidium at the Seventh Comintern Congress.

101 Arvo Tuominen, in *Bol'shaia sovetskaia entsiklopediia*, Vol. LVII (Moscow: Ogiz, 1936), p. 603. Tuominen states that the Manner-Malm opposition was joined by the remnants of the ultraleft group led by E. Rahja. It should, however, be noted that both Manner and Malm attacked that brand of left extremism which found expression in the Finnish League of Red Soldiers and which was, presumably, supported by Rahja. K. Manner, in *Proletaari*, No. 6 (56), June 1931, pp. 28-29; H. Malm, "Ei oikealle eikä vasemmalle," in *Vapaus*, April 23, 1932, p. 1.

102 *Kommunisti*, No. 19 (103), October 15, 1932, p. 884; *ibid.*, No. 4 (112), February 28, 1933, p. 183.

103 *Suomen sosialidemokraattisen puoluetoimikunnan pöytäkirjat*, July 28, 1930; Hugo M. Ahokanta to author, April 27, 1962.

104 Communists formed their own trade union movement, the Finnish Red Trade Union Organization (*Suomen Punainen Ammattijärjestö*), which worked underground and had very few members. Tuominen, *Kremlin*, p. 266; Arvo Tuominen to author, October 2, 1962; Jaakko Kivi to author, April 26, 1962; Hj. Långström to author, September 13, 1962; Hugo M. Ahokanta to author, April 27, 1962.

of the Finnish Communist Party called for a broad, united trade union movement,[105] saying that Communists should join the Confederation of Trade Unions, although only in a revolutionary sense.[106] The central committee plenum still endorsed a united front from below. The plenum continued to refer to Social Democratic leaders as "Social Fascists," and it viewed the maneuvers of the left wing in the Social Democratic Party as *the most insidious means of Social Democracy to support the Fascist dictatorship.*"[107]

A year later the change initiated in 1933 was carried further. In order to achieve unity in the trade union

[105] Arvo Tuominen, in *Vapaus*, September 5, 1935, p. 2.

[106] *Työmies* (SKP:n äänenkannattaja), No. 2, 1933, p. 2. Members of the Communist Party were ordered to establish "revolutionary trade union opposition groups" (*VAO:n ryhmiä*) in the Social Democratic trade union organizations.

[107] *Suomen kommunistinen puolue*, pp. 416-417. The left wing in the Social Democratic Party was not at this time a homogeneous grouping. It included such diverse personalities as Cay Sundström, Mikko Ampuja, Johan Helo, Karl Wiik, Rieti Itkonen, and Väinö Hupli. A common denominator was found in the struggle against right-wing Socialism, personified by Väinö Tanner, and in the struggle against Tanner's "dictatorial" control of party affairs. For further details, see the following: Hupli, in *Suomen Sosialidemokraatti*, December 9, 1926, p. 6; Tanner, in *Kansan Lehti*, December 23, 1927, pp. 1, 4; Itkonen, in *Suomen Sosialidemokraatti*, January 8, 1928, p. 6; Tanner, in *Kansan Lehti*, January 12, 1928, pp. 4-5; Itkonen, in *Suomen Sosialidemokraatti*, January 17, 1928, pp. 3-4; Wiik, in *ibid.*, February 1, 1928, p. 5; Sundström, in *ibid.*, June 16, 1928, p. 2; Wiik, in *ibid.*, November 22, 1928, p. 6; Wiik, in *ibid.*, January 10, 1929, pp. 1, 6; Hupli, in *ibid.*, September 15, 1929, pp. 5-6; Tanner, in *ibid.*, November 7, 1929, p. 5; Wiik, in *ibid.*, November 10, 1929, p. 6; editorial, in *Kansan Työ*, November 19, 1929, p. 2; editorial, in *ibid.*, November 20, 1929, p. 2; Tanner, in *Suomen Sosialidemokraatti*, November 21, 1929, pp. 4-5; Wiik, in *ibid.*, November 21, 1929, p. 5; Wiik, in *Suomen sosialidemokraattisen puolueen viidennentoista edustajakokouksen pöytäkirja*, p. 132; Ampuja, in *Suomen Sosialidemokraatti*, January 7, 1926, p. 4; Ampuja, in *ibid.*, April 3, 1928, p. 6.

movement, Communists were now willing to accept a united front from *above*.[108] A plenum of the central committee of the Communist Party proclaimed that there was a difference between Fascism and Social Fascism. The plenum supported cooperation with the Social Democratic left wing, saying that the left wing should be forced to demonstrate whether it was willing in deeds, not just words, to join the fight against Fascism. In certain instances the concept of a united front could even extend to the Social Democratic Party "in its entirety."[109] The Communists were only one step away from the "Popular Front" declared in 1935 at the Seventh Comintern Congress. The Popular Front would unite Communists, Socialists, and some members of the bourgeoisie in a worldwide struggle against the Fascist danger. But emigrant Finnish Communists, many of whom had risen to high positions in the party and state apparatus of Soviet Karelia, discovered that their security was endangered not by Fascism but by the reign of terror unleashed after the assassination in December 1934 of Stalin's heir apparent.[110]

[108] *Suomen Punainen Ammattijärjestö*, November 1934, p. 8.

[109] *Suomen kommunistinen puolue*, pp. 458, 466-467, 469, 473. The plenum was held in the summer of 1934. *SKP taistelujen tiellä*, Vol. III (Helsinki: Yhteistyön kirjapaino, 1947), p. 34. Several months earlier, in April, the French Communist Party had been instructed by Moscow to carry out a united front from above. Franz Borkenau, *European Communism* (New York: Harper & Brothers, 1953), pp. 122-123.

[110] The assassination of S. M. Kirov still remains shrouded in mystery, but there is general agreement that Stalin himself was in some way connected with the conspiracy.

CHAPTER SIX

National Deviation: Soviet Karelia

IN April 1918 it was apparent that the Finnish Civil War could end only in defeat for the Reds. The question of a retreat to Soviet Russia had become, therefore, an issue of major importance. The prevailing sentiment among Finnish Reds was that their forces should be evacuated to Eastern Russia,[1] whereas Edvard Gylling, an opponent of revolution, although a member of the revolutionary government, urged that resettlement be undertaken in Soviet Karelia. Karelia, which from ancient times has been considered an ethnological whole but which by the early seventeenth century, following repeated military conflict between the great northern powers, had been divided into Finnish Karelia and Russian Karelia, acted like a magnet. Even objections voiced by E. D. Stasova, secretary of the Russian Communist Party, could not sway Gylling.[2] The latter, an expert on agrarian matters and a former chairman of

[1] Oskari Tokoi, *Maanpakolaisen muistelmia* (Helsinki: Tammi, 1959), p. 224.

[2] *Ibid.*, p. 224; Kalle Lepola, in *Vapaus*, November 30, 1931, p. 2; Eero Haapalainen, in *Suomen Työmies*, June 13, 1923, p. 5. Ten days after the outbreak of the Finnish Civil War, the revolutionary government decided that Gylling should be asked to assume the duties of Minister of Finance; on March 8, 1918, he was formally named a member of the revolutionary government in charge of financial matters. *Suomen kansanvaltuuskunnan pöytäkirjat*, February 6, 1918, 8:30 P.M.; *Syyttäjistön arkisto* C a 7 (Valtionarkistossa). Gylling's opposition to revolution, discussed in chapter

Parliament's Board of Overseers for the Bank of Finland,[3] saw the settlement of Finnish Reds in Soviet Karelia as the first step in the development of a backward area hitherto regarded as a place suitable only for exile. Two years later, in 1920, Gylling would gain the support of Lenin, but in the interim Finnish Reds were widely scattered on both sides of the Ural Mountains. Gylling emigrated to Sweden.

Early in 1920 a small group of Finnish emigrants under the leadership of Jaakko Mäki was sent from Petrograd to Soviet Karelia with instructions to launch a program of agitation and propaganda among the non-Russian nationals. Late in March 1920 this program was formalized when a Karelian-Murmansk Department of the Central Bureau of Finnish Organizations of the Russian Communist Party (b) [*VKP (b) :n Suomalaisten Järjestöjen Keskustoimiston Karjalan-Muurmannin osasto*] was established.[4] The task of this department was to administer the agitation and propaganda

---

three, weathered the storm of civil war. In 1920, when his colleagues were advocating violence as the only means to establish proletarian rule, Gylling saw the possibility of, and expressed a preference for, social revolution brought about by parliamentary means. *Suomen työväen vallankumous 1918: Arviota ja itsekritiikkiä* (Leningrad: Kirja, 1928), p. 105.

[3] It is shocking to find Gylling falsely described by one American author as an ex-burglar. C. Jay Smith, Jr., *Finland and the Russian Revolution 1917-1922* (Athens: University of Georgia Press, 1958), p. 56.

[4] Jaakko Mäki, in *Punainen Karjala*, July 10, 1925, p. 5; Mäki, in *ibid.*, November 30, 1931, p. 3. The Central Bureau had been established in December 1919 in accordance with a decision made by the central committee of the Russian Communist Party; in 1924 the Central Bureau was liquidated. *Vapaus*, January 19, 1921, p. 2; *Kommunisti*, No. 5 (65), May 1930, p. 190. Perhaps the most notable achievement of the Central Bureau was the setting up in

work among the Finnish-speaking inhabitants of Soviet Karelia,[5] and Mäki, as secretary of the department, recommended to the central authorities that more extensive political and economic work be undertaken in Soviet Karelia.[6]

At this time Edvard Gylling proposed to leading figures in the Russian Communist Party that the internal affairs of Karelia be organized on the basis of autonomy.[7] Gylling was asked to come to Soviet Russia, and in May 1920 he met Lenin.[8] They agreed that Gylling should draw up a plan for an autonomous republic;[9] on the basis of this plan a decree establishing the Karelian Workers' Commune (*Karjalan Työkansan Kommuuni*) was issued on June 7, 1920, by the All-Russian Central Executive Committee (VTsIK) of the

---

January 1922 of a party school for Finns. In the fall of that year the school became one of two sections in the Petrograd Division of the Communist University for Western Minority Nationalities. The first rector of the Petrograd Division was Yrjö Sirola. *Vapaus*, January 29, 1927, p. 2; *ibid.*, September 22, 1922, p. 3; *ibid.*, April 24, 1923, p. 3; *ibid.*, June 13, 1925, p. 1; *Kommunisti*, No. 5 (29), May 1927, pp. 209-211.

[5] Jaakko Mäki, in *Punainen Karjala*, July 10, 1925, p. 5. According to the Russian census of 1920, there were about 2,000 Finnish-speaking inhabitants in Soviet Karelia. Edvard Gylling, in *Suomen Työläinen*, October 20, 1921, p. 2.

[6] Jaakko Mäki, in *Punainen Karjala*, November 30, 1931, p. 3; *ibid.*, November 6, 1932, p. 4. In the fall of 1917 Mäki had been a chairman of the Finnish Social Democratic parliamentary group.

[7] Eero Haapalainen, in *Suomen Työmies*, June 13, 1923, p. 5; Jaakko Mäki, in *Punainen Karjala*, November 30, 1931, p. 3.

[8] Edvard Gylling, in *Pravda*, July 3, 1935, p. 2.

[9] Yrjö Sirola, present during the discussion with Lenin, had—unlike Gylling—doubts about the wisdom of setting up an autonomous Karelian republic. Yrjö Sirola, in J. E. Latukka, ed., *Lenin suomalaisten muistelmissa* (Leningrad: Kirja, 1925), p. 11; Iu. Sirola, "Vospominaniia o Lenine," *Proletarskaia revoliutsiia*, No. 1 (96), January 1930, p. 83.

Congress of Soviets.[10] The decree also set up a three-member Revolutionary Committee, whose members included Edvard Gylling (chairman), Jaakko Mäki, and Vasilii Kudzhiev, to deal with administrative matters and to lay the groundwork for a Congress of Karelian Soviets.[11]

Late in June 1920—after having collected in Petrograd men, money, and a printing press—Gylling and Mäki traveled north to Petroskoi (Petrozavodsk).[12] There they met Kudzhiev, and the three-member Revolutionary Committee continued north along the Murmansk railroad in search of a capital for the Karelian Workers' Commune.[13] The search took them as far north as Kemi (Kem'), but in the end they returned to Petroskoi even though it was considered a reactionary city and too Russian.[14] The decision to make Petroskoi the capital of the Karelian Workers' Commune meant that there would be

[10] Edvard Gylling, in *Pravda*, July 3, 1935, p. 2.

[11] *Kymmenen vuotta Neuvosto-Karjalaa 1920-1930* (Petroskoi: AKSNT:n Toimeenpaneva Keskuskomitea, 1930), p. 9; Jaakko Mäki, in *Punainen Karjala*, July 10, 1925, p. 5. The Revolutionary Committee was later enlarged and then in February 1921 replaced by a Karelian Central Executive Committee. The elected chairman of the Central Executive Committee was Edvard Gylling. Jaakko Mäki, in *Punainen Karjala*, July 4, 1935, p. 3; Edvard Gylling, in *Suomen Työmies*, March 16, 1921, p. 6; *Kymmenen vuotta*, p. 61; E. Haapalainen, "Neuvosto-Karjala XV-vuotias," in *Sosialistinen Kalenteri vuodelle 1935* (Leningrad: Kirja, 1935), p. 59.

[12] Jaakko Mäki, in *Punainen Karjala*, July 10, 1925, p. 5; Mäki, in *ibid.*, November 30, 1931, p. 3; Mäki, in *ibid.*, July 4, 1935, p. 2; Edvard Gylling, in *Suomen Työmies*, March 16, 1921, p. 6.

[13] Jaakko Mäki, in *Punainen Karjala*, July 4, 1935, p. 2.

[14] Eero Haapalainen, in *Suomen Työmies*, June 13, 1923, p. 5; Jaakko Mäki, in *Punainen Karjala*, November 30, 1931, pp. 3-4. In 1926 the population of Petroskoi was approximately 90 percent Russian (*ibid.*, July 28, 1927, p. 2); there is no indication from the population data examined by the author that in 1920 this percentage was substantially different.

two administrative centers in the same city, for the Executive Committee of Aunus (Olonets) county was already located there.[15]

The boundaries of the Karelian Workers' Commune had not been fixed by the decree of June 7, 1920, and the Revolutionary Committee soon began to discuss this question with the Executive Committee of Aunus county. A special joint committee was established to deal with the boundary issue, but no agreement could be reached. The Aunus Executive Committee wanted to see the border drawn solely on the basis of nationality, whereas the Revolutionary Committee advocated economic boundaries.[16] On August 4, 1920, a decree issued by the All-Russian Central Executive Committee and the Council of People's Commissars (Sovnarkom) of the RSFSR settled the matter to the satisfaction of the Revolutionary Committee.[17] Parts of Aunus, Petroskoi, Kemi, and Poventsa (Povenetskii) counties were included in the Karelian Workers' Commune. The Aunus Executive Committee continued, however, to demand national borders even after the central authorities had given their backing to the Revolutionary Committee.[18]

This difference of opinion over the territorial composition of the Karelian Workers' Commune was just one aspect of a larger conflict concerning the purpose and necessity of the Karelian Workers' Commune. Aunus county officials, and particularly V. Kudzhiev,

[15] Jaakko Mäki, in *ibid.*, July 4, 1935, p. 2.

[16] Edvard Gylling, in *Suomen Työmies*, March 16, 1921, p. 6; *Sovetskaia Kareliia: ocherki partiinogo, sovetskogo i kul'turnogo stroitel'stva AKSSR* (Moscow-Leningrad: OGIZ, 1933), p. 53, note 1.

[17] Edvard Gylling, in *Suomen Työmies*, March 16, 1921, p. 6.

[18] *Sovetskaia Kareliia*, p. 53, note 1. Detailed information on the boundaries of the Karelian Workers' Commune can be found in Mauno Jääskeläinen, *Itä-Karjalan kysymys* (Porvoo: WSOY, 1961), p. 284.

considered the Karelian Workers' Commune a temporary phenomenon which would pass into oblivion as
soon as an agreement establishing peace in Karelia
could be reached between Finland and Soviet Russia.[19]
Kudzhiev envisioned a rapid liquidation of the Karelian Workers' Commune, in which he was a leading
figure, and the reincorporation of its territories into
the counties from which they had been separated.[20] The
dispute was soon resolved by fiat. After the Eighth All-
Russian Congress of Soviets, held in late 1920, the All-
Russian Central Executive Committee ordered the Aunus
Executive Committee to move its offices from Petroskoi;[21] in October 1922 Aunus county with all its
administrative organs was abolished.[22] In October 1923,
in accordance with a decree issued by the All-Russian

[19] Edvard Gylling, in *Suomen Työmies*, March 16, 1921, p. 6;
Jaakko Mäki, in *Punainen Karjala*, July 10, 1925, p. 6; Mäki, in
ibid., November 30, 1931, pp. 3-4. In February 1918 Gustaf Mannerheim, commander in chief of the Finnish Civil Guard, declared
that he would not put his sword in its scabbard until the question
of East Karelia was settled. This statement was followed in March
1918 by an attack on Soviet Karelia in the region of Uhtua
(Ukhta). In April 1919 Finnish forces again crossed the Soviet-
Finnish border in a drive on the cities of Aunus and Petroskoi
(Petrozavodsk). A peace treaty between Finland and Soviet Russia
was signed in October 1920, but in November of the following
year, charging that Soviet Russia had not lived up to certain provisions of the treaty, Finnish Whites resumed the offensive in
Eastern Karelia. Details on these military operations can be found
in Jääskeläinen, *op.cit.*, pp. 93-99, 173-174, 206-233, 319-321. For
a thorough analysis of the ideological issue involved, namely, the
formation of a Greater Finland, see Marvin Rintala, *Three Generations: The Extreme Right Wing in Finnish Politics* (Bloomington: Indiana University Press, 1962).

[20] Jaakko Mäki, in *Punainen Karjala*, July 10, 1925, p. 6; Mäki,
in *ibid.*, November 30, 1931, p. 4.

[21] Edvard Gylling, in *Suomen Työmies*, March 16, 1921, p. 6.

[22] *Kymmenen vuotta*, p. 88; Jaakko Mäki, in *Punainen Karjala*,
July 4, 1935, p. 3.

Executive Committee on July 25, 1923, the Fourth All-Karelian Congress of Soviets proclaimed the transformation of the Karelian Workers' Commune into the Autonomous Karelian Soviet Socialist Republic.[23]

On the basis of a census taken in 1920 it is estimated that at the end of 1923 the population of the seven counties in the Autonomous Karelian Republic was 210,211.[24] The national composition of some counties (Poventsa and Puudosi) was almost exclusively Russian, whereas in others (Aunus and Uhtua) it was overwhelmingly Karelian. Finns, accounting for less than one per cent of the total population of Soviet Karelia, were located primarily in the county of Petroskoi.[25]

[23] *Sovetskaia Kareliia*, p. 66. The terms of peace ending the Russo-Finnish War of 1939-1940 increased the population and area of the Autonomous Karelian Soviet Socialist Republic, and on March 31, 1940, it was transformed into the Karelo-Finnish Soviet Socialist Republic. In June 1956 the Karelo-Finnish Soviet Socialist Republic was reincorporated into the RSFSR as an autonomous republic.

[24] *Statisticheskii obzor 1923-1924 g.: Tilastollinen katsaus v. 1923-1924* (Petrozavodsk: Izdanie statisticheskogo upravleniia AKSSR, 1925), introduction, p. 13. Moving from north to south the seven counties, comprising an area considerably larger than that which was included in the Karelian Workers' Commune by the decree of August 4, 1920, were as follows: Uhtua (Ukhtinskii), Kemi (Kemskii), Paadene (Padanskii), Poventsa (Povenetskii), Puudosi (Pudozhskii), Petroskoi (Petrozavodskii), and Aunus (Olonetskii). In 1927 the counties, subdivided into fifty-five rural villages, were abolished in favor of a new administrative system based on *raions* (districts).

[25] *Ibid.*, introduction, pp. 13-15, part one, p. 27; *Nekotorye dannye o rabote karel'skogo pravitel'stva* (Petrozavodsk: Gos. Tipografiia im. P. F. Anokhina, 1929), p. 3; *Kymmenen vuotta*, p. 60. At the end of 1923 Russians accounted for 55.7 percent, Karelians for 42.8 percent, of the total population in the Autonomous Karelian Republic. Of the 1,051 Finns in the Republic at the end of 1923, 548 resided in the county of Petroskoi.

153

An already difficult nationality question became more complicated in November 1924 when a rural district (*volost'*) inhabited mainly by Veps was added to the Autonomous Karelian Republic.[26]

One of the central, and most difficult, problems confronting the architects of a nationality policy in Soviet Karelia was the question of a written language for the Karelians.[27] The problem in stark simplicity was the absence of a unified "Karelian language."[28] In northern Karelia (Uhtua) dialects very close to pure Finnish were spoken. In central Karelia (Paadene-Kemi) the similarity was less pronounced, although the dialects bore a resemblance to Finnish. In southern Karelia (Aunus) it was Russian which had left an imprint on the speech of the Karelians.[29] There were, moreover, Karelians in the southern area ("Lyydiköt") whose language had been influenced by the dialect of the Veps, which, in

[26] *Krasnaia Kareliia*, November 21, 1924, p. 3; *Sovetskaia Kareliia*, p. 119. According to the Russian census of 1920, the combined population of this rural district (Soltjärvi-Sheltozerskaia) and one other (Latva-Ladvinskaia) was 10,276. *Statisticheskii*, p. iv. In 1926, also a census year, the population of Soltjärvi was 8,858, Latva 4,295. *Punainen Karjala*, July 28, 1927, p. 2. The 1926 census reported that there were 8,587 Veps—as compared with 2,327 Finns, 100,781 Karelians, and 153,967 Russians—within the Autonomous Karelian Republic. *Karelo-Murmanskii krai*, No. 7 (July), 1928, p. 34.

[27] *Punainen Karjala*, October 8, 1927, p. 1; *ibid.*, November 27, 1930, p. 3; *ibid.*, November 30, 1931, p. 1.

[28] *Ibid.*, January 13, 1925, p. 1; *Krasnaia Kareliia*, May 6, 1937, p. 3; *ibid.*, December 18, 1937, p. 3.

[29] *Punainen Karjala*, January 13, 1925, p. 1; *ibid.*, December 8, 1931, p. 3; K. Rovio, "Kielikysymys Neuvosto-Karjalan kansallisuuspolitiikassa," *Kommunisti*, No. 8 (80), August 1931, pp. 382-383. A Russian text of the Rovio article can be found in *Karelo-Murmanskii krai*, No. 1-2 (January-February), 1931, pp. 16-21.

154

turn, was considered a linguistic link between Finnish and Estonian.[30]

The authorities in Soviet Karelia had three alternatives. The Karelians would have to adopt as a written language Russian, Finnish, or a special, as yet nonexistent, Karelian literary language.[31] The formation of a Karelian literary language was rejected as unnecessary and impractical since all the spoken Karelian dialects had many points in common with Finnish.[32] The choice was narrowed to either Russian or Finnish. By 1923 the problem had at least in principle been solved.[33] Finnish and Russian had been proclaimed the official state languages,[34] which meant, in effect, that the literary language of the Karelians was to be Finnish.[35] As

[30] *Krasnaia Kareliia*, December 18, 1937, p. 3; *Punainen Karjala*, January 13, 1925, p. 1. In spite of this linguistic affinity, Finnish was a foreign language to the Veps. They understood Russian. Rovio, "Kielikysymys," pp. 382-383.

[31] Rovio, "Kielikysymys," pp. 376-377.

[32] *Ibid.*, p. 380; H. Rautio, in *Kommunisti*, No. 6, June 15, 1925, p. 263. One professor of linguistics has written that the Karelian dialects and Finnish bear a relationship which is similar to that which exists between Polish and Russian. D. V. Bubrikh, in *Krasnaia Kareliia*, September 21, 1937, p. 2.

[33] *Punainen Karjala*, November 7, 1928, p. 4.

[34] Edvard Gylling, in *Pravda*, July 3, 1935, p. 2; *Suomen Työmies*, July 31, 1923, p. 1; *Kommuna*, October 7, 1921, p. 2; L. Letonmäki, *Karjalan historia* (Leningrad: Kirja, 1931), pp. 159-160; *Kolmannen yleiskarjalaisen työläisten, talonpoikain ja puna-armeijalaisten neuvostojen edustajakokouksen pöytäkirja. Kokous pidetty Petroskoissa lokakuun 2-7 p:nä v. 1922* (Petroskoi: Aluekirjapaino, 1922), p. 36; *Punainen Karjala*, November 7, 1928, p. 4; *ibid.*, May 26, 1929, p. 1. When a Karelian army was formed, in the summer of 1925, the troops were obliged to know general command words in both Finnish and Russian. The language used in the ranks, however, was Finnish. *Kymmenen vuotta*, pp. 163-164; *Sosialistinen Kalenteri*, p. 160.

[35] *Kymmenen vuotta*, p. 234; Kustaa Rovio, in *Punainen Karjala*, November 30, 1931, p. 1.

Kustaa Rovio, first secretary of the Karelian party apparatus from 1929 to 1935, later noted: If Russian *had* been made the language for the Karelians, the formation of an autonomous republic would have been nonsensical.[36]

The solution to the language problem had an explosive impact on the school system in Soviet Karelia. Of the four hundred and twelve schools existing in 1920, only thirty-three were located in areas considered Karelian in composition. In none of the thirty-three was Finnish the language of instruction.[37] Russian reigned supreme. After the formation of the Karelian Workers' Commune, however, some Finnish schools were established. In 1921 the Second All-Karelian Congress of Soviets voted to enlarge the network of Finnish-language schools;[38] the following year the budget for Russian schools was cut in order to finance the development of Finnish schools.[39] Resistance to this new policy was strong. Some influential figures who, like V. Kudzhiev, were later labeled Great Russian chauvinists, challenged the necessity of the Finnish language in Soviet Karelia and urged that Finnish schools be closed.[40] The opposition discovered, however, that it was struggling against superior forces. In the winter of 1922 the People's Commissar of Nationalities, Joseph V. Stalin, threw his weight behind Edvard Gylling and "Karelization"

[36] Rovio, "Kielikysymys," p. 385. From December 1927 until shortly before he was elected secretary of the Karelian *Obkom* of the Russian Communist Party, in July 1929, Rovio had been rector of the Petrograd Division of the Communist University for Western Minority Nationalities. *Punainen Karjala*, July 4, 1929, p. 1.

[37] *Punainen Karjala*, June 22, 1935, p. 2; *Vapaus*, July 2, 1935, p. 3.

[38] *Kolmannen yleiskarjalaisen*, p. 19.

[39] *Kymmenen vuotta*, p. 85.

[40] *Sovetskaia Kareliia*, pp. 252-253; *Punainen Karjala*, December 10, 1929, p. 2.

(*karjalaistuttaminen*).[41] The overall policy was described by Gylling as an attempt to make the Karelians feel at home.[42] Another leading figure in the Karelian state apparatus was more explicit: "Karelization means that the Karelian dialects have civil rights everywhere, that Karelians in all offices and meetings will be able to explain their business in their own dialect. But if one thinks of Karelization as meaning that one wants to use the Karelian dialects, which often are mixed up with Russian words more than half of the time, as a literary language, then Karelization is naturally irrational."[43]

In 1924 the Central Executive Committee of the Autonomous Karelian Republic issued a detailed decree regarding the policy of Karelization.[44] In the school system Karelization meant that:

1. In those areas inhabited by Karelians who use only a Karelian dialect and who, in general, do not know Russian, school work must be organized in the Finnish language;

2. In those areas where the Karelian population also speaks Russian, the population must decide for itself whether school work will be conducted in Russian or Finnish. In either case instruction must be organized in such a way that the other language is used and the students learn to write it. One must also see to it that the spoken language of the population, Karelian, is not foreign to the teachers and that with

41 Edvard Gylling, in *Pravda*, July 3, 1935, p. 2.

42 Gylling, in *Punainen Karjala*, March 22, 1927, p. 3.

43 Santeri Nuorteva, in *ibid.*, January 27, 1925, p. 2.

44 *Kommunisti*, No. 6, June 15, 1925, p. 264; *Sovetskaia Kareliia*, p. 189; *Krasnaia Kareliia*, October 7, 1924, p. 1.

it they can satisfy the cultural needs of the population.[45]

A man later reviled as a Finnish nationalist wrote more candidly in the leading journal of the Finnish Communist Party that Karelization of the school system had as its real aim the liquidation of Russian-language schools in Karelian areas.[46] Karelization meant a transformation of all these Russian schools into Finnish-language schools.[47] In 1931 the goal was achieved. All schools in Karelian areas of the Autonomous Karelian Republic, numbering approximately two hundred and seventy-five,[48] were operating in Finnish.[49] Not even in the Aunus *raion*, where a decade earlier half of the Karelians had understood Russian,[50] were there Russian-language schools.[51]

Official jubilation over the successful Karelization of the school system was dampened by the emergence at this time of a threat to the very foundation of the nation-

[45] *Punainen Karjala*, January 13, 1925, p. 1.

[46] H. Rautio, "Karjalan suomenkielisten koulujen kehityksestä," *Kommunisti*, No. 6, June 15, 1925, p. 264.

[47] *Punainen Karjala*, February 3, 1931, p. 2.

[48] *Kommunisti*, No. 5 (89), March 1932, p. 219. At the end of 1931 there were, in all, some five hundred schools in Karelia.

[49] *Vapaus*, July 2, 1935, p. 3; *Punainen Karjala*, June 22, 1935, p. 2.

[50] Rovio, "Kielikysymys," pp. 382-383.

[51] *Punainen Karjala*, February 3, 1931, p. 2. By 1928-1929 only about 22 percent of the schools in the Aunus *raion* had been organized on the basis of Finnish. *Ibid.*, April 1, 1928, p. 1. The rapid transformation which occurred by 1931 was in keeping with a June 1929 resolution of the central committee of the Russian Communist Party, which called for an increased tempo in the Karelization of the party, state, trade union, and cooperative apparatus, as well as of schools and cultural institutions. *Sovetskaia Kareliia*, p. 94. It is interesting to note that during the period 1929-1931 even Veps, who were originally so hostile to Finnish, began to study in Finnish schools. Rovio, "Kielikysymys," p. 383.

ality policy in Soviet Karelia. In August 1929 the Karelian *Obkom* and Control Committee had declared that
to develop a special Karelian literary language would
be not only unnecessary and impractical, but also reactionary.[52] This view was not shared in certain influential circles outside of the Autonomous Karelian
Republic. At a conference held in Moscow in 1930 it
was proposed that a written language be formed for the
thousands of Karelians located near Moscow in the
Tver (Kalininskaia) *oblast*; the impression conveyed in a
press release about the conference was that the language
should also be introduced in the Autonomous Karelian
Republic. The leaders in Soviet Karelia were put on
the defensive. Attention was called to the fact that Tver
Karelians who had moved to Soviet Karelia were managing without difficulty; it was suggested that before
proceeding with the development of a new literary language, Karelians in the Tver *oblast* should first try to
use Finnish as their written language.[53] The first secretary of the Karelian *Obkom*, Kustaa Rovio, then stated
that from both a linguistic and political point of view
the language problem in Karelia had been correctly resolved.[54] Moscow was not, however, in full agreement.
The Russian Academy of Sciences charged that the
nationality policy in Soviet Karelia was one of Finnization;[55] on April 25, 1931, the Presidium of the Council

[52] *Sovetskaia Kareliia*, p. 254; Rovio, "Kielikysymys," p. 378.

[53] *Punainen Karjala*, May 23, 1930, p. 2. It is estimated that in
1937 there were over 150,000 Karelians in the Tver *oblast*. *Krasnaia Kareliia*, May 15, 1937, p. 3. The leading figure behind the
formation of a Karelian literary language was Professor D. V.
Bubrikh.

[54] Rovio, "Kielikysymys," p. 384.

[55] *Krasnaia Kareliia*, February 11, 1939, p. 2. The charge was
made in 1931; N. Ia. Marr appears to have been personally involved in the matter.

of Nationalities of the All-Russian Central Executive Committee ordered the government of the Autonomous Karelian Republic to begin work on the formation of a Karelian literary language.[56] Petroskoi lodged a protest with the central committee of the Russian Communist Party, and on June 30, 1931, the Politburo of the central committee revoked the order which had called for the establishment of a Karelian literary language.[57] The line taken by the Karelian party organization on the language question was pronounced sound, but a literary language was, nonetheless, developed in 1931 for Karelians in the Tver *oblast*.[58]

The debate on the language question took place while the First Five Year Plan, with its program of rapid industrialization, was in full swing throughout the Soviet Union, and it was apparent that the nationality policy in the Autonomous Karelian Republic could suffer as much from the new economic policy as from the formation of a Karelian literary language. The pertinent fact was that the industrial proletariat in Soviet Karelia was almost exclusively Russian.[59] The Karelians were mainly small farmers, more backward than their Russian neighbors. Even before the era of five year plans the number of Russians moving annually to the Autonomous Karelian Republic was between four and five

[56] *Punainen Karjala*, December 8, 1931, p. 3.

[57] *Ibid.*, December 8, 1931, p. 3; *ibid.*, December 7, 1931, p. 4.

[58] D. V. Bubrikh, in *Krasnaia Kareliia*, September 21, 1937, p. 3; Bubrikh, in *ibid.*, December 18, 1937, p. 3. In 1937 a Karelian *okrug* (circuit) was set up in the Tver (Kalininskaia) *oblast*. The *okrug* had a population of 163,000 (about 62 percent were Karelians) and was composed of five *raions*. *Krasnaia Kareliia*, May 15, 1937, p. 3; *ibid.*, September 24, 1937, p. 3.

[59] Kustaa Rovio, in *Punainen Karjala*, August 17, 1929, p. 3.

thousand, causing a decline in the non-Russian percentage of the total population.[60] And with forced industrialization there was a danger that Russians would soon account for a much greater percentage of the total population.[61] In August 1929 Kustaa Rovio announced to a joint meeting of the Karelian *Obkom* and Control Committee that the formation of a national proletariat was one of the most important tasks of the nationality policy in Soviet Karelia and that this was particularly so during the period when new factories and sawmills were being constructed.[62] He pointed out that Russians already employed in factories could not be fired, but he urged that preference be given to national workers (Karelians, Finns, and Veps) when hiring men for new jobs. Rovio proposed that a national university, drawing students from the Tver and Leningrad *oblasts* as well as from Karelia, be established in Petroskoi in order to provide a cadre of skilled, national labor.[63]

In 1930 the question of a national proletariat was discussed in more detail.[64] It was not until 1931, however, that a final resolution to the problem was reached. In March 1931 Edvard Gylling, then chairman of the

[60] Editorial, in *ibid.*, October 8, 1927, p. 1; Edvard Gylling, in *ibid.*, March 31, 1931, p. 1; *ibid.*, July 28, 1927, p. 1.

[61] *Sovetskaia Kareliia (Neuvosto-Karjala)*, No. 8-10, 1931, p. 156.
[62] *Punainen Karjala*, August 18, 1929, p. 3.

[63] *Ibid.*, August 17, 1929, p. 3. Rovio's proposal was approved by the *Obkom* and Control Committee. In March 1932 a Communist University was opened in Karelia; at the end of the year, in accordance with a decision of the central committee of the Russian Communist Party, the university became an Agricultural Institute. *Ibid.*, August 24, 1929, p. 4; *ibid.*, July 17, 1934, p. 1; *Sovetskaia Kareliia*, p. 267.

[64] Edvard Gylling, in *Punainen Karjala*, July 5, 1935; *Sovetskaia Kareliia*, p. 195.

Karelian Council of People's Commissars,[65] addressed
the Third Joint Plenum of the Karelian *Obkom* and
Control Committee. He noted that the figure for yearly
immigration into Soviet Karelia had risen to between
seven thousand and seventy-five hundred and that this
had occurred without any special organization or leadership. Gylling added that surplus labor in the countryside was being exhausted.[66] Labor for industry, whether
drawn from rural areas in Soviet Karelia or from other
parts of the Soviet Union, was becoming scarce.[67] In
1929 about sixty thousand laborers had been brought
into Soviet Karelia for seasonal forestry work; in 1930
the number had fallen to ten thousand.[68] To cope with
these problems the Third Joint Plenum of the Karelian
Obkom and Control Committee decided that a standing
labor force should be created.[69] It would be used primarily in sawmills and lumbering,[70] on which the economy of Soviet Karelia rested, as well as in roadbuilding

[65] When the Autonomous Karelian Soviet Socialist Republic was
founded in 1923, a reorganization of the government apparatus
took place. Gylling, who until that time had been president of the
Central Executive Committee, was elected chairman of the newly
formed Council of People's Commissars. He held the latter post
for twelve years. Gylling was also a member of the Karelian and
Leningrad *obkom* bureaus as well as the Karelian party secretariat.

[66] *Punainen Karjala*, March 31, 1931, p. 1.

[67] Edvard Gylling, in *ibid.*, July 22, 1930, p. 2; Kustaa Rovio, in
ibid., March 15, 1931, p. 4; *ibid.*, June 29, 1934, p. 2.

[68] Edvard Gylling, in *ibid.*, November 15, 1931, p. 1. Forestry
work was generally considered part of "industry." *Ibid.*, November
23, 1936, p. 1.

[69] *Ibid.*, December 7, 1931, p. 4; *ibid.*, November 29, 1932, p. 3;
ibid., December 6, 1932, p. 2.

[70] Edvard Gylling, in *ibid.*, January 4, 1931, p. 1; Gylling, in
ibid., January 9, 1935, p. 1. This is also indicated by the phrase
usually used to describe the standing labor force: *vakinaiset
(vakituiset) metsätyöläiskaaderit*.

and construction work.[71] The standing labor force would be settled in labor colonies (*uutisasutuksia*) ;[72] it would consist of sixteen thousand men.[73] Of the sixteen thousand, at least 75 percent were to be national elements: Karelians, Tver Karelians, Ingrians, Finns, and Veps.[74] An Immigration Bureau was set up and given the task of recruiting the standing labor force from territories within the Soviet Union and from the United States and Canada.[75]

The solution reached by the Third Joint Plenum of the Karelian *Obkom* and Control Committee proved to be a solution only on paper. Already in October 1931 the Karelles Lumber Trust, the largest trust in Soviet Karelia,[76] was reprimanded for sending into purely national *raions* nonnational standing cadres.[77] It had been planned that in 1931 the Immigration Sector of the Karelles Trust would provide 11,300 members of the standing labor force, but by the end of

71 Edvard Gylling, in *ibid.*, May 23, 1935, p. 1.

72 Kustaa Rovio, in *ibid.*, March 15, 1931, p. 4; *ibid.*, January 3, 1932, p. 3; Edvard Gylling, in *ibid.*, May 23, 1935, p. 1.

73 Edvard Gylling, in *ibid.*, March 31, 1931, p. 1; *ibid.*, December 7, 1931, p. 4; *ibid.*, January 3, 1932, p. 3; Kustaa Rovio, in *ibid.*, January 20, 1932, p. 2.

74 *Ibid.*, January 3, 1932, p. 3; Kustaa Rovio, in *ibid.*, January 20, 1932, p. 2; *ibid.*, February 21, 1932, p. 2; *ibid.*, November 29, 1932, p. 3. There were approximately 27,000 Veps in the Leningrad *oblast*. *Krasnaia Kareliia*, June 11, 1937, p. 3.

75 *Punainen Karjala*, October 6, 1935, p. 1. For information on the Finnish population in America, see A. William Hoglund, *Finnish Immigrants in America, 1880-1920* (Madison: University of Wisconsin Press, 1960).

76 *Punainen Karjala*, December 2, 1932, p. 3. Forestry work in Soviet Karelia was at this time done under the supervision of three lumber trusts: Karelles, Sevsaptranles, and Lenles.

77 *Ibid.*, July 22, 1933, p. 3. Of the nineteen *raions* existing in Soviet Karelia in 1931, ten were Karelian in composition. Edvard Gylling, in *ibid.*, January 4, 1931, p. 1.

the year it had succeeded in recruiting only 3,785 men. An analysis of the national composition of the 3,785 laborers was even more indicative of failure: 45 per cent were Russians, 28 per cent Karelians, 17.5 per cent Finns, and 8.5 per cent Germans from the Lower Volga. The remaining 1 per cent included Tatars, Mongolians, Chuvash, and Kirghiz.[78] The record elsewhere in Soviet Karelia offered no balm. In a general survey of the situation the director of the Karelian Immigration Bureau stated in April 1932 that only 6,000 standing cadres had been recruited during the previous year. Many of the 6,000 had come for no longer than two or three years; of the total number only 35 per cent were Karelians or Finns. The Director quipped that a chorus in nine languages could be formed from the standing labor force.[79] The attempt to set up a national proletariat did not succeed,[80] but even in failure Moscow saw the first signs of a national deviation.

[78] *Ibid.*, January 3, 1932, p. 3.

[79] *Ibid.*, April 27, 1932, p. 4. A voice from the crowd shouted that the chorus should be led by the Immigration Bureau.

[80] *Ibid.*, October 23, 1932, p. 3. In 1934 Kustaa Rovio stated that the standing labor force was not worth mentioning. *Ibid.*, September 10, 1934, p. 1. In 1935 Edvard Gylling stated that the task of forming a standing labor force was being poorly carried out. *Ibid.*, January 9, 1935, p. 1. There was, moreover, no proportional decline in Soviet Karelia's Russian population. On the contrary, the Russian percentage of the total population figure continued to increase. In 1931 it was 58.9 per cent; in 1933 it was 60.3 per cent. A great influx of Russians and other nonnational elements occurred in 1932. *Sovetskaia Kareliia (Neuvosto-Karjala)*, No. 8-10, 1931, p. 152; *Bol'shaia sovetskaia entsiklopediia*, Vol. XXXI (Moscow: Ogiz, 1937), p. 514; Upravlenie Narodno-Khoziaistvennogo Ucheta Karel'skoi ASSR (Karjalan ASNT:n Kansantalouden Luettelointihallinto), *Perepis' naseleniia AKSSR (Karjalan ASNT:n väenlasku) v. 1933 g.*, vypusk III julkaisu (Petrozavodsk: Izdanie UNKhU AKSSR, 1935), pp. 16-17.

In October 1932 workers who had emigrated to Soviet Karelia from capitalist countries were accused of having brought with them many misleading and erroneous conceptions about the dictatorship of the proletariat.[81] It was, moreover, asserted in the spring of 1933 that American immigrants refused even to advise a Russian, a Karelian, or a "Finnish Finn" on technological matters. With Yankee pride the Americans chased them all away as backward and bungling elements. Immigrants from Finland also came under fire. They believed in a wonder-working quality, Finnish *sisu,* and felt that one Finn was the equivalent of ten Russians.[82] It was not long before a more direct attack on the standing labor force was launched. In July 1933 the Leningrad *Obkom,* before which the Karelian party organization was accountable,[83] criticized the Karelian *Obkom* for wanting to send only national labor into national *raions.* Party leaders in Soviet Karelia were rebuked for advocating a policy which fostered withdrawal into a national shell. The main danger in the Autonomous Karelian Republic and all other parts of the Soviet Union was, however, still Great Russian chauvinism and not local nationalism.[84]

In November 1933 a significant change in the nationality policy of the Soviet Union was proclaimed. The occasion chosen for the announcement was a joint plenum of the central committee and central control committee of the Ukrainian Communist Party (b). Following the report of S. V. Kossior, first secretary of the Ukrainian Party and a full member of the Politburo of

81 *Punainen Karjala,* October 28, 1932, p. 1.
82 *Ibid.,* April 27, 1933, p. 2.
83 *Ibid.,* October 6, 1935, p. 2.
84 *Ibid.,* July 22, 1933, p. 3.

the Russian Communist Party, a resolution was approved in which it was stated that although Great Russian chauvinism was the main danger in the Soviet Union as a whole, the chief danger in the Ukraine and certain other Soviet republics was local chauvinism.[85] A month later the Sixth Joint Plenum of the Karelian *Obkom* and Control Committee met, and, taking his cue from Kossior, the Chairman of the Karelian Purge Commission stated that the main danger in Soviet Karelia was local nationalism.[86] This view was not, however, shared by all those present. Edvard Gylling protested, as did Kustaa Rovio.[87] The resolution which dealt with the report delivered by the chairman of the Purge Commission indicated that opposition to Moscow was strong. Precedence was given neither to the struggle against Great Russian chauvinism nor to the struggle against local nationalism.[88] This modest victory was short-lived. Within a matter of days the Leningrad party apparatus exerted pressure on the Karelian *Obkom*;[89] in the final resolutions of the Sixth Joint Plenum local chauvinism was declared the main danger in the Autonomous Karelian Republic.[90] The stage was set for a sweeping purge

[85] *Ibid.*, December 3, 1933, p. 3.

[86] P. E. Bushuev, in *ibid.*, December 24, 1933, p. 2.

[87] *Ibid.*, October 11, 1935, p. 2.

[88] *Ibid.*, December 28, 1933, p. 2.

[89] P. Hyppönen, in *ibid.*, October 11, 1935, p. 2; Pentti Renvall, "Neuvosto-Karjalan suomalaisuuden kriisin alkuvaiheista," *Historiallinen Aikakauskirja*, 1944, p. 87.

[90] *Punainen Karjala*, January 10, 1934, p. 1. Edvard Gylling and Kustaa Rovio found it expedient to fall in step with the new line. Rovio, in *ibid.*, January 2, 1934, p. 3; Gylling, in *ibid.*, January 4, 1934, p. 3. It was later asserted that when Rovio and other members of the Karelian *Obkom* were forced to acknowledge local nationalism as the main danger in the Autonomous Karelian Republic, they did so only in words. P. Hyppönen, in *ibid.*, October 11, 1935, p. 2.

166

of "nationalists," which, apparently due to a temporary crisis within the highest organs of the Russian Communist Party,[91] was delayed for a year.

In the spring of 1935 the third secretary of the Leningrad *Obkom*, P. A. Irklis, attacked local nationalism in Karelia.[92] The central committee of the Russian Communist Party then established a commission to examine and report on the work of the Karelian party organization. This report, which included a condemnation of the theory that a standing labor force, national in composition, should be "imported" from other parts of the Soviet Union and from abroad,[93] was discussed at the August 1935 plenum of the Karelian *Obkom*[94] Detailed information about the plenum was not released, but on August 22 it was announced that Kustaa Rovio had been replaced by P. A. Irklis as first secretary of the party.[95] A month later, on September 26, the Leningrad *Obkom* resolved that Rovio and the Karelian *Obkom* Bureau in its entirety had distorted the nationality policy of Lenin and Stalin.[96] Within a few days the Fifth Plenum of the Karelian *Obkom* met.

At the Fifth Plenum a full scale attack on "nationalists" was launched by M. S. Chudov, a secretary of the

[91] In 1934 Stalin was engaged in a behind-the-scenes struggle with advocates of "moderation." Leonard Schapiro, *The Communist Party of the Soviet Union* (New York: Random House, 1960), pp. 396-400; George F. Kennan, *Russia and the West under Lenin and Stalin* (New York: Mentor Books, 1962), pp. 283-285.

[92] *Punainen Karjala*, April 21, 1935, p. 2. A noted authority has written that the attack on "national deviation" throughout the Soviet Union, including Karelia, began in mid-1937. Zbigniew K. Brzezinski, *The Permanent Purge* (Cambridge: Harvard University Press, 1956), pp. 79, 81.

[93] *Punainen Karjala*, September 16, 1935, p. 1.

[94] *Ibid.*, August 20, 1935, p. 1.

[95] *Ibid.*, August 22, 1935, p. 1.

[96] *Ibid.*, October 5, 1935, p. 1.

167

Leningrad *Obkom*, and by P. A. Irklis. Irklis, as he had done on another recent occasion, criticized the standing labor force and stated that the Karelian Immigration Bureau had outlived its usefulness.[97] The central issue under discussion at the Fifth Plenum, the language question, was dealt with in detail by Chudov. He charged that Russian was being undermined by the stress on Finnish and that in some schools Russian was not even taught. The Karelian *Obkom*, Chudov continued, had permitted a mechanical attitude toward the language question and had not taken into consideration the national and linguistic peculiarities of different *raions*: Russian *raions*, the Vep *raion*, and *raions* where dialects of central and southern Karelia were spoken.[98] Following the reports of Chudov and Irklis, the plenum approved a resolution which in most respects was a carbon copy of the Leningrad attack.[99] The full significance of the Fifth Plenum did not go unnoticed. Some members of the Karelian *Obkom* stated that since a drive against Finns had begun, it would be best to leave Soviet Karelia. It was whispered that Leningrad wanted to put an end to Karelian independence and turn the autonomous republic into a colony.[100]

Edvard Gylling had been attacked by Chudov,[101] but, unlike Kustaa Rovio, Gylling was not mentioned by

---

[97] *Ibid.*, October 6, 1935, p. 1; *ibid.*, September 16, 1935, p. 1.

[98] *Ibid.*, October 5, 1935, p. 1. Edvard Gylling asked the Commissar of Education whether it was true that courses in Russian were not offered in some schools; the latter replied that such was the case in certain schools in three *raions*: Kiestinki, Repola, and Kalevala. *Ibid.*, October 11, 1935, p. 3.

[99] The resolution appeared in *ibid.*, October 3, 1935, pp. 1-2.

[100] Renvall, "Neuvosto-Karjalan," pp. 102-103. Irklis stated that speeches about the loss of Karelian independence were speeches of class enemies. *Punainen Karjala*, October 6, 1935, p. 2.

[101] *Ibid.*, October 5, 1935, p. 1.

name in the resolutions of the Fifth Plenum. This reprieve was short. At a meeting of the Karelian Central Executive Committee on November 5, 1935, Gylling was relieved of his duties as chairman of the Council of People's Commissars.[102] P. E. Bushuev, chairman in 1933 of the Karelian Purge Commission and a secretary in the party apparatus of the city of Leningrad, was elected in his stead. Moscow had chosen a Tver Karelian to replace a Finn.[103] In view of the language controversy of 1931, which had ended in the formation of a Karelian literary language for Tver Karelians but not for Karelians in the Autonomous Karelian Republic, it was not difficult to foresee the next step in the campaign against Finnish "nationalists" in Soviet Karelia.

Early in 1936 the complaint was voiced that Karelians in the Autonomous Karelian Republic could not get ahead with merely Finnish literature and the Finnish language.[104] In November 1936, at the Eleventh All-Karelian Congress of Soviets, one member of the Karelian *Obkom* Bureau urged that direction be given to the development of a written Karelian language.[105] In the spring of the following year a draft constitution, based on the Stalin Constitution of 1936, was prepared for the Autonomous Karelian Republic. Paragraph twenty-four of the draft constitution stated that all laws approved by the Supreme Soviet of the Autonomous

---

102 *Ibid.*, November 10, 1935, p. 2. Following their ouster Gylling and Rovio were called to Moscow, where, on July 25, 1937, they were imprisoned. Arvo Tuominen, *Kremlin kellot* (Helsinki: Tammi, 1957), pp. 366, 371. Details about their fate still remain secret, although in 1956 both Gylling and Rovio were rehabilitated. Ville Pessi, in *Työkansan Sanomat*, June 28, 1956, p. 4.

103 *Punainen Karjala*, November 27, 1935, p. 1.

104 *Ibid.*, February 5, 1936, p. 2.

105 P. Hyppönen, in *ibid.*, November 24, 1936, p. 2.

Karelian Soviet Socialist Republic would be published in Finnish, Russian, and Karelian.[106] When the constitution was ratified, on June 17, 1937, P. A. Irklis elaborated on the significance of paragraph twenty-four: "It means that in Karelia there will be not only two state languages, as has been the case until now, but three—Karelian, Finnish, and Russian. This, comrades, means that a Karelian literary language will be formed in Soviet Karelia."[107] On August 21-22 a linguistic conference convened in Petroskoi to discuss the scientific and practical questions involved in the formation of a written Karelian language.[108]

In September of the same year, as part of a coordinated attack on "nationalist deviation" throughout the Soviet Union, two articles appearing in *Pravda* riveted attention to the question of a Karelian literary language. *Pravda* charged that bourgeois nationalists in Soviet Karelia arrogantly scorned a written Karelian language and were attempting to Finnicize the working population of Karelia.[109] It was asserted that the Karelian Central Executive Committee, in defiance of paragraph twenty-four of the Karelian constitution, was obstructing the development of the third state language.[110] *Pravda* declared, furthermore, that there was great need for a Karelian-language newspaper.

[106] *Ibid.*, April 18, 1937, p. 1.

[107] *Ibid.*, June 17, 1937, p. 2.

[108] *Ibid.*, August 24, 1937, p. 4. Professor D. V. Bubrikh, a leading figure behind the formation in 1931 of a literary language for Tver Karelians, delivered a paper at the Petroskoi conference.

[109] *Pravda*, September 9, 1937, p. 4. The *Pravda* article can also be found in *Punainen Karjala*, September 10, 1937, p. 1, and *Vapaus*, September 14, 1937, p. 2.

[110] *Pravda*, September 11, 1937, p. 2. See also *Punainen Karjala*, September 12, 1937, p. 1, and *Vapaus*, September 15, 1937, p. 2.

On September 26-27, 1937, the Karelian *Obkom* met to discuss the *Pravda* articles.[111] P. A. Irklis, who, like P. E. Bushuev, had become a traitor and turncoat, a loathsome viper, and an agent of German-Finnish Fascism, was removed as first secretary.[112] The plenum agreed with Moscow that a newspaper in Karelian was a necessity;[113] on October 10 it was announced that a unified alphabet, based on the Russian rather than the Latin alphabet, had been formed for Karelians in Soviet Karelia and for Tver Karelians.[114] On January 1, 1938, shortly after all Finnish-language publications in the Soviet Union had been banned, the first issue of a Karelian-language newspaper appeared.[115]

The last act in the Karelian tragedy was being performed. In July 1938 the Supreme Soviet of the Autonomous Karelian Soviet Socialist Republic altered the constitution so that Soviet Karelia had only two state languages: Karelian and Russian.[116] For the education system this meant that the language of instruction in schools located in non-Russian *raions* would no longer be Finnish. In the lower forms it would be Karelian, in the upper forms Russian.[117] Russification in Soviet

111 *Punainen Karjala*, September 30, 1937, p. 1.

112 *Ibid.*, September 12, 1937, p. 1; *ibid.*, September 30, 1937, p. 1.

113 *Ibid.*, September 30, 1937, p. 1.

114 *Krasnaia Kareliia*, October 10, 1937, p. 3; *ibid.*, October 30, 1937, p. 3; *ibid.*, January 3, 1938, p. 2. Tver Karelians, who had had a literary language of their own since 1931, were forced to abandon the Latin alphabet.

115 *Ibid.*, January 1, 1938, p. 1; Arvo Tuominen, *Neuvostoliitto Leninin perinnön vartijana* (Stockholm: Tryckeriaktiebolaget tiden, 1941), p. 59. Publication of the two major Finnish-language newspapers in the Soviet Union, *Punainen Karjala* and *Vapaus*, stopped in the fall of 1937.

116 *Krasnaia Kareliia*, July 28, 1938, pp. 1-2.

117 *Ibid.*, October 2, 1937, p. 2; *ibid.*, February 1, 1938, p. 1; *ibid.*, April 4, 1938, p. 3; *ibid.*, July 28, 1938, p. 2.

Karelia faced only one more hurdle. The relationship between Russian and Karelian had to be defined in more explicit terms. This occurred early in 1939, when there was no longer any need of a stick, a Karelian literary language, with which to beat Finnish "nationalists." A prominent member of the Russian Academy of Sciences asserted that those who had developed the Karelian literary language in 1937-1938 were advocates of Finnization.[118] The central authorities in Soviet Karelia stated that neither the Karelians in their republic nor the Karelians in the Tver *oblast* could understand the unified literary language. New directions for the formation of a written Karelian language were issued:

1. A Karelian literary language must be formed which will be understood, above all, by Karelians in the Karelian Republic;

2. The language must be freed from Finnicisms, archaic words, and invented terms and forms;

3. Under no circumstances should the Karelian language be artificially torn from Russian; it must, on the contrary, be *drawn closer* to Russian wherever such a step is legitimate and natural;

4. All grammatical forms must be reexamined, taking into account *all* the dialects existing in Karelia.[119]

After two decades of change the language question in Soviet Karelia was back where it had been immediately following the Bolshevik Revolution. Russian was the language for all. At the end of this cycle thousands, in-

118 N. I. Meshchaninov, in *ibid.*, February 11, 1939, p. 2.
119 *Ibid.*, March 27, 1939, p. 3.

cluding the Old Guard of the Finnish Communist Party, lost their lives.[120] Finnish Communists, persecuted in the Soviet Union and driven underground in Finland, were without power or influence on the eve of the Second World War. But a remarkable revitalization of Finnish Communism was soon an accomplished fact.

[120] It is significant that in the January 1933 census there were 12,084 Finns in Soviet Karelia, whereas by January 1939 the number had fallen to approximately 9,000. The former figure is cited in *Sovetskaia Kareliia*, p. 119; the latter figure is derived from data presented in *Krasnaia Kareliia*, June 3, 1939, p. 2, and *ibid.*, July 28, 1938, p. 2. The fact that the borders of Soviet Karelia were altered during the period 1933-1939 cannot account for the decline in the Finnish population. The only major border change came in 1938 when the Kantalahti (Kandalakshskii) *raion*, with a Finnish population of several hundred, was detached from the Autonomous Karelian Republic and included in the Murmansk *oblast*. *Krasnaia Kareliia*, July 28, 1938, p. 2; *Sovetskaia Kareliia*, p. 119.

CHAPTER SEVEN

Finnish Communism Reborn

FOR three and one-half years, first in 1939-1940 and then in 1941-1944, Finland was at war with the Soviet Union. Twice Finland suffered defeat. It is astonishing, therefore, that in the first parliamentary election in postwar Finland members of the Communist Party were able to capture forty of the two hundred seats.[1] In explaining this paradox, a logical point of departure is the year 1931. It was then that the first issue of *Soihtu*, a journal of the Academic Socialist Society, appeared. The early leitmotivs of the journal were best expressed in the articles written by the editor-in-chief, Cay Sundström. Sundström rejected Communism but stated that it should be kept in mind that the Soviet Union was also attempting to build Socialism. He demanded more freedom within the Finnish Social Democratic Party. Finally, with the specter of Fascism and its German variant, National Socialism, before him, Sundström urged that Social Democracy define its position on the issue of democracy and dictatorship.[2]

[1] *SKP taistelujen tiellä*, Vol. III (Helsinki: Yhteistyön kirjapaino, 1947), p. 52; L. A. Ingul'skaia, "Rabochii klass finliandii i demokratizatsiia strany (1944-1948 gg.)," in I. M. Maiskii, ed., *Rabochee dvizhenie v skandinavskikh stranakh i finliandii* (Moscow: Izdatel'stvo Nauka, 1965), pp. 151, 169. The forty Communists were elected on lists of the Finnish People's Democratic League (SKDL); nine non-Communists were also elected as part of the SKDL parliamentary group.

[2] Cay Sundström, in *Soihtu*, No. 6, December 1932, p. 11; Sundström, in *ibid.*, No. 7, November 6, 1933, p. 141. See also the 1934 issues of this journal.

With the passage of time *Soihtu* became more extreme both in its attitude toward the right-wing leadership of the Finnish Social Democratic Party and in its tolerance of Soviet Russia. The party had developed, so it seemed, a cancerous growth. At a meeting of the party executive committee on May 10, 1937, treatment commensurate with the diagnosed malady was administered. The Academic Socialist Society was expelled from the party; Social Democrats were forbidden to cooperate with *Soihtu*; two members of the editorial board of *Soihtu*, Mauri Ryömä and Raoul Palmgren, were separated from the party; three others, Cay Sundström, Kaisu-Mirjami Rydberg, and Ahti Myrsky, received severe warnings. Only Karl Wiik and Johan Helo had risen in protest.[3] For Wiik, a leading figure in the Finnish Social Democratic Party both before and after the Civil War, the decision of the executive committee was symptomatic of an even more serious illness than that with which it was designed to cope. He wrote that in a democracy minorities, too, have rights.[4]

It was at this time that the Social Democratic Party, disregarding its official program,[5] sanctioned a large increase in defense expenditures. Non-Socialists rejoiced and saw in this move an end to the revolutionary side of Finnish Social Democracy. Karl Wiik, described by the right as "Finland's Karl Marx" and by the left as

[3] *Suomen sosialidemokraattisen puoluetoimikunnan pöytäkirjat*, May 10, 1937; Karl Wiik and Johan Helo, in *ibid.*, April 5, 1937.

[4] K. H. Wiik, "Puolueemme vasemmiston sananvapaus tämän jälkeen," in *Suomen Sosialidemokraatti*, May 15, 1937, p. 6.

[5] Väinö Tanner, *Itsenäisen Suomen arkea* (Helsinki: Tammi, 1956), p. 280; *Suomen sosialidemokraattinen työväenliike 1899-1949* (Helsinki: KK:n kirjapaino, 1949), p. 290. Leaders of the Social Democratic Party considered the program obsolete. They were confident that in recognition of this fact the next party congress would give them a vote of confidence.

"the conscience of the Finnish labor movement,"[6] concluded that the party had become subservient to the bourgeoisie.[7] He opposed what he called "the armaments psychosis"; it made rational discussion of events impossible.[8] In April 1938 first contact with the Finnish government was made by the Soviet Union on an issue which would challenge the rational powers of Finnish politicians as no issue had done since the Civil War. The Finnish Foreign Minister was informed of the Soviet desire to obtain "guarantees" that Finland, many of whose educated class were captivated by Fascism,[9] would not side with Germany in a war against the Soviet Union.[10]

In the spring and fall of 1939 the Soviet government was more specific. It desired certain Finnish territory, with or without compensation, in order to protect Leningrad.[11] Both Väinö Tanner, leader of the Finnish Social Democratic Party, and Karl Wiik, chief

[6] Erkki Räikkönen, in *Kustaa Vaasa*, No. 2, March 22, 1939, p. 37; R. P. [Raoul Palmgren], in *Vapaa Sana*, June 30, 1946, p. 7.

[7] K. H. Wiik, "Kuutosryhmän historia," in *Vapaa Sana*, January 6, 1946, p. 6; K. H. Wiik, *Näkökohtia sos.-dem. puolueessa v:n 1941 alussa vallitsevasta tilanteesta*, p. 1.

[8] K. H. Wiik, *Kuka hajoittaa? Kuka yhdistää?*, p. 4.

[9] Marvin Rintala, "An Image of European Politics: The People's Patriotic Movement," *Journal of Central European Affairs*, Vol. XXII, No. 3 (October 1962), pp. 308-316; Marvin Rintala, *Three Generations: The Extreme Right Wing in Finnish Politics* (Bloomington: Indiana University Press, 1962), pp. 221-243.

[10] Max Jakobson, *The Diplomacy of the Winter War* (Cambridge: Harvard University Press, 1961), p. 9.

[11] Gustaf Mannerheim, chairman of the Defense Council, and J. K. Paasikivi, chosen by the Finnish government in October 1939 to negotiate with the Russians, shared the opinion that territory for the defense of Leningrad was a legitimate demand which should be satisfied. J. K. Paasikivi, *Toimintani Moskovassa ja Suomessa 1939-41*, Vol. 1 (Porvoo: WSOY, 1958), pp. 2, 52; Jakobson, *op.cit.*, pp. 63-64.

176

figure in the Social Democratic opposition, urged that the Finnish government make concessions.[12] There was, however, a gulf between the two men. Wiik argued that agreement with the Soviet Union, even on unsatisfactory terms, was a necessity. The alternative might be a war which Finland would fight alone.[13] On November 26, 1939, four days before the outbreak of the Winter War, Wiik again expressed his apprehensions. They were dismissed by Tanner as nothing but pessimism.[14] Tanner, like the Finnish nation as a whole,[15] did not expect the Soviet Union to attack. The absence of a Soviet ultimatum specifying a date on which war would begin led Tanner to believe that the fall negotiations, in which he played a leading role, were nothing more than a "friendly discussion."[16] Even after bombs had begun to fall, Tanner doubted that hostilities had commenced;

[12] Tanner's conciliatory attitude toward the Russians is noted in Jakobson, *op.cit.*, p. 159; Paasikivi, *op.cit.*, I, 11, 56-57, 85. Paasikivi adds, however, that Tanner was not willing to go so far as he on the question of concessions.

[13] Karl Wiik, in *Suomen sosialidemokraattisen eduskuntaryhmän pöytäkirjat*, November 16, 1939; Wiik, in *Suomen sosialidemokraattisen eduskuntaryhmän valmistavan valiokunnan ja puoluetoimikunnan yhteisten kokousten pöytäkirjat*, November 7, 1939. The similarity between the views of Wiik and Gustaf Mannerheim is striking. In November 1939 Mannerheim told J. K. Paasikivi: "We cannot expect effective aid from anyone. We must, therefore, do all in our power to avoid war with the Soviet Union. Agreement with the Soviet Union must be reached. Although a military base on Finland's shore would be deplorable, some island, for instance Jussarö or some other, must be offered to the Russians in order to reach an agreement." Mannerheim, as paraphrased in Paasikivi, *op.cit.*, I, 101. The Finnish government, as is well known, refused to consider any major concessions to the Soviet Union.

[14] *Suomen sosialidemokraattisen puolueneuvoston pöytäkirjat*, November 26, 1939, p. 9.

[15] Paasikivi, *op.cit.*, I, 57, 99, 114.

[16] Väinö Tanner, in *Suomen sosialidemokraattisen puolueneuvoston*, April 7, 1940, liite 7, p. 22.

the bombs were just a continuation of the "war of nerves."[17]

On December 1, 1939, the formation of a new Finnish government was announced. Included in the Cabinet were three members of the executive committee of the Social Democratic Party: Väinö Tanner, Väinö Salovaara, and Mauno Pekkala. Tanner, who had been Minister of Finance in 1937-1939, became Foreign Minister. His initial efforts as Foreign Minister were directed toward a reopening of negotiations with the Soviet Union, but when it appeared possible that the Russians might finally negotiate, late in January 1940, Tanner began to haggle.[18] He was not willing to remove the one serious obstacle to Finnish-Soviet agreement; he would not grant the Soviet Union a naval base at the mouth of the Gulf of Finland.[19] The fine showing of the Finnish army had created, as a leading member of the Cabinet later wrote, a false sense of security.[20] This bubble of optimism soon burst.

On February 1, 1940, Soviet armies launched a full-scale attack on the Karelian Isthmus. Within ten days there had been a breach in the Finnish defense line.[21] On February 12 the Cabinet's Foreign Affairs Com-

[17] Väinö Tanner, *Olin ulkoministerinä talvisodan aikana* (Helsinki: Tammi, 1951), p. 150. One must agree with J. K. Paasikivi, Finland's greatest statesman, that foreign policy was not really Tanner's forte. Paasikivi, *op.cit.*, I, 13, 57.

[18] *Ibid.*, I, 118.

[19] Tanner, *Olin*, p. 207; Jakobson, *op.cit.*, p. 211. Even Gustaf Mannerheim, who had advocated concessions to the Soviet Union in the fall of 1939, now considered it difficult to concede a base at the mouth of the Gulf of Finland. Tanner, *Olin*, p. 203; Paasikivi, *op.cit.*, I, 135.

[20] Paasikivi, *op.cit.*, I, 135, 144-146, 155.

[21] *Ibid.*, I, 146-147, 152; Jakobson, *op.cit.*, p. 225.

178

mittee, which had not met since December 2, 1939,[22] was called together by Tanner. He concealed the fact that he had been in touch with Moscow; his approach was one of presenting theoretical possibilities.[23] Tanner now urged that Finland accede to Soviet demands for a base at the mouth of the Gulf of Finland.[24] He was supported by Prime Minister Ryti and J. K. Paasikivi, both of whom, along with Tanner, knew of the January peace overture,[25] but was opposed by three other members of the committee.[26] This debate came, in any event, too late.[27]

On February 13 Tanner received a message from the Soviet Foreign Minister. The Soviet Union now wanted Hanko, the entire Karelian Isthmus, and part of the area north of Lake Ladoga.[28] Tanner did not bother to present this message to the Cabinet or to its Foreign Affairs Committee. His ardor for peace had been

[22] Jakobson, *op.cit.*, pp. 222, 224.

[23] *Ibid.*, p. 224; Tanner, *Olin*, p. 247. The six members of the Foreign Affairs Committee were Ryti, Tanner, Paasikivi, Niukkanen, Hannula, and Söderhjelm.

[24] Tanner, *Olin*, p. 248; Paasikivi, *op.cit.*, I, 147.

[25] Of the three only Paasikivi had been willing in January 1940 to grant the Soviet Union a naval base at the mouth of the Gulf of Finland. Tanner, *Olin*, p. 207. During his long political life, dating back to the turn of the century, Paasikivi rarely deviated from the principle that Finland should be willing to make necessary concessions to Russia. See John H. Hodgson, "The Paasikivi Line," *The American Slavic and East European Review*, Vol. XVIII, No. 2 (April 1959), pp. 145-173; Allan A. Kuusisto, "The Paasikivi Line in Finland's Foreign Policy," *The Western Political Quarterly*, Vol. XII, No. 1 (March 1959), pp. 37-49.

[26] Tanner, *Olin*, p. 252; Paasikivi, *op.cit.*, I, 148. President Kallio, who attended the Foreign Affairs Committee meeting, supported Tanner.

[27] Paasikivi, *op.cit.*, I, 148.

[28] *Ibid.*; Jakobson, *op.cit.*, p. 233.

dampened by the new demands.[29] On February 22 Molotov informed the Finnish chargé d'affaires in Stockholm that the Soviet Union would, as of that date, settle for nothing less than Hanko, the Karelian Isthmus and Viipuri (Finland's second largest city), the northeastern part of Lake Ladoga and Sortavala, and a mutual defense treaty.[30] On February 23 the Foreign Affairs Committee met to discuss the Soviet demands. Two days later the Cabinet was called together; Tanner outlined two alternatives. War could be continued with foreign (Swedish or Allied) aid, or Finland could sue for peace on terms approximating those offered by the Soviet government.[31] Minister Pekkala, chairman of the Social Democratic parliamentary group, was a strong supporter of the second alternative.[32] Minister Salovaara, vice-chairman of the executive committee of the Social Democratic Party, chose the first path. He wanted to continue the war on the strength of Allied promises to send men, materiel, and money.[33] The position of the leader of the Social Democratic Party, Tanner, was ambivalent. He called for peace but at the same time hoped for foreign aid.[34] On February 28, following a two-day visit to Sweden, Tanner finally took a firm stand. He stated at a meeting of the Cabinet that there was no longer any choice. Finland would have to accept

[29] Jakobson, *op.cit.*, p. 234.

[30] Paasikivi, *op.cit.*, I, 148.

[31] *Ibid.*, I, 152-154; Tanner, *Olin*, p. 286.

[32] Paasikivi, *op.cit.*, I, 155; Tanner, *Olin*, p. 286; J. Niukkanen and M. Pekkala, in *Valtiopäivät 1940 pöytäkirjat*, Vol. I (Helsinki: Valtioneuvoston kirjapaino, 1940), p. 554.

[33] Paasikivi, *op.cit.*, I, 155-156; Tanner, *Olin*, p. 286; M. Pekkala, in *Suomen sosialidemokraattisen puolueen yhdeksännentoista edustajakokouksen pöytäkirja* (Helsinki: Työväen kirjapaino, 1946), p. 55.

[34] Tanner, *Olin*, pp. 301-302; Paasikivi, *op.cit.*, I, 153-154.

the conditions of peace dictated by the Soviet Union.[35] At the end of February Tanner faced up to reality and began to drive hard for peace on Soviet terms.[36] On March 12, 1940, a peace treaty was signed.[37]

It is unjust to charge, as did a bourgeois member of the Cabinet's Foreign Affairs Committee,[38] that Väinö Tanner alone was responsible for the direction of Finnish foreign policy during the Winter War. There is, however, a grain of truth in the assertion. Tanner has acknowledged that he did not consider the question of peace with the Soviet Union a matter for the Cabinet or its Foreign Affairs Committee. It was, accordingly, dealt with by only two, or three, men.[39] Shortly after the signing of the March Peace Treaty, members of the Social Democratic opposition demanded that Tanner lift the veil of secrecy surrounding wartime events. Johan Helo,

[35] Tanner, *Olin*, p. 302; Paasikivi, *op.cit.*, I, 158-159. A pessimistic military report by Marshal Mannerheim soon caused Väinö Salovaara to follow the lead of his party colleague. Paasikivi, *op.cit.*, I, 161.

[36] Paasikivi, *op.cit.*, I, 118. Tanner was so forceful in gaining the support of the Social Democratic parliamentary group for peace on Soviet terms that one leading figure in the party thought that Tanner, although he got what he wanted, had committed political suicide. Sylvi-Kyllikki Kilpi to author, January 15, 1963.

[37] A complete text of the treaty can be found in Jakobson, *op.cit.*, pp. 261-266. The treaty did not call for a mutual defense alliance. The Kremlin, on its own initiative, had abandoned that demand. Paasikivi, *op.cit.*, I, 198.

[38] U. H. [Uuno Hannula], in *Pohjolan Sanomat*, June 28, 1940, p. 2. Hannula, of all the Cabinet members, was the most determined opponent of peace with the Soviet Union.

[39] Väinö Tanner, in *Suomen sosialidemokraattisen puolueneuvoston*, November 7, 1943. See also Jakobson, *op.cit.*, pp. 222, 225. The three figures were Tanner, Ryti, and Paasikivi. Tanner's inclination to say two, rather than three, men probably stems from the fact that Paasikivi's views were not always endorsed by the "inner circle," i.e. by Tanner and Ryti.

an alternate member of the executive committee, wanted to know whether everything possible had been done to avoid war.[40] Karl Wiik noted that Finnish politicians had been intoxicated by early military victories and that Tanner had boasted as late as February that the Soviet Union would not dictate peace to Finland.[41] Wiik and Helo urged that the past be discussed in order to learn for the future. Tanner, however, considered such a discussion premature in view of the unstable world situation.[42]

At a meeting of the executive committee on July 19, 1940, Tanner proposed that Social Democratic presses refuse to print a newspaper, *Vapaa Sana*, which Karl Wiik, in an attempt to circumvent party censorship,[43] was seeking to publish. Tanner was supported by the executive committee,[44] but this resolution did not prevent publication of the weekly. *Vapaa Sana* appeared for the first time on July 24, 1940, and brought together a diverse group of well-known Social Democrats: Karl Wiik, Johan Helo, Yrjö Räisänen, Mikko Ampuja, Cay Sundström, and K.-M. Rydberg. These figures, con-

[40] Johan Helo, in *Suomen sosialidemokraattisen puolueneuvoston*, April 7, 1940, pp. 15-16.

[41] Karl Wiik, in *ibid.*, April 7, 1940, p. 9. See also Paasikivi, *op.cit.*, I, 118.

[42] Karl Wiik and Johan Helo, in *Suomen sosialidemokraattisen puolueneuvoston*, April 7, 1940, pp. 8, 16; Väinö Tanner, in *ibid.*, July 28, 1940, p. 53. It is interesting to note that Tanner's view was shared by Prime Minister Ryti. Ryti, in *Helsingin Sanomat*, July 5, 1940, p. 3.

[43] This point is stressed in a letter from Karl Wiik to Edward Huttunen, dated October 7, 1940, and in *Vapaa Sana*, August 9, 1940, p. 3.

[44] *Suomen sosialidemokraattisen puoluetoimikunnan*, July 19, 1940, p. 49. Reference was made to the precedent set in 1937 when the executive committee prohibited any form of cooperation with the journal *Soihtu*.

trary to the picture generally presented,[45] were tied together by more than just a hatred of Väinö Tanner. Two factors united the group: first, the view that Social Democrats must think and act independently of the bourgeoisie, and second, the struggle against such slogans as "a fight to the last man" and "not an inch."[46] The program advanced in the first issue of *Vapaa Sana* was summed up in three words: Socialism, Internationalism, Peace.[47]

For a more detailed exposition of the program and its underlying premises, one must turn to the writings of Karl Wiik. Wiik, the principal figure in the *Vapaa Sana* group, was troubled by the drift to the right in the orientation of the Social Democratic Party.[48] In his eyes the party leadership in 1939 had gone over to the bourgeoisie. Wiik argued that both the material and spiritual (*aatteelliset*) interests of the workers had been sacrificed to the bourgeoisie in that year.[49] The Winter War, he asserted, could have been averted if the workers had remained an independent political force.[50] The fact that the party supported censorship and war-

[45] The standard interpretation was first expressed in Vanha vasemmistolainen, *Avoin kirje Sasu Punaselle, K. H. Wiikille, Johan Helolle ym. Vapaan Sanan toimitusneuvoston jäsenille* (Helsinki: Työväen kirjapaino, 1940), pp. 3, 14. It was recently repeated to the author by a man who, at the time of writing, is a member of the executive committee of the Social Democratic Party. K.-A. Fagerholm to author, February 8, 1963.

[46] Mikko Ampuja, *Pajasta parlamenttiin* (Helsinki: Tammi, 1947), pp. 258-259.

[47] Editorial, in *Vapaa Sana*, July 24, 1940, p. 1.

[48] Anna Wiik to author, February 4, 1963.

[49] Mimeographed letter from Karl Wiik to members of the executive council of the Social Democratic Party, December 16, 1940, p. 1; Wiik, *Näkökohtia*, p. 1.

[50] Karl Wiik, in *Suomen sosialidemokraattisen puolueneuvoston*, July 28, 1940, p. 25.

time restrictions even after peace had been restored was seen by Wiik as a sign of party submission to the bourgeoisie.[51] Wiik did not reject all cooperation with the bourgeoisie, but he demanded that it be temporary, that it meet a specific situation, and that it be in the interests of both the workers and the bourgeoisie.[52] These criteria had existed on at least one occasion in recent history, on November 30, 1939, when Finland was called upon to defend herself against the Soviet attack.[53] What Wiik was striving for was a return to a party resolution made in 1930: "In order to achieve or facilitate class cooperation one must not sacrifice, by covering up contrasts between the bourgeois and labor classes or by concealing the difference in the final aims of the bourgeois parties and the Social Democratic Party, the self-esteem and independent thinking of the working class."[54] Wiik warned that one must not lose sight of the final goal, Socialism, when cooperating with the bourgeoisie.[55] The actions of Karl Wiik can be understood only in the light of his devotion to this end.

In 1935 Wiik, as party secretary, had urged that Finnish Social Democrats unmask Fascism, also in its domestic (*Isänmaallinen Kansanliike*) form, as a desperate attempt to save capitalism from destruction. He had argued that the struggle against Fascism was a struggle

[51] Mimeographed letter from Karl Wiik to members of the executive council of the Social Democratic Party, December 16, 1940, p. 3; Wiik, *Näkökohtia*, pp. 1-2.

[52] Wiik, *Kuka*, p. 4; K. H. Wiik, "Sosialidemokratian rappeutumisen syyt," in *Sosialistisen eduskuntaryhmän kirjeitä*, No. 8, June 12, 1941, liite, p. 4.

[53] Karl Wiik, in *Suomen sosialidemokraattisen puolueneuvoston*, April 7, 1940, p. 11.

[54] Wiik, *Kuka*, p. 9; Wiik, *Näkökohtia*, p. 2.

[55] Wiik, *Näkökohtia*, p. 2.

against capitalism; only Socialism offered salvation.[56] Five years later Wiik repeated this view. Fascism was a form of degenerate capitalism; only Socialist workers could conquer Fascism because they alone were struggling against capitalism in its entirety.[57] With the fall of France in June 1940 Socialism became even more meaningful for Wiik. He considered it likely that two dictatorial systems, Fascism and Bolshevism, would emerge victorious in the European war.[58] Of the two, Wiik preferred the latter. He argued that Fascism was an integral part of capitalism and consequently could not become democratic. Bolshevism, on the other hand, had destroyed capitalism and not only could, but indeed would be forced to, turn to the path of democracy. The very fact that the Soviet Union would eventually become involved in a military conflict with a Fascist Europe meant, Wiik thought, that Finland's independence would be guaranteed. In anticipation of the great resolution (*suurratkaisu*), the Soviet Union would seek peace on her northwestern frontier.[59] For Wiik the greatest danger and greatest evil was, in short, Fascism.[60]

In the summer of 1940 Soviet troops had occupied the three Baltic states; it was widely feared that Finland would soon suffer a similar fate.[61] For many Finns Ger-

---

[56] Karl Wiik, in *Suomen Sosialidemokraatti*, April 23, 1935, p. 2.

[57] Wiik, *Kuka*, p. 5.

[58] *Ibid.*, p. 6; Karl Wiik, in *Vapaa Sana*, August 2, 1940, p. 2.

[59] Wiik, *Kuka*, pp. 6-7.

[60] *Ibid.*, p. 5; mimeographed letter from Karl Wiik to the executive committee of the Social Democratic Party, November 29, 1940, p. 1.

[61] Even J. K. Paasikivi, who probably understood the Russians better than any other Finn, was apprehensive. The fate of the Baltic countries was always in his mind; he thought it likely in August 1940 that the Soviet leaders wanted to annex Finland. Paasikivi, *op.cit.*, II, 62, 82.

man military might seemed to be the only hope.[62] Karl Wiik was alarmed by this infatuation with Germany, and he pondered about the path which Finnish Social Democracy would choose.[63] With the foundation on August 28, 1940, of a new Social Democratic association, *Raivaajat* (Trail Blazers), it appeared that at least a segment of the party had decided to follow the lead of the Finnish bourgeoisie. This was revealed in the program endorsed by members of *Raivaajat*:

> In the present critical period, important and decisive for the working class and our whole nation, it is *imperative that our country's independence [itsenäisyys ja riippumattomuus] be protected* and that those aspirations which in this respect might become dangerous be repressed with a heavy hand. Ultimately our nation will weather its ordeal only on its own, with the aid of a *spiritual and material fitness for defense.* Cognizant of all this we must, however, reexamine *without prejudice* and *in a pertinent manner* our relations with the so-called government-controlled states. Reform work in the Soviet Union has always been attentively observed in the Finnish labor movement. It is extremely important to the whole nation that our labor movement adopt an attitude free from all prejudice also toward the reform work carried out by the German and Italian nations, trying to become acquainted with it objectively but emphasizing at the same time that the Finnish nation itself must find those means and methods which it must use to realize a brighter future.[64]

[62] Arvi Korhonen, *Barbarossa-suunnitelma ja Suomi* (Porvoo: WSOY, 1961), pp. 51, 53, 88, 296; Paasikivi, *op.cit.*, II, 209.

[63] Letter from Karl Wiik to Huugo Lehtinen, July 30, 1940.

[64] *"Raivaajat" kutsuu Sinua rakentamaan yhteisvoimin 'hengen ja käden' työllä vapaata ja voimakasta Suomea* (Helsinki: Työväen

COMMUNISM REBORN

The association's secretary spoke even more openly:

> We must take heed of the signs of the time and must open our eyes to all that is happening around us because it is useless to struggle against the course of events. We must be ready with as little friction as possible to slip into the new channel which will be open to us in the reborn Europe. That part of our nation which supports Social Democracy cannot remain aloof from this development. It must, on the contrary, take part without prejudice in this process of development. The alternative is that the opinion of Finnish Social Democrats may not be sought, and we may lose what we have achieved through long and purposeful labor.[65]

Karl Wiik could find no trace of Socialism, Internationalism, or Peace in the program of *Raivaajat*. What he saw was the prevailing German form of Socialism:

---

kirjapaino, 1940), p. 2; also in *Suomen Sosialidemokraatti*, August 30, 1940, p. 8. According to one leading member of *Raivaajat*, U. U. Utrio, a split occurred at the founding meeting of the association over the attitude to be taken toward Nazi Germany and Fascist Italy. U. U. Utrio to author, January 18, 1963. The chairman of *Raivaajat* denies that the association was German-oriented, but he admits that Germany tried to interpret the existence of *Raivaajat* as a sign that there was a faction within the Finnish Social Democratic Party which was sympathetic to Germany. Kalle Lehmus to author, January 31, 1963.

65 Kullervo Kulmala, in *Suomen Sosialidemokraatti*, September 13, 1940, p. 6. The chairman of *Raivaajat* also referred to Finland and the reborn Europe. He wrote: "We want to belong, along with Scandinavia, to the new Europe which will be born after the war has ended." Kalle Lehmus, in *Suomen Kuvalehti*, No. 33, August 17, 1940, p. 849. One should not overlook the fact that in August 1940 Denmark and Norway were occupied countries.

National Socialism.[66] Membership in the association was small,[67] but, as Wiik pointed out,[68] inspiration for the foundation of *Raivaajat* had come from circles close to the leadership of the Social Democratic Party. Kalle Lehmus, organizational secretary (*järjestösihteeri*) of the party, was chairman of *Raivaajat*.[69] Its secretary, Kullervo Kulmala, was also secretary of the large consumers' cooperative (*Elanto*) of which Väinö Tanner was managing director.[70]

[66] Mimeographed letter from Karl Wiik to the executive committee of the Social Democratic Party, November 29, 1940, p. 1; mimeographed letter from Karl Wiik to members of the executive council of the Social Democratic Party, December 16, 1940, p. 2. Some Social Democrats not in opposition to the party leadership appear to have agreed with Wiik. See "Asemamme ja tehtävämme," in *Kansan Voima*, May 5, 1941, p. 2.

[67] One leading figure in *Raivaajat* has stated that the association had only about twenty members. Vilho Toivari to author, February 13, 1963.

[68] Mimeographed letter from Karl Wiik to members of the executive council of the Social Democratic Party, December 16, 1940, pp. 2, 4; mimeographed letter from Karl Wiik to the executive committee of the Social Democratic Party, November 29, 1940, p. 1; Wiik, *Kuka*, p. 7; mimeographed letter from K. H. Wiik, M. Ampuja, Cay Sundström, and K.-M. Rydberg to the executive committee of the Social Democratic Party, September 25, 1940, p. 3.

[69] On October 8, 1940, Sylvi-Kyllikki Kilpi, a member of the executive committee of the Social Democratic Party, told her husband that it seemed as if Lehmus was becoming a Nazi. Eino Kilpi, editor-in-chief of *Suomen Sosialidemokraatti*, agreed. Sylvi-Kyllikki Kilpi, *Päiväkirjamuistiinpanot*, October 8, 1940. See also the entries for September 24 and November 18, 1940. A leading figure in *Raivaajat* has stated that Lehmus was sympathetic toward Nazism. U. U. Utrio to author, January 18, 1963.

[70] The executive board (*johtokunta*) of *Raivaajat* included ten men: Kalle Lehmus, Yrjö Kilpeläinen ("Jahvetti"), Kullervo Kulmala, Jorma Tuominen, Karl-Johan Harvala, Jussi Ahokas ("Juhokas"), Toivo Hänninen, Untamo Utrio, Vilho Toivari, and Väinö Leskinen. *"Raivaajat" kutsuu*, pp. 3-4; *Suomen Sosialidemokraatti*, August 29, 1940, p. 7; *Ylioppilaslehti*, No. 3, October 19, 1940, p. 43.

188

A major aim of *Raivaajat* was the expulsion of the *Vapaa Sana* group from the Social Democratic Party;[71] on August 29, 1940, the new association sent a letter to the executive committee demanding that steps be taken against the group.[72] On September 20, 1940, the party secretary, referring to the *Raivaajat* letter, urged that the executive committee expel from the party the six members of the editorial board of *Vapaa Sana*.[73] One week later a final decision was reached when Mauno Pekkala proposed that an extraordinary party congress be called to resolve the matter. He stated that he did not always agree with those who were now threatened with expulsion from the party but that this fact did not give him the right to demand that they be thrown "over-

[71] Kalle Lehmus to author, January 31, 1963. A second goal was to convince Finnish workers of the need for military preparedness. Vilho Toivari to author, February 13, 1963. The importance of this goal is reflected in the fact that four members of the executive board of *Raivaajat* (Lehmus, Tuominen, Leskinen, and Kulmala) occupied leading positions in the Finnish League of Brothers-in-Arms (*Suomen Aseveljien Liitto*). These men were also the inspiration behind the formation in November 1940 of a workers' regiment (*Sörkän rykmentti*) within the bourgeois Civil Guard.

[72] Mimeographed letter from Karl Wiik to the executive committee of the Social Democratic Party, November 29, 1940, p. 1; mimeographed letter from Karl Wiik to the executive council of the Social Democratic Party, December 16, 1940, pp. 1-2; *Sosialistisen eduskuntaryhmän kirjeitä*, No. 1, November 30, 1940, p. 3.

[73] *Suomen sosialidemokraattisen puoluetoimikunnan*, September 20, 1940, liite 23. In his opening indictment of the *Vapaa Sana* group the party secretary, Aleksi Aaltonen, repeated word for word the charges which had been made in the *Raivaajat* letter. Mimeographed letter from Karl Wiik to the executive council of the Social Democratic Party, December 16, 1940, p. 1; mimeographed letter from Karl Wiik to the executive committee of the Social Democratic Party, November 29, 1940, p. 1; mimeographed letter from K. H. Wiik, M. Ampuja, Cay Sundström, and K.-M. Rydberg to the executive committee of the Social Democratic Party, September 25, 1940, p. 3.

board," because in a party as large as the Social Democratic Party there should, in his opinion, be as great a
freedom to criticize as possible. A second compromise
proposal was made by Kaarlo Harvala. He stated that the
fate of the *Vapaa Sana* group should be determined by
the executive council and not by the executive committee
in view of the fact that two members of the latter organ,
Karl Wiik and Johan Helo, would be directly affected
by the decision.[74] The party secretary, on the other hand,
was adamant. He demanded that the executive committee
without further delay use its power of expulsion.[75] On
the final vote, between the proposals of the party secretary and Harvala, five of the nine full members of the
executive committee (Väinö Tanner, Aleksi Aaltonen,
Väinö Salovaara, Sylvi-Kyllikki Kilpi, and Gunnar
Andersson) supported immediate expulsion. The other
four (Kaarlo Harvala, Karl Wiik, Mauno Pekkala, and
J. W. Keto) voted in favor of postponing the matter
until it could be taken up by the executive council. It
was, therefore, by a margin of one vote that the fateful
decision was made.[76] Bourgeois advocates of National
Socialism in Finland pointed, with unconcealed delight,
to the significance of this decision: "The Winter War
has cleared the atmosphere to such an extent that the

[74] Mauno Pekkala, in *Suomen sosialidemokraattisen puoluetoimikunnan*, September 27, 1940, liite 25; Kaarlo Harvala, in *ibid.*,
September 27, 1940, p. 73.

[75] On July 28, 1940, the executive council had delegated its
power of expulsion to the executive committee. *Suomen sosialidemokraattisen puolueneuvoston*, July 28, 1940, p. 63.

[76] *Suomen sosialidemokraattisen puoluetoimikunnan*, September
27, 1940, p. 74. Others present at this meeting of the executive
committee were Johan Helo and Raf. Paasio (alternate members
of the executive committee) and Kalle Lehmus. A purge in the
lower ranks of the party followed soon after the executive committee had declared the *Vapaa Sana* leaders *personae non grata*.

Social Democratic Party now criticizes its own program so radically that straight off, without batting an eye, it expels those who still dare to espouse the old party program."[77]

The fact that the *Vapaa Sana* group had been placed outside of the Social Democratic Party did not mean the end of their newspaper. On the contrary, interest in *Vapaa Sana* continued to grow. Its circulation surpassed that of the chief newspaper of the Social Democratic Party, *Suomen Sosialidemokraatti*.[78] National Socialists noted that if Wiik and his supporters were permitted to continue sowing their "poison" in the struggle for the soul of Finnish labor, the leaders of the Social Democratic Party would soon be generals without an army.[79] Tanner, the strong man in the party, apparently agreed. In the summer he had stated that to let the newspaper *Vapaa Sana* exist would be almost the same as leading the Social Democratic Party to suicide.[80]

The campaign against the *Vapaa Sana* group was stepped up in the fall of 1940 with the distribution of two pamphlets originating in influential Social Democratic circles. The first pamphlet, written, presumably, by a former Communist who had been an important figure in the Finnish Trade Union Organization,[81]

[77] *Kustaa Vaasa*, No. 2, November 15, 1940, p. 12.

[78] Kustaa Vilkuna, *Sanan valvontaa. Sensuuri 1939-1944* (Helsinki: Otava, 1962), p. 29; *Vapaa Sana*, No. 5, August 23, 1940, p. 3; *ibid.*, No. 6, August 30, 1940, p. 1.

[79] *Kustaa Vaasa*, No. 1, September 5, 1940, p. 10.

[80] Väinö Tanner, in *Suomen sosialidemokraattisen puolueneuvoston*, July 28, 1940, p. 57.

[81] Mimeographed letter from Karl Wiik to the executive committee of the Social Democratic Party, November 29, 1940, p. 2. In the summer of 1940 Kalle Lehmus had been in touch with Arvo Tuominen; Lehmus proposed that Tuominen, then living in

charged that the friendship shown by the *Vapaa Sana* group for the Soviet Union was almost without parallel in Finnish history.[82] The author of the second pamphlet, using the pseudonym Lenni Lindström, went even further. He drew no distinction between the *Vapaa Sana* group and Communist leaders of the recently formed Finnish-Soviet Society of Peace and Friendship. Wiik, Helo, and Sundström were depicted as "Finnish attorneys for Russian imperialism."[83] They were, the author charged, working for the destruction of Finland in order to erect in its stead a Soviet Republic.[84] The members of

---

Sweden, be utilized by the Social Democratic Party in the struggle against the *Vapaa Sana* group. Sylvi-Kyllikki Kilpi, *Päiväkirja-muistiinpanot*, August 22, 1940.

[82] Vanha vasemmistolainen, *op.cit.*, p. 6.

[83] Lenni Lindström, *Mitä ryömäläisyys tarjoaa Suomen työväen-luokalle?*, p. 3. This pamphlet was distributed by Kalle Lehmus. *Vapaa Sana*, August 4, 1945, p. 3; mimeographed letter from K. H. Wiik and Cay Sundström to the speaker of Parliament, May 19, 1941, p. 3. The author, whose name has never been revealed, is still alive. Kalle Lehmus to author, February 4, 1963. The Finnish-Soviet Society of Peace and Friendship, to which reference is made in the pamphlet, was formed on May 22, 1940, by Communists and left-wing Socialists. The first executive board included Mauri Ryömä (chairman), Allen Järvenpää, Aimo Rikka, Elvi Sinervo, Lauri Vilenius, Irja Palmgren, and Aune Laurikainen. Göran von Bonsdorff, "Suomi-Neuvostoliitto-Seura ja sen edeltäjät," in *10 vuotta Suomen ja Neuvostoliiton ystävyyttä* (Pori: Satakunnan Yhteisvoima Oy, 1954), p. 39. The author has come across no evidence indicating that members of the editorial board of *Vapaa Sana* belonged to the Finnish-Soviet Society. Wiik, it should be noted, protested against those who sought to equate the *Vapaa Sana* group *(viikiläisyys)* with the Communist leaders of the Finnish-Soviet Society *(ryömäläisyys)*. Mimeographed letter from Karl Wiik to the executive council of the Social Democratic Party, December 16, 1940, pp. 1, 5.

[84] Introduction to the Swedish summary of the Lindström pamphlet. Referred to in a mimeographed letter from K. H. Wiik and Cay Sundström to the speaker of Parliament, May 19, 1941, pp. 1-2.

the editorial board of *Vapaa Sana*, motivated by a desire to secure for themselves "several Commissar positions," were "marionettes in the hands of the Comintern and Russian imperialists."[85]

On July 30, 1941, shortly after Finland had become a cobelligerent with Germany in the Second World War, Väinö Tanner accused the *Vapaa Sana* group, which now included six members of Parliament,[86] of calculating on a Soviet conquest of Finland. He stated that Communists and the so-called Six would have to be crushed.[87] In August 1941 the city manager of Helsinki (Johan Helo) and the Six (Karl Wiik, Mikko Ampuja, Yrjö Räisänen, Cay Sundström, Kaisu-Mirjami Rydberg, and Väinö Meltti) were arrested. The following year they were convicted of treason (*valtiopetos*) and sentenced to prison.[88] The voice of dissidence had been silenced, but

[85] Lindström, *op.cit.*, pp. 11, 15.

[86] In April 1941 Väinö Meltti joined Wiik, Ampuja, Räisänen, Rydberg, and Sundström in what was known as the Socialist Parliamentary Group (*Sosialistinen Eduskuntaryhmä*). *Suomen sosialidemokraattisen puoluetoimikunnan*, May 23, 1941, p. 31, and liite 11. Helo, the seventh important figure in the *Vapaa Sana* group, was not a member of Parliament.

[87] Väinö Tanner, in *Suomen Sosialidemokraatti*, July 31, 1941, p. 3. In October 1940 Tanner had stated that in the secret thoughts of the *Vapaa Sana* group was hidden the hope that in foreign policy Finland would choose the Baltic path. Väinö Tanner, in *ibid.*, October 4, 1940, p. 9. An English scholar has written that Tanner "was in that dangerous state of mind which sees everyone who calls for better relations with the USSR as a hidden communist or a potential traitor." Anthony F. Upton, *Finland in Crisis, 1940-1941: A Study in Small-Power Politics* (Ithaca: Cornell University Press, 1965), p. 156.

[88] In its judgment of September 15, 1942, the Finnish Supreme Court sentenced Ampuja, Helo, Meltti, Rydberg, and Räisänen to three years in prison. The sentences for Wiik and Sundström were heavier: five years for the former, six for the latter. Ensio Hiitonen, *Vääryyttä oikeuden valekaavussa* (Hyvinkää: Hyvinkään kirjapaino,

only temporarily. During the course of Finland's "Continuation War" with the Soviet Union a new opposition was born within the ranks of the Finnish Social Democratic Party. The issues raised were those of war and peace.

The Continuation War, unlike the Winter War, was not merely a defensive response to Soviet aggression. The fact that German troops had been in western and northern Finland since September 1940 makes it unreasonable to suppose that the Finnish military and the Finnish government expected, or wanted, to remain neutral in the event of hostilities between Germany and the Soviet Union.[89] When Operation Barbarossa was set in motion, on June 22, 1941, there was little question as to where Finland stood. On that date Hitler declared that German forces in Norway were standing together (*im Bunde*) with Finnish troops,[90] although it was not until four days later, following Soviet air attacks, that the Finnish government proclaimed the existence of a state of war. Väinö Tanner, Minister of Finance during the Continuation War and a member of the Cabinet's Foreign Affairs Committee,[91] has stated that Finland

1953), pp. 473-474. The imprisonment of the *Vapaa Sana* group has been described by the President of Finland as "a travesty of justice" (*oikeusmurha*). President Urho Kekkonen to author, January 9, 1963.

[89] This is suggested, unwittingly, by a noted Finnish historian when he writes in a scholarly apology for his country's cobelligerency with Germany that Finland was in the dilemma of having to choose either the Soviet Union or Germany. Korhonen, *op.cit.*, p. 322. That a third alternative existed is the central theme of Upton, *op.cit.*, pp. 234, 248, 275. See also Paasikivi, *op.cit.*, II, 220; C. Leonard Lundin, *Finland in the Second World War* (Bloomington: Indiana University Press, 1957), pp. 101-112.

[90] Korhonen, *op.cit.*, p. 323; Lundin, *op.cit.*, p. 109; Upton, *op.cit.*, p. 282.

[91] Tanner was Minister of Commerce and Industry in 1941-1942;

would have launched her own attack even if the Soviet Union had not taken the initiative.[92] Most Finns believed that Germany would defeat the Soviet Union with lightning speed.[93] Väinö Tanner, sharing this belief,[94] noted with unconcealed pleasure in the early days of the war that Finland was no longer alone.[95] The optimism existing in bourgeois and Social Democratic circles was reflected in a radio speech delivered by the Socialist speaker of Parliament, Väinö Hakkila, on July 20, 1941: "The only difference is that in our present struggle there is not the same despair and inequality which characterized the Winter War. We are not alone. That nation in Europe which is the most fit for battle and the most efficient, the German nation, is now crushing with its steel army our traditional, ever treacherous and ever deceitful enemy. Therefore, our gloomy winter war now continues as bright as summer and with victory

---

Minister of Finance in 1942-1944. From 1941 until 1944 he was a member of the Cabinet's Foreign Affairs Committee.

[92] Väinö Tanner, in *Suomen sosialidemokraattisen puolueneuvoston*, November 30, 1941, liite 2, p. 5. Tanner thought that either public opinion or a German attack from Finnish territory would have caused Finland to resume hostilities with the Soviet Union. Väinö Tanner, in *Suomen Sosialidemokraatti*, December 19, 1945, p. 5. These two factors are also noted by Korhonen, *op.cit.*, pp. 322, 336, although his major theme is that Finland was forced into war by aggressive acts of the Soviet Union. Upton, *op.cit.*, pp. 266-267, 269, 275, 285, 292-293, presents conclusive evidence that in the absence of the Soviet air attacks of June 25, 1941, Finnish troops would nonetheless have first supported Germany's northern operations and then, on July 10, launched a major offensive.

[93] Paasikivi, *op.cit.*, II, 212; Korhonen, *op.cit.*, pp. 339-340.

[94] Väinö Tanner, in *Suomen Sosialidemokraatti*, Sepember 15, 1941, p. 2; Tanner, in *Suomen sosialidemokraattisen eduskuntaryhmän*, October 22, 1942.

[95] Tanner, *Itsenäisen*, p. 318.

a certainty."[96] Although he rejected the idea of a "Greater Finland," Hakkila considered it only just that Finland's borders be extended eastward as compensation for all her sufferings. In an Order of the Day, Marshal Mannerheim had been more explicit regarding Finnish war aims. He had stated: "The freedom of Karelia and the Greater Finland is the goal that beckons us in this mighty whirl of historical events."[97] Early in September 1941, having regained the territory lost as a result of the Winter War, the Finnish army moved across the old border. By mid-September Finland had, as Väinö Tanner remarked, repossessed her former territory "with interest."[98]

Late in 1941 there was little to indicate that Finland had miscalculated when she became a cobelligerent with Germany. Opposition to the alignment did, nonetheless, exist. In the executive committee of the Social Democratic Party criticism came from Mauno Pekkala and J. W. Keto. They did not share Tanner's conviction that German military might was invincible;[99] they advo-

[96] Väinö Hakkila, in *Suomen Sosialidemokraatti*, July 21, 1941, p. 2.

[97] Lundin, *op.cit.*, p. 127. It was asserted in government circles that the Order of the Day was merely an attempt by Mannerheim to sustain the fighting spirit of Finnish soldiers. Mauno Pekkala, in *Suomen sosialidemokraattisen puolueneuvoston*, November 7, 1943, liite 6, p. 2. A clear indication that the Order of the Day was not merely psychological in nature can be found in Upton, *op.cit.*, p. 284.

[98] Väinö Tanner, in *Suomen Sosialidemokraatti*, September 15, 1941, p. 2. It should be noted that Tanner himself consistently opposed Finnish designs on Soviet Karelia.

[99] Mauno Pekkala, in *Suomen sosialidemokraattisen eduskunta-ryhmän valmistusvaliokunnan pöytäkirjat*, April 16, 1941, 12:30 P.M.; Pekkala, in *ibid.*, May 15, 1941; *Suomen sosialidemokraattisen puolueneuvoston*, November 30, 1941, p. 6; J. W. Keto, in *Suomen*

cated the signing of a separate peace treaty with the Soviet Union.[100] Germany's shift to the defensive on the Eastern Front in the winter of 1942-1943 was not accompanied, contrary to what one might expect, by a reconciliation of views within the party executive committee. Pekkala and Keto were more convinced than ever of German defeat and of the importance of a separate peace.[101] They argued that the key to Finnish independence lay in the attitude which England and the United States would take at the peace conference.[102] Tanner, however, disagreed with the opposition on all points. He admitted that the military situation had changed but was not sure that this spelled defeat for Germany.[103] He considered Germany, moreover, the sole power capable of providing Finland with immediate protection against her one enemy.[104] Only those who

---

sosialidemokraattisen puoluetoimikunnan, January 9, 1942; Keto, in *Suomen sosialidemokraattisen puolueen yhdeksännentoista,* p. 66.

[100] Mauno Pekkala, in *Suomen sosialidemokraattisen puoluetoimikunnan,* January 9, 1942; Mauno Pekkala and J. W. Keto, in *ibid.,* January 16, 1942. Tanner stated in September 1941 that it would be senseless to make peace with a country doomed to destruction. Väinö Tanner, in *Suomen Sosialidemokraatti,* September 15, 1941, p. 2.

[101] Mauno Pekkala, in *Presidentin valitsijamiesten sosialidemokraattisen valitsijamiesryhmän kokousten pöytäkirjat,* February 13, 1943; J. W. Keto, in *Suomen sosialidemokraattisen puolueneuvoston,* February 14, 1943, liite 7, p. 14; Keto, in *Suomen sosialidemokraattisen puoluetoimikunnan,* September 10, 1943; Keto, in *Suomen sosialidemokraattisen puolueneuvoston,* November 7, 1943, liite 4, p. 1; Pekkala, in *ibid.,* November 7, 1943, liite 6, pp. 3, 6.

[102] J. W. Keto, in *Suomen sosialidemokraattisen puolueneuvoston,* February 14, 1943, liite 7, p. 24; Mauno Pekkala, in *ibid.,* November 7, 1943, liite 6, p. 4.

[103] Väinö Tanner, in *Suomen sosialidemokraattisen puoluetoimikunnan,* September 10, 1943; Tanner, in *Suomen sosialidemokraattisen puolueneuvoston,* November 7, 1943, liite 2, p. 4.

[104] Väinö Tanner, in *Suomen sosialidemokraattisen puolueneuvos-*

were not independence men (*itsenäisyysmiehiä*) could advocate a speedy peace with the Soviet Union.[105]

The issue of peace was lifted from the realm of theoretical discussion and placed in the category of concrete questions early in 1944 when the Soviet Union informed the Finnish government that peace hinged upon two factors. Finland would have to acknowledge the border established in March 1940 and Finland would have to agree to expel all German forces from her territory. Väinö Tanner stated that to approve these peace terms would be almost the same as sticking one's head straight into the hangman's noose.[106] Tanner no longer believed in German victory, but he was convinced that German defeat was not an imminent matter.[107] He asserted,

---

ton, November 30, 1941, liite 2, p. 5; Tanner, in *ibid.*, November 7, 1943, liite 2, p. 14. Tanner appears to have believed, at least in 1940, that only dismemberment of Soviet Russia could offer Finland permanent security. See Wiik, *Kuka*, p. 7; letter from Karl Wiik to Huugo Lehtinen, July 30, 1940.

[105] Väinö Tanner, in *Suomen sosialidemokraattisen puoluetoimikunnan*, November 6, 1943. Tanner was convinced that the Red Army would not halt until Tsarist patrimony had been reclaimed. Paasikivi, *op.cit.*, II, 179; Väinö Tanner, in *Suomen sosialidemokraattisen puolueneuvoston*, April 7, 1940, liite 7, p. 23. This had not, however, been Tanner's view at the time of the Winter War. Paasikivi, *op.cit.*, I, 11. In retrospect one can argue that an early peace with the Soviet Union was what preserved Finnish independence in the postwar period. If Finland had waited longer than September 1944 to conclude an armistice agreement, she might very well have been dealt with as were the East European nations. In 1944, however, the Soviet government found it expedient for military and political reasons to bring to a close the northern campaign.

[106] Väinö Tanner, in *Suomen sosialidemokraattisen puolueneuvoston*, April 11, 1944, liite 7, p. 8. For details concerning the peace terms, see Väinö Tanner, *Suomen tie rauhaan 1943-44* (Helsinki: Tammi, 1952), pp. 178, 231-232.

[107] Väinö Tanner, in *Suomen sosialidemokraattisen eduskuntaryhmän*, February 10, 1944; Tanner, in *ibid.*, March 14, 1944;

moreover, that Finland had not yet lost her war with the Soviet Union.[108] Under the circumstances he considered it advisable to postpone peace. Tanner argued that in the ensuing months Soviet influence and power within the Allied camp would be weakened. A rift might even develop, he thought, between the Soviet Union and her Western Allies.[109]

The Social Democratic opposition did not find Tanner's remarks convincing or reassuring. J. W. Keto called it pure fantasy (*vapaan käden runoutta*) to think that relations between Russia and the Western Powers would deteriorate during the war to such an extent that the latter would champion Finnish interests in a way which would provide Finland with a means of obtaining more favorable peace terms.[110] He noted also that it was self-deception inspired by dreams of victory to assume that the Finnish army could resist Soviet attacks until the position of the Western Allies vis-à-vis the Soviet Union had become stronger.[111] Both Keto and

Tanner, in *Suomen sosialidemokraattisen puolueneuvoston*, April 11, 1944, liite 7, p. 10.

[108] Väinö Tanner, in *Suomen sosialidemokraattisen puolueneuvoston*, April 11, 1944, liite 7, p. 8. In March 1944 Mannerheim had informed Tanner and other members of the Cabinet that the Red Army could, if the Soviet Union so desired, drive into Finland. Mannerheim cautioned those who believed that the Soviet Union was not capable of launching an attack. Tanner, *Suomen*, p. 207.

[109] Väinö Tanner, in *Suomen sosialidemokraattisen puolueneuvoston*, November 7, 1943, liite 2, p. 14; Tanner, in *ibid.*, April 11, 1944, liite 7, p. 10; Tanner, in *Suomen sosialidemokraattisen eduskuntaryhmän*, February 10, 1944.

[110] J. W. Keto, in *Suomen sosialidemokraattisen puolueneuvoston*, April 11, 1944, liite 8, p. 5. Keto speculated that in ten or twenty years there might be a world war between the Western Allies and the Soviet Union, but this did not, he argued, offer Finland a solution to her immediate problem.

[111] J. W. Keto, in *ibid.*, November 7, 1943, liite 4, p. 6.

Mauno Pekkala warned, moreover, that a rejection of Soviet peace terms would erase the last traces of English and American sympathy for Finland.[112] These arguments were endorsed by five of the nine full members of the party executive committee but dismissed as inconsequential by the executive council and the parliamentary group.[113] On April 12, 1944, Social Democratic and bourgeois members of Parliament supported the Cabinet in its view that peace on the terms offered by the Soviet Union was impossible.

What has been described by Mauno Pekkala as the logical outcome of Finland's foreign policy then occurred.[114] On June 26, 1944, President Ryti pledged in a letter to Hitler that neither he, Ryti, nor a Cabinet named by him would sign a separate peace with the Soviet Union, making Finland an ally of Germany in the World War.[115] The Ryti Agreement aggravated the

[112] J. W. Keto, in *Suomen sosialidemokraattisen puoluetoimikunnan*, February 11, 1944; Mauno Pekkala, in *Valtiopäivät 1944 pöytäkirjat*, Vol. III (Helsinki: Valtioneuvoston kirjapaino, 1945), p. 36. In December 1941 Great Britain had declared war on Finland. The United States, however, had not yet severed diplomatic relations with the Finnish government.

[113] See the letter from J. W. Keto, Mauno Pekkala, Gunnar Andersson, and Sylvi-Kyllikki Kilpi to the executive committee, March 17, 1944, in *Suomen sosialidemokraattisen puoluetoimikunnan*, March 22, 1944, liite 11; Eino Kilpi, in *ibid.*, February 11, 1944; Eino Kilpi, in *Suomen sosialidemokraattisen puolueneuvoston*, April 11, 1944, liite 10, pp. 2, 6-7; *Suomen Sosialidemokraatti*, August 27, 1943, pp. 1-2; Keto, in *ibid.*, September 9, 1943, p. 3; *Suomen sosialidemokraattisen puolueneuvoston*, April 11, 1944; *Suomen sosialidemokraattisen eduskuntaryhmän*, March 14, 1944; *ibid.*, April 12, 1944. Tanner accused J. W. Keto, M. Pekkala, S.-K. Kilpi, E. Kilpi, and G. Andersson of using their majority power in the executive committee wantonly. Väinö Tanner, in *Suomen sosialidemokraattisen puolueneuvoston*, April 11, 1944, liite 7, p. 11.

[114] Mauno Pekkala, in *Suomen sosialidemokraattisen eduskuntaryhmän*, June 29, 1944.

[115] Mauno Pekkala, in *ibid.*, June 29, 1944; Tanner, *Suomen*,

split within the Social Democratic Party. All Social Democrats opposed the pact, but there was disagreement over whether Social Democrats should resign from the Cabinet in protest. Tanner thought it best for the country that they remain in the government. He was outvoted in the executive committee, but the parliamentary group, acting against the advice of its preparatory committee *(valmistava valiokunta)*, gave Tanner the support he needed. One leading member of the Social Democratic Party, at home neither in the Tanner nor the Pekkala-Keto camp, asserted in 1945 that the Social Democratic opposition never would have become so strong if the parliamentary group had recalled its men from the Cabinet.[116] The necessity of peace was, however, inescapable. On August 1, 1944, Ryti submitted his resignation. Three days later Parliament elected Marshal Mannerheim, characterized by the leading figure in postwar Finnish politics as the only man who could have led Finland out of the war,[117] to succeed Ryti. On August 8 a new Cabinet was formed; on August 17 Mannerheim informed the German Marshal Wilhelm Keitel that he did not consider himself bound by Ryti's letter to Hitler. On August 25 the Finnish government inquired whether the Soviet Union would be willing to receive a delegation empowered to discuss an armistice or peace. Four days later the Soviet government replied in the affirmative on the condition that Finland first sever diplomatic relations with Germany and demand the immediate withdrawal of Ger-

---

p. 306. The complete text of the Ryti letter can be found in Lundin, *op.cit.*, p. 216; Tanner, *Suomen*, p. 305. The letter led the United States, on June 30, 1944, to break diplomatic relations with Finland.

116 K.-A. Fagerholm, in *Suomen Sosialidemokraatti*, January 30, 1945, p. 4.

117 J. K. Paasikivi, *Paasikiven linja*, I (Porvoo: WSOY, 1956), p. 69.

man troops from her territory.[118] The Finnish government complied with Soviet wishes. An armistice agreement was signed on September 19, 1944, in Moscow.[119]

Implicit in the Armistice Agreement was recognition of the legal status of the Finnish Communist Party. On October 4-5, 1944, Communists held a nationwide conference, representing some two thousand party members,[120] in Helsinki. Aimo Aaltonen was elected party chairman, Ville Pessi general secretary. This meeting marked, as Pessi has noted, the beginning of a new stage in the history of both the Finnish Communist Party and the Finnish labor movement.[121] The Social Democratic Party now had a legal competitor for the allegiance of Finnish workers.[122] Late in 1944 J. W. Keto and Mauno Pekkala warned that the working class was critical of the Social Democratic leadership and that Communists could gain a monopoly position in the Finnish labor movement.[123] To prevent the growth of Communism at the expense of Social Democracy, Keto and Pekkala considered it imperative that the Social Democratic

[118] Tanner, *Suomen*, pp. 358-359, 366-368.

[119] The Armistice Agreement can be found in *ibid.*, pp. 403-414; Anatole G. Mazour, *Finland between East and West* (New York: D. Van Nostrand Company, Inc., 1956), pp. 249-259.

[120] Hertta Kuusinen, in *SKP:n vuosikirja*, Vol. xi (Helsinki: Yhteistyön kirjapaino, 1955), p. 8; Hertta Kuusinen, in *Kipinastä tuli syttyi* (Helsinki: Yhteistyön kirjapaino, 1958), p. 218. Another Communist source states that in the fall of 1944 the Finnish Communist Party had only 1,500 members. I. Rozdorozhnyi, "40 let Kompartii Finliandii," *Agitator*, No. 17 (September), 1958, p. 36.

[121] Ville Pessi, in *Kymmenvuotias liitto* (Helsinki: SKDL, 1954), p. 59.

[122] On October 15, 1944, the Finnish Communist Party was officially proclaimed a legal party. *Vapaa Sana*, November 7, 1944, p. 4.

[123] J. W. Keto and Mauno Pekkala, in *Suomen sosialidemokraattisen puoluetoimikunnan*, September 22, 1944.

Party be renovated. They proposed that as a first step the Social Democrats most closely associated with the question of war responsibility withdraw from party life.[124] Keto and Pekkala also urged that the base of the Social Democratic Party be broadened to include all workers who supported democracy and Finnish independence. Included in this category, they argued, were the *Vapaa Sana* group and the *Suomen Työmies* ("those who totter") group.[125]

For Väinö Tanner these proposals were merely a cloak behind which the opposition was concealing its bid for power.[126] He saw no reason to compete with the Communists and stated that it would be an error to enlarge the base of the party with elements which, he asserted, did not approve of the principles and tactics of Social Democracy.[127] Tanner could find no room in the Social Democratic Party for the Communist (*sic*) *Suomen Työmies* group; leaders of the *Vapaa Sana* group could be taken back into the party but only on certain

[124] J. W. Keto and Mauno Pekkala, in *Suomen Sosialidemokraatti*, October 21, 1944, p. 4. The opposition pointed in particular to Väinö Tanner, Väinö Hakkila, and Väinö Salovaara. J. W. Keto, in *Suomen sosialidemokraattisen puolueneuvoston*, October 22, 1944, liite 4, p. 2.

[125] J. W. Keto and Mauno Pekkala, in *Suomen Sosialidemokraatti*, October 21, 1944, p. 4; Keto and Pekkala, in *Suomen sosialidemokraattisen puoluetoimikunnan*, September 22, 1944; Keto, in *Suomen sosialidemokraattisen puolueneuvoston*, October 22, 1944, p. 23, and liite 4, pp. 2-3. Five of the seven leading figures in the *Vapaa Sana* group had been released from prison in the spring and summer of 1944; Karl Wiik and Cay Sundström had to await the signing of the Armistice Agreement. In November 1944 Wiik, Sundström, Rydberg, Meltti, Ampuja, and Räisänen were permitted to return to Parliament. Hiitonen, *op.cit.*, pp. 476-477.

[126] Väinö Tanner, in *Suomen sosialidemokraattisen puolueneuvoston*, October 22, 1944, liite 6, p. 8.

[127] Väinö Tanner, in *Suomen sosialidemokraattisen puoluetoimikunnan*, September 22, 1944.

conditions.[128] The executive council on October 22, 1944, agreed, as did the party congress held a month later, with Tanner.[129] The impact of this attitude toward internal party reform was far-reaching. On October 24, 1944, two Socialist ministers informed the

[128] Väinö Tanner, in *Suomen sosialidemokraattisen puolueneuvoston*, October 22, 1944, liite 6, p. 6. Whether or not the leaders of the *Vapaa Sana* group wanted to return to the Social Democratic Party is a question which must be raised. The answer is perhaps to be found in the fact that of the seven figures only one, Kaisu-Mirjami Rydberg, in 1945, joined the Communist Party. Kaisu-Mirjami Rydberg, in *SKP taistelujen tiellä*, III, 218. In a speech delivered on October 21, 1944, Yrjö Räisänen stated that what the *Vapaa Sana* group wanted was not a new party but rather reforms within the Social Democratic Party. Yrjö Räisänen, in *Suomen Sosialidemokraatti*, October 22, 1944, p. 4.

[129] *Suomen sosialidemokraattisen puolueneuvoston*, October 22, 1944, p. 24; *Suomen sosialidemokraattisen puolueen yhdeksännentoista*, pp. 313, 316, 318-319. Sylvi-Kyllikki Kilpi, shortly before the vote in the executive council, predicted that if a compromise enabling the *Vapaa Sana* group to return to the Social Democratic Party were not found, the group would draw closer to the Communists. Sylvi-Kyllikki Kilpi, in *Suomen sosialidemokraattisen puolueneuvoston*, October 22, 1944, p. 22. At the party congress it was resolved that the *Vapaa Sana* group could be taken back into the Social Democratic Party only if the group agreed to obey party rules, the party program, and decisions of the party organs. Karl Wiik responded by charging that it was not the *Vapaa Sana* group which had acted contrary to the rules and program of the party. He considered it shameful (*hävytön*) that the party should dictate conditions to the *Vapaa Sana* group. Wiik did, however, see in the compromises reached at the party congress a ray of hope for the future. K. H. Wiik, in *Vapaa Sana*, No. 7B, December 20, 1944, p. 1. Tanner, at his own request, was not elected by the party congress to the executive committee. The new executive committee included K.-A. Fagerholm and Eero A. Wuori, key personalities in what one might call a moderate opposition group, as well as Mauno Pekkala and J. W. Keto. Among the other members of the executive committee were Jorma Tuominen, who had been a leading figure in *Raivaajat*, and Aleksi Aaltonen. It should, moreover, be noted that Keto, vice-chairman of the party since 1943, was elected to the executive committee only as an alternate member.

Social Democratic parliamentary group that the decisions of the executive council had made their position in the Cabinet, as appointed representatives of the parliamentary group, extremely difficult.[130]

The Cabinet crisis which ensued ended on November 17, 1944, with the formation of a new government. Included in the Cabinet were Mauno Pekkala, Johan Helo, and, for the first time in Finnish history, a member of the Communist Party.[131] Prime Minister Paasikivi justified the presence of a Communist in the Cabinet on the grounds that it would take into consideration, in advance, the political situation which would be reflected in the March 1945 parliamentary election.[132] Mauno Pekkala saw no danger in the presence of one Communist in the Cabinet. He noted that it would, on

[130] Letter from K.-A. Fagerholm and Eero A. Wuori, in *Suomen sosialidemokraattisen eduskuntaryhmän valmistavan valiokunnan kokousten pöytäkirjat*, October 25, 1944, liite 1.

[131] The Communist Yrjö Leino became the second Minister for Social Affairs. In April 1945, following a parliamentary election, Leino was given the post of Minister of the Interior; he was later relieved of his duties by the President of Finland. See Hodgson, "The Paasikivi Line," pp. 156-157; Yrjö Leino, *Kommunisti sisäministerinä* (Helsinki: Tammi, 1958), pp. 119-120, 255-257. In the spring of 1948 Leino was instrumental in thwarting what may have been an attempt to overthrow the Finnish government. He warned the commander of Finnish defense forces, General Aarne Sihvo, that there was serious unrest in both right-wing and left-wing quarters. The necessary precautions were then taken by President Paasikivi, General Sihvo, and the chief of police in Helsinki. Leino, *op.cit.*, pp. 249-255; Aarne Sihvo, in *Helsingin Sanomat*, March 16, 1958, p. 7. An account based on dispatches in the *New York Times* has been written by Hans Peter Krosby, "The Communist Power Bid in Finland in 1948," *Political Science Quarterly*, June 1960, pp. 229-243.

[132] Väinö Tanner, in *Suomen sosialidemokraattisen eduskuntaryhmän*, November 15, 1944. Tanner was reporting to the parliamentary group on talks which he and others had had with Paasikivi.

205

the contrary, deprive the Communist Party of a good election trump[133] as uppermost in the minds of all was the coming election campaign. This was particularly true in the case of Finnish Communists, who, on October 29, 1944,[134] had been instrumental in forming the Finnish People's Democratic League (*Suomen Kansan Demokraattinen Liitto*).

Cooperating with the Communists in the formation of the Finnish People's Democratic League (SKDL) were the seven leaders of the *Vapaa Sana* group.[135] On November 2, 1944, Karl Wiik was elected chairman and Cay Sundström vice-chairman of the Great Committee (*Suuri Toimikunta*) of the SKDL.[136] The immediate task of this committee was the preparation of statutes and a program. For Wiik this meant only one thing: Socialism.[137] Wiik's open enthusiasm for Socialism was not, however, shared by members of the Communist Party.[138] Hertta Kuusinen, daughter of Otto Kuusinen and chairman of the SKDL parliamentary group from 1945 until 1966, feared that by mentioning Socialism in the SKDL program many people who might otherwise

[133] Mauno Pekkala, in *ibid.*, November 15, 1944.

[134] Hertta Kuusinen, in *SKP taistelujen tiellä*, Vol. VIII (Helsinki: Yhteistyön kirjapaino, 1952), p. 69; Kusti L. Kulo, in *Kymmenvuotias*, p. 6; Leino, *op.cit.*, pp. 28-29.

[135] Kusti L. Kulo, in *Kymmenvuotias*, pp. 7-8; Väinö Meltti to author, January 22, 1963; Johan Helo to author, June 8, 1962.

[136] *Vapaa Sana*, November 7, 1944, p. 1. The secretary, Tyyne Tuominen, was the wife of a leading Communist.

[137] Anna Wiik to author, September 14, 1962, February 4, 1963, and February 19, 1963; letter from Karl Wiik to Huugo Lehtinen, April 9, 1945. Wiik hoped to make of the SKDL a united Marxist labor party. Letter from Karl Wiik to Väinö Nieminen, March 18, 1945.

[138] Olavi Borg, *Suomen puolueideologiat* (Porvoo: WSOY, 1964), p. 43. Communist authorities censored articles written by Wiik. Anna Wiik to author, September 14, 1962, and February 4, 1963.

support the league would be driven away.[139] For Communists the main slogan was simply democracy.[140] This conflict between Wiik and the Communists, which led to his sudden replacement as chairman of the SKDL,[141] was concisely summarized in a letter which

[139] *Vapaa Pohjola*, April 4, 1946, p. 4; letter from Karl Wiik to a Swedish friend, January 5, 1945. Presumably, Hertta Kuusinen was thinking primarily of the small farmers. Statistics for the seven postwar parliamentary elections reveal that in certain election districts the SKDL has been a strong competitor for the farm vote. The Communist Party, it should be noted, has never been able to make much headway in the countryside. In 1928, 86 per cent of the party's members were workers and only 14 per cent small farmers. Yrjö Sirola, in *Työmies* (Sup.), September 5, 1928, p. 3. Thirty years later the picture was roughly the same. Rozdorozhnyi, "40 let," p. 36. If prewar experiences reflect the postwar situation, the Communist Party has also found it difficult to gain the support of Swedish-speaking Finnish workers. *Suomen kommunistinen puolue. Puoluekokousten, konferenssien ja keskuskomitean plenumien päätöksiä*, Vol. I (Leningrad: Kirja, 1935), p. 422. The SKDL, on the other hand, has had considerable success. In the 1948 parliamentary election about 14,000 Swedish-speaking Finnish workers voted for the SKDL; about 20,000 cast ballots for the Social Democratic Party. Göran von Bonsdorff, *Suomen poliittiset puolueet* (Helsinki: Tammi, 1957), p. 45.

[140] Letter from Karl Wiik to Väinö Nieminen, March 18, 1945; *Vapaa Pohjola*, April 4, 1946, p. 4; Ingul'skaia, "Rabochii klass," p. 150. In the 1962 parliamentary election the watchword was still Democracy. See *Ajan puntari*, No. 1 (January), 1962, p. 7. The importance of stressing Democracy, not Socialism, is reminiscent of a remark made in the 1920s by Otto Kuusinen: For us this slogan, a Workers' Government, is nothing more than a secret name for a dictatorship of the proletariat. We need it in order to gain the support of unripe workers. Otto V. Kuusinen, in *Kommunisti*, No. 7-8 (July-August), 1925, p. 318.

[141] Early in November 1944 Wiik traveled to Stockholm with his wife. This temporary absence from Finland was the reason later given by Communists for the naming of a new SKDL chairman. Anna Wiik to author, February 14, 1963. It was under the new chairman, Cay Sundström, that the SKDL really began to function as an organization. Tyyne Tuominen, in *Vapaa Sana*, November 23, 1945, p. 3.

Wiik wrote to a friend in Pietarsaari: "I know that some are hesitant and think that the bourgeoisie can be more easily defeated if one is silent about Socialism and speaks only about democracy. For me, Socialism is the most important thing; one must not sell (*kaupustella*) it in order to win a few bourgeois votes."[142] Wiik informed the Great Committee that if the SKDL wanted him on its lists in the parliamentary election, he would agree only on the condition that he be permitted to appear as a *Socialist* in his election speeches, his parliamentary speeches, and in all his activity.[143]

On December 22, 1944, as the parliamentary election drew nearer, the question of cooperation with the SKDL was raised in the executive committee of the Social Democratic Party by J. W. Keto, Mauno Pekkala, and K.-A. Fagerholm. They feared that the bourgeois parties would have combined lists and saw in a Social Democratic-SKDL election bloc (*vaaliliitto*) the means of meeting such a challenge.[144] They argued that cooper-

---

[142] Letter from Karl Wiik to a friend in Pietarsaari, January 2, 1945. Wiik was also discontented with the Communists for their failure to demand that the Finnish army be purged of "Fascist elements." The Communists apparently wanted to avoid all wrangles while trying to set the SKDL up on a firm base. Anna Wiik to author, February 14, 1963.

[143] Letter from Karl Wiik to the SKDL:n toimikunnalle, January 5, 1945. On the same day Wiik left for Ostrobothnia (northwestern Finland) with the intention of preaching Socialism in such a manner that it would reverberate throughout the province. Letter from Karl Wiik to a Swedish friend, January 5, 1945.

[144] Letter (dated December 22, 1944) from Mauno Pekkala, J. W. Keto, and K.-A. Fagerholm to the executive committee of the Social Democratic Party, in *Suomen sosialidemokraattisen puoluetoimikunnan*, January 3, 1945, liite 1. A brief but excellent description of the system controlling the distribution of parliamentary seats in Finland has been written by Jan-Magnus Jansson, "Post-war Elections in Finland," *Bank of Finland Monthly Bulletin*, Vol. XXXVI, No. 4 (April 1962), pp. 22-27.

ation between the Social Democrats and the SKDL would, in any case, prevent votes from being wasted and increase labor's representation in Parliament.[145] The fact that an election coalition with the SKDL would involve collaboration not only with the *Vapaa Sana* group but also with Communists did not distress them. All three men felt that the principles of the Communist Party had changed fundamentally in the 1930s and especially during the Second World War.[146] The Social Democratic executive committee was not, however, receptive to their proposal that a letter calling for an election coalition be sent to the SKDL. In a 5 to 4 vote on January 3, 1945, the committee refused to take the initiative.[147]

On January 13 the overture was made by the SKDL. In an "open letter" to the Social Democratic Party an election bloc was proposed on the basis of five points:

[145] *Suomen sosialidemokraattisen puoluetoimikunnan,* January 3, 1945, liite 1. A classic example of votes being wasted occurred in the 1962 parliamentary election. Only two members of the Social Democratic League *(Sosialidemokraattinen Liitto),* a party formed by dissident Social Democrats, were elected to Parliament, although the league received about 100,000 votes. By way of contrast, fourteen members of the Swedish People's Party were elected with a total popular vote of 148,000. This incongruity is examined by Onni Rantala, in *Uusi Suomi,* February 17, 1962, p. 6.

[146] *Suomen sosialidemokraattisen puoluetoimikunnan,* January 3, 1945, liite 1. The nature of postwar Finnish Communism was an issue discussed in some detail at the November 1944 Social Democratic Party congress. J. W. Keto, in *Suomen sosialidemokraattisen puolueen yhdeksännentoista,* pp. 239-240; Sylvi-Kyllikki Kilpi, in *ibid.,* p. 241; Väinö Tanner, in *ibid.,* pp. 231, 242; Eero A. Wuori, in *ibid.,* p. 236.

[147] *Suomen sosialidemokraattisen puoluetoimikunnan,* January 3, 1945. Voting with Keto, Pekkala, and Fagerholm was Eero A. Wuori. The majority included Onni Hiltunen, Unto Varjonen, Martta Salmela-Järvinen, Jorma Tuominen, and Emil Skog.

1. War "responsibles" [*sotasyylliset*] such as Tanner, Hakkila, Salovaara, and Aaltonen must not be candidates.

2. Those elected to Parliament must cooperate closely to prevent Fascist activity and to bring about the removal of Fascists and persons sympathetic to them from our country's leading political and civic jobs as well as from administrative and other offices.

3. Wage reductions must be fought. Energetic steps designed to raise the real wages of workers to the 1938-39 level must be taken.

4. Facilities owned by the Social Democratic Party must be put at the disposal of the SKDL and all its member organizations.

5. A comprehensive program for improvement in the living standard [*elinehdot*] of small farmers must be launched.[148]

At a meeting of the Social Democratic executive committee on January 21, Mauno Pekkala proposed that the conditions be accepted and that the executive committee request the four Social Democrats named in the SKDL letter not to stand as candidates in the parliamentary election.[149] Pekkala received the full support of J. W. Keto and, with some reservations, that of K.-A. Fagerholm and Eero A. Wuori.[150] Once again, how-

[148] *Suomen sosialidemokraattisen puoluetoimikunnan*, January 19, 1945, liite 2. The five points are quoted in *Suomen sosialidemokraattinen*, p. 349.

[149] Mauno Pekkala, in *Suomen sosialidemokraattisen puoluetoimikunnan*, January 21, 1945.

[150] J. W. Keto, in *ibid.*, January 19 and 21, 1945. Fagerholm stated that the executive committee did not have the right to remove candidates from the election lists. K.-A. Fagerholm, in *ibid.*, January 19, 1945. Fagerholm and Wuori wanted the executive committee to discuss the matter with the four Socialists mentioned in

ever, they were a minority. The executive committee in a 5 to 4 vote rejected an election coalition with the SKDL.[151]

On January 29 a declaration issued in the name of the central committee of the Social Democratic opposition (*Sosialidemokraattisen Opposition Keskustoimikunta*), of which J. W. Keto was chairman and Mauno Pekkala a member, announced that the opposition had joined the SKDL in an election coalition.[152] The Social Democratic executive committee reacted swiftly. On February 12 a resolution urging the executive council to expel Pekkala and Keto from the executive committee was approved.[153] Three days later the executive council removed them from the executive committee and ordered the "ground organizations"

the SKDL letter before reaching a final decision. K.-A. Fagerholm and Eero A. Wuori, in *ibid.*, January 21, 1945. See also K.-A. Fagerholm, in *Suomen Sosialidemokraatti*, January 30, 1945, pp. 4-5; Mauno Pekkala, in *ibid.*, February 4, 1945, pp. 6-7; Fagerholm, in *ibid.*, February 7, 1945, p. 4. Both Wuori and Fagerholm did, however, support Pekkala's proposal after the executive committee voted to settle the matter immediately.

151 *Suomen sosialidemokraattisen puoluetoimikunnan*, January 21, 1945. In the majority were O. Hiltunen, M. Salmela-Järvinen, U. Varjonen, E. Skog, and E. Pusa.

152 *Vapaa Sana*, January 29, 1945, p. 1. Other members of the central committee were K. Kulo (vice-chairman), E. Hiitonen (secretary), S. Winter (secretary), J. Hämäläinen, S. Jacobsson, V. Laine, E. Peuranen, Y. Ruutu, R. Svento, and N. Wälläri. *Vapaa Pohjola*, February 22, 1945, p. 2. The central committee indicated in its declaration that the opposition did not intend to resign from the Social Democratic Party. This led K.-A. Fagerholm to speculate that members of the opposition elected to Parliament might join the Social Democratic parliamentary group. K.-A. Fagerholm, in *Suomen sosialidemokraattisen puoluetoimikunnan*, February 12, 1945. For details concerning the history of the central committee, see *Vapaa Sana*, March 15, 1945, p. 4.

153 *Suomen sosialidemokraattisen puoluetoimikunnan*, February 12, 1945.

(*perusjärjestöt*) to expel from the party all those joining the SKDL election bloc.[154] A clean break was thus
made on the eve of the parliamentary election.[155] On
March 17-18, 1945, the Finnish populace went to the
polls.

With 23.5 per cent of the total popular vote the
SKDL won forty-nine of the two hundred seats in Parliament. The Social Democratic parliamentary group
was larger, but for Social Democrats this offered no con-
solation. The Social Democratic Party had lost thirty-
five of its eighty-five seats. Many who had previously
voted Social Democratic cast ballots in 1945 for the
SKDL.[156] Although it is difficult to depict in numerical
terms the role which the *Vapaa Sana* leaders and the
Social Democratic opposition played in the SKDL
victory,[157] one can hardly overestimate the importance

[154] *Suomen sosialidemokraattisen puolueneuvoston*, February 15,
1945, p. 35.

[155] K.-A. Fagerholm had proposed that the matter be postponed
until after the election. Fagerholm, in *ibid.*, February 15, 1945,
pp. 16, 35; Fagerholm, in *Suomen sosialidemokraattisen puoluetoimikunnan*, February 12, 1945. Fagerholm supported what was known
as the Social Democratic *Party* opposition. *Suomen Sosialidemokraatti*, March 11, 1945, pp. 1-2. Fagerholm's group wished to em-
phasize the fact that it, too, was in opposition but that its candidates in the parliamentary election would be found on lists of
the Social Democratic Party.

[156] A Finnish political scientist concludes from a rise in electoral
participation (66.6 per cent in 1939, 74.9 per cent in 1945) that
before 1945 many supporters of the extreme left abstained from
voting. He also notes, however, that the SKDL made real headway
at the expense of the Social Democrats. Jansson, "Post-war Elections," p. 25. The distribution of parliamentary seats in the 1945
election was as follows: Social Democratic Party 50, SKDL 49,
Agrarian League 49, National Coalition Party 28, Swedish People's
Party 14, National Progressive Party 9, and Swedish Left 1.

[157] In 1946 the chairman of the Social Democratic Party stated
that the Social Democratic opposition had caused the party to lose

of these two groups. Together they accounted for some 130,000 of the 398,618 votes cast for the SKDL.[158] Five members of the *Vapaa Sana* group and four of the Social Democratic opposition were elected to Parliament.[159] In numerous instances the Communist Party, the third major group in the SKDL election coalition, rode in on the coattails of Socialist candidates.[160] Socialists gave to the SKDL an air of respectability, and Finnish Communists, with good reason, have insisted throughout the postwar period that the chairman of the SKDL be a left-wing Socialist. The election of 1945 set a

---

between six and eight parliamentary seats. Onni Hiltunen, in *Suomen sosialidemokraattisen puolueen kahdennenkymmenennen edustajakokouksen pöytäkirja* (Helsinki: Työväen kirjapaino, 1948), p. 5.

[158] *Vapaa Pohjola*, July 25, 1946, p. 6. Attention should be called to the fact that membership in the SKDL has always fallen far short of the number of votes cast for the SKDL at election time. In the fall of 1945, membership in the SKDL is reputed to have been around 100,000. Tyyne Tuominen, in *Vapaa Sana*, November 23, 1945, p. 3. Official Communist sources assert that in late 1945 membership in the Communist Party, the hard core of the SKDL, was 20,000. *SKP taistelujen tiellä*, III, 53; *SKP:n vuosikirja*, XI, 42; Ingul'skaia, "Rabochii klass," p. 138. Communist Party membership in 1951 and 1958 is said to have been 50,000. *SKP:n vuosikirja*, XI, 42; Hertta Kuusinen, in *Pravda*, August 30, 1958, p. 3; Rozdorozhnyi, "40 let," p. 36.

[159] These nine members of Parliament were K. H. Wiik, Y. Räisänen, J. Helo, C. Sundström, K.-M. Rydberg, M. Pekkala, R. Svento, Y. Manninen, and V. Lehtonen. On March 22, 1946, figures from the *Vapaa Sana* group and the Social Democratic opposition formed the Socialist Unity Party (*Sosialistinen yhtenäisyyspuolue*). Informative articles on this party, which for nine years was a member organization of the SKDL, can be found in *Vapaa Sana*, March 23, 1946, pp. 1, 4; *Vapaa Pohjola*, March 28, 1946, pp. 1, 4, 8; *ibid.*, April 4, 1946, p. 8; Ensio Hiitonen, "Karvaita kokemuksia," *Sosialistinen Aikakauslehti*, No. 10 (October), 1953, pp. 392-395; *Vapaa Sana*, March 26, 1955, p. 9; *ibid.*, March 29, 1955, p. 11.

[160] *Vapaa Pohjola*, July 25, 1946, p. 6.

pattern for the future. Communist strength in postwar Finland was established. It has been carried forward by a combination of factors: an established pattern of voting behavior, the right-wing orientation of the Social Democratic Party, and, particularly in northern Finland, depressed economic conditions.

CHAPTER EIGHT

Conclusion

THE fundamental problem confronting leaders of the Finnish labor movement, Socialists as well as Communists, has been how to cope with both nationalism and the doctrine of class warfare. A simple geographic fact explains the magnitude of this problem. Finland, a small country, shares a long common frontier with an expansive Great Power. Finnish nationalism has been periodically stimulated by Tsar and Commissar.

In 1899, with his February Manifesto, Tsar Nicholas II formally endorsed Russification in Finland. In the same year the Finnish Labor Party was formed, marking the firm establishment on Finnish soil of Socialist ideas. Thus was posed at an early date the dilemma of Finnish labor. Initially, emphasis was on national liberation from Russian oppression rather than on deliverance from the ruling classes. Some Social Democrats in their attempt to combat Russification became advocates of cooperation with the bourgeoisie. Accused of class conciliation, these Socialists received a rebuff from their party in the wake of the 1905 general strike. The Fifth Congress of the Finnish Social Democratic Party, held in 1906, was a victory for the doctrine of class struggle. This did not, however, mean that there was now less interest in the fight for national liberation. It meant merely that Socialists were to carry on their fight divorced from that of the bourgeoisie.

When the Tsar, in 1910, signed legislation which had evoked from one delighted member of the State Duma the exclamation *finis Finlandiae!* the question of co-operation between Social Democrats and members of the bourgeoisie again became a source of heated discussion. The debate took on added poignancy with the outbreak of the First World War. By 1915 many Finns were looking to Germany for aid in the struggle against Tsarist rule. The Finnish Social Democratic Party was sympathetic, but hesitant, toward this activism. Not until the March Revolution was the party extricated from a delicate situation. With the formation of the Provisional Government in Russia, hopes were high among Finnish Social Democrats that a satisfactory settlement of the Finnish question could be achieved through negotiation.

When Kerenskii visited Finland in March 1917, leading Finnish Socialists proposed full internal independence for Finland. Only foreign affairs would remain under Russian control. But within a matter of days the Socialist memorandum was rejected. The Provisional Government was willing to repeal legislation enacted during the era of Russification; it would not, however, take any further action. All major issues, including the Finnish question, were to be resolved by the Constituent Assembly. The Provisional Government was firm, but so were Finnish Socialists. They now turned to the Finnish Parliament, where, as a result of an election held the previous year, they had a majority.

Finnish Socialists proposed that Parliament assume all powers, with the exception of control over foreign affairs and military matters, which had been the prerogative of the Tsar. By a vote of 136 to 55 this declaration of internal independence was approved. On July 31,

1917, the Provisional Government made its counter-move. The Finnish Parliament was dissolved. Socialists considered members of the bourgeoisie partially responsible for this turn of events, and class conflict in Finland quickened. When leaders of the bourgeois parties temporarily shelved their political differences and a Parliament with a non-Socialist majority was elected in October 1917, class antipathy crystallized.

A new element was injected into an already explosive situation when the Bolsheviks seized power in Russia. Feeling the pull of revolution, Finnish workers declared a general strike in support of their own demands for social reform and independence. The strike achieved the desired end, social reform and the assumption by Parliament of the Tsar's former powers, but in the process many workers rejected the authority of both the state and the Social Democratic Party executive committee. Violence was on the upswing, causing the gulf between Socialist and non-Socialist to widen. After January 12, 1918, when Parliament authorized use of the bourgeois Civil Guard to restore law and order in Finland, conciliation was impossible. Many Socialists, particularly those in the Red Guard, regarded this legislation as a declaration of class war by the bourgeoisie.

On January 19, 1918, the first serious clash between the Civil Guard and the Red Guard occurred. Six days later the Social Democratic executive committee, not wanting to abandon the masses and hoping to prevent anarchy, voted to seize power in southern Finland by revolutionary means. The commander in chief of the Civil Guard, Gustaf Mannerheim, decided on the same day to initiate military action in central western Finland (Etelä-Pohjanmaa): the die was cast. During the night of January 27-28 hostilities commenced in both central western and southern Finland. For the Reds it was Civil War; for the Whites, a War of Independence.

The nature of this war continues to be a subject of dispute. The bourgeoisie remains convinced that Finnish Socialists wanted to put an end to Finnish independence with the assistance of Russian troops stationed in Finland. In fact, however, this was not the case. Leaders of the Finnish Social Democratic Party opposed the use of Russian troops in Finland's internal affairs; the Soviet government, for its part, was not able to offer extensive aid. Finnish Socialists were anxious to have their revolution judged apart from the Bolshevik Revolution to obtain some form of an international guarantee for Finnish independence. They feared that the Bolshevik regime in Russia would soon be supplanted by a government less willing to recognize Finnish independence. One must, therefore, reject the notion that the armed conflict of January—May 1918 was a War of Independence. It was clearly a Civil War in which class struggle and nationalism were closely interwoven themes.

An immediate result of the White victory in the Civil War was the emergence of two parties, one representing right-wing Socialism and the other Bolshevism, in competition for the allegiance of Finnish workers. On August 29, 1918, Finnish Socialists who had sought refuge in Soviet Russia formed the Finnish Communist Party. Meanwhile, in Finland, the chastened Social Democratic Party was resurrected under the aegis of revisionism. The new line of Finnish Social Democracy found its most outspoken leader in the person of Väinö Tanner. For Tanner the task of Finnish Socialists was to split the bourgeoisie and foster the development of a radical bourgeois faction. A small Center Group of

Socialists demanded an emphasis on class struggle and warned against turning the Social Democratic Party into what Communists and left-wing Socialists charged it already was, a bourgeois reform party; but this group was ineffectual. The Finnish Social Democratic Party was cast in a permanent mold shaped by Väinö Tanner.

Right-wing Socialism was viewed in Petrograd by the central committee of the Finnish Communist Party as a serious danger, and in the spring of 1919 Otto Kuusinen was sent to Helsinki with orders to cut the ground out from under Tanner's policy of class conciliation. Finnish workers were to boycott elections, destroy Parliament, shun the trade union movement, and prepare for a new armed struggle which would establish an iron dictatorship of the proletariat. Kuusinen soon discovered, however, that this line was at variance with the mood of Finnish labor. He was a general without troops. Therefore, against a central committee majority and well in advance of the decisions spelled out at the Third Congress of the Communist International, Kuusinen abandoned the policy of left extremism. In what proved to be an effective approach, Finnish workers opposed to right-wing Socialism were urged to join forces in a united front. Communists and left-wing Socialists proceeded to wrest control, from the Social Democratic Party, of the Finnish Trade Union Organization, the Social Democratic League of Women, the Youth League, the Workers' Temperance League, and the Workers' Athletic Union. Failing to capture the Social Democratic Party itself, Communists and left-wing Socialists founded the Socialist Workers' Party. Membership in the latter soared while that of the former plummeted.

The Finnish Communist Party could claim a substantial victory. It soon became clear, however, that

Moscow's grip on the radical left was not firm. In December 1924 local Communists and left-wing Socialists refused to put forward Otto Kuusinen as their candidate in the presidential election to be held the following year. They chose, instead, a prominent trade union figure who openly fought against emigrant interference in Finland's internal affairs. Opposition to Moscow intensified after the Sixth Congress of the Communist International. Finnish trade unionists, in particular, rejected the new revolutionary line. In May 1929, at the Eighth Congress of the Finnish Trade Union Organization, even the most trusted Communists failed to obey orders from the Politburo of the Finnish Communist Party. By the end of 1929 leading Communists and left-wing Socialists had joined hands in formal opposition to Moscow. In their newspaper, *Suomen Työmies*, they demanded that Finnish workers be masters in their own house. For Moscow this was a serious challenge, but the nascent split within the Communist Party was liquidated almost immediately when legislation legally proscribing the party was passed at the behest of Finnish admirers of Benito Mussolini.

The totalitarian Lapua movement put an end to "leader opportunism" within the Finnish Communist Party, but at the same time it gave rise to a left deviation among both local and emigrant Communists. Left sectarianism in Finland was prevalent at the rank-and-file level of organization; in the Soviet Union it reached into the highest echelons of the party. Finnish Communists continued, nonetheless, to view right opportunism as the principal threat to their movement. Stalin concurred, although for him right opportunism in the Finnish Communist Party had a special meaning. He saw this deviation as "nationalism" among emigrant Finns in Soviet Karelia.

In July 1933 the Leningrad *Obkom*, headed by Stalin's so-called heir apparent, Kirov, criticized Finnish leaders of the Autonomous Karelian Republic for discriminating against Great Russians. A few months later local nationalism formally replaced Great Russian chauvinism as the main "danger" in Soviet Karelia. The follow-up came in 1935 when Kustaa Rovio, first secretary of the Karelian *Obkom*, and Edvard Gylling, the most prominent figure in the history of Soviet Karelia, were purged as Finnish "nationalists." Foremost among the charges emanating from Leningrad was that Russian, one of the two state languages, was being undermined by an unhealthy emphasis on Finnish. Leningrad had a remedy for this fundamental problem. A literary Karelian language, the development of which had long been opposed by Finnish emigrants as not only unnecessary but also reactionary, was introduced in Soviet Karelia. By 1938 it had supplanted Finnish as the second state language. During the following year the procreators of this new written language were themselves attacked as proponents of Finnization. At a great sacrifice of life, including the lives of the Old Guard of the Finnish Communist Party, Great Russian control in Soviet Karelia had by the outbreak of the Second World War been reestablished.

Persecuted in the Soviet Union and driven underground in Finland, Finnish Communists were a minuscule group with little or no influence when the world conflagration began. Wartime events, however, led to a new power configuration. In 1944 a Communist entered the Cabinet for the first time in Finnish history; in 1945 Communists were elected to forty of the two hundred seats in Parliament. Behind this remarkable success story was the inability of the Finnish Social Democratic Party to strike a satisfactory balance between nationalism and Marxism. In the late 1930s eminent Socialists had begun to see eye to eye with the bourgeoisie on matters of national defense. After the Soviet attack on Finland in November 1939, the distinction between Socialist and bourgeois leaders was all but obliterated. Class struggle was sacrificed to the demands of nationalism.

K. H. Wiik, a member of the executive committee of the Finnish Social Democratic Party for over two decades, protested against this drift to the right in party policy. He charged that party leaders had lost sight of the final goal, Socialism, and that the working class was no longer an independent political force. He argued, moreover, that Fascism was a more serious threat to Finnish independence than was Bolshevism. Recognizing the attraction which the banners raised by Wiik had for Finnish workers, the Social Democratic executive committee—dominated by Väinö Tanner and under the influence of men who were seeking a place for Finland in the reborn Europe of National Socialism—expelled Wiik from the party. In August 1941, shortly after Finland had become a cobelligerent with Germany, Wiik was arrested. Also arrested were his best-known supporters: five Members of Parliament and the city manager of Helsinki. In 1942 these seven excommunicated Socialists were convicted of treason against the state. The voice of dissidence had been silenced, if only temporarily.

By the end of 1941 two members of the party executive committee, Mauno Pekkala and J. W. Keto, were already taking issue with their colleagues—especially

Väinö Tanner—who considered German military might invincible and who saw Germany as the only power capable of frustrating Soviet designs on Finland. Pekkala and Keto viewed with skepticism the likelihood of German victory in the World War. They supported a separate peace treaty between Finland and the Soviet Union; they argued that the key to Finnish independence lay in the attitude which England and the United States would take at the final peace conference. As Finland's war with the Soviet Union dragged on, this rift within the inner circles of the Social Democratic Party became more pronounced. In the spring of 1944 it became irreparable when the party, prodded by Tanner, joined with bourgeois parties in a rejection of Soviet peace terms. The alternative which Finland chose was a more intimate association with Germany. Harsh facts of reality soon, however, forced even the most ardent opponents of a separate peace to conclude that it was a necessity. On September 19, 1944, an armistice agreement was signed between Finland and the Soviet Union.

The cessation of armed hostilities was accompanied by the legalization of the Finnish Communist Party. Although its membership in the fall of 1944 was small, the prospects for growth were good, due to the critical attitude of Finnish workers toward the Social Democratic Party. Mauno Pekkala and J. W. Keto recognized this danger and urged that the Social Democratic Party be renovated. At a crucial meeting in October 1944 they proposed that Väinö Tanner retire from politics and that the base of the party be broadened to include the group led by Karl Wiik as well as the group which in 1929-1930 had severed its ties with the Finnish Communist Party. Neither proposal was accepted, with far-reaching consequences.

On October 29, 1944, Finnish Communists, in an astute election move, organized the Finnish People's Democratic League (SKDL). Cooperating with the Communists were Karl Wiik—the first of four Socialist chairmen of the SKDL—and his six prominent associates. In January 1945 the SKDL received an additional boost when Mauno Pekkala and J. W. Keto announced that in the coming election they, too, would support the SKDL and not the Social Democratic Party. On March 17-18, 1945, Finns went to the polls. Of the total popular vote, 23.5 per cent was cast for the SKDL. Forty-nine SKDL candidates, including a disproportionately large number of Communists, were elected to Parliament. The outcome of the election was unquestionably a triumph for the SKDL, and, more specifically, for the Finnish Communist Party. In the manipulation of popular slogans, such as Democracy, and in the skillful utilization of rifts within the Social Democratic Party, Communists found a formula for establishing themselves as a significant force in postwar Finland.

EPILOGUE

FOR many observers the presence of a large Communist group in the Finnish Parliament is a paradox. How is it possible that a Communist party can be so strong in a country which fought the Soviet Union twice during the Second World War, first in 1939-1940 and again in 1941-1944, and which is an independent, democratic nation? The preceding pages, an attempt to answer this question, end with an analysis of an election which took place over two decades ago, but even the six elections since 1945 can be explained through reference to the 1945 election. The first postwar election set a pattern for the future.

Continuity is indicated by the percentage of the popular vote and the number of parliamentary seats obtained by the Finnish People's Democratic League.

Year	Percentage of Popular Vote	Seats (out of 200)
1945	23.5	49
1948	20.0	38
1951	21.6	43
1954	21.6	43
1958	23.2	50
1962	22.0	47
1966	21.2	41

One is struck by the fact that in all seven elections the SKDL has received at least one fifth of the popular vote, although the number of seats won by the SKDL shows slightly more fluctuation than does the percentage of popular vote. The explanation for this higher rate of change rests with the system of proportional representation used in Finland.[1] Also, of the four largest parties (SKDL, Social Democratic Party, Agrarian/Centrist Party, and National Coalition Party), only the Agrarian/Centrist Party, with a fluctuation of eight seats over the twenty-one-year period, shows more stability in terms of representation. In 1966, as in earlier postwar elections, the SKDL received its chief support from four election districts *(vaalipiirit)*, two of which constitute the northern half of the country—which as far back as 1932 was described by the Communists as the area most firmly under their control.[2] Continuity in the postwar period is also shown by the fact that the vast majority of SKDL representatives in Parliament are members of the Communist Party: 40 of 49 in the first election and 37 of 41 in the most recent election.[3]

Why have approximately half a million Finnish voters repeatedly cast ballots for the SKDL in the post-

[1] Striking evidence of one peculiarity in the Finnish system is provided by the case of the Social Democratic League of Workers and Small Farmers, which in the election of 1962 obtained two seats with 100,396 votes, while in the 1966 election, in an election coalition with the SKDL, it was able to win seven seats with only 61,-830 votes.

[2] *Suomen kommunistinen puolue. Puoluekokousten, konferenssien ja keskuskomitean plenumien päätöksiä,* Vol. 1 (Leningrad: Kirja, 1935), p. 386; *Kommunisti,* No. 19 (103), October 15, 1932, p. 884. See also Ilkka Hakalehto, "Kommunistinen liike," in Päiviö Tommila, ed., *Kaksi vuosikymmentä Suomen sisäpolitiikkaa 1919-1939* (Porvoo: WSOY, 1964), pp. 113-114; Ilkka Hakalehto, *Suomen kommunistinen puolue ja sen vaikutus poliittiseen ja ammatilliseen työväenliikkeeseen 1918-1928* (Porvoo: WSOY, 1966), pp. 128, 198-200.

[3] The figure 37 comes from the party bureau, although the liberal newspaper *Helsingin Sanomat,* May 8, 1966, p. 17, reports that 38 of the 41 representatives are members of the Communist Party.

war period? This continuity is most likely explained by the fact that once party identification is established, it is, as V. O. Key noted in a study of American politics, to a degree independent of factors often thought to be determinative of partisan loyalty.[4] In other words, there is a high probability that a voter will be consistent in voting once party identification has been created. A recent study by a Finnish political scientist, Pertti Pesonen, indicates that this hypothesis holds true for Finland. Writing about the election of 1958, Pesonen states: "Party affiliation was demonstrated in general to be a sufficiently permanent characteristic that party choice at election time cannot be explained without reference to its development. Particularly in a two-party system, but apparently also in Finland's multiparty system, many voters always support the same party and perhaps even the party choice of their parents."[5] A political sociologist, Erik Allardt, appears to support this supposition in one of the few serious studies of contemporary Finnish Communism. From ecological research he concludes that Communist support is to a large extent explained by traditions.[6] It would, therefore, seem that the most

[4] V. O. Key, Jr., *Politics, Parties, and Pressure Groups,* fourth edition (New York: Thomas Y. Crowell Company, 1958), pp. 234-235.

[5] Pertti Pesonen, *Valtuutus kansalta* (Porvoo: WSOY, 1965), p. 348.

[6] Erik Allardt, "Social Sources of Finnish Communism: Traditional and Emerging Radicalism," *International Journal of Comparative Sociology,* Vol. v, No. 1 (March 1964), pp. 68-69. See also Erik Allardt, "Patterns of Class Conflict and Working Class Consciousness in Finnish Politics," in Erik Allardt and Yrjö Littunen, eds., *Cleavages, Ideologies and Party Systems: Contributions to Comparative Political Sociology* (Turku: Transactions of the Westermarck Society, Vol. x, 1964), p. 127. Tradition as the major source of Communist support in one of the four election districts most favorably inclined toward the SKDL is a central theme of a book

important election in postwar Finland was that of 1945, which established party identification and a tradition for future generations.

The outcome of the 1945 election, a resounding victory for the Communist-dominated SKDL, has been traced in chapter seven to the failure of the Social Democratic Party to dissociate itself from the past and accept the necessity of reform to the left. The party, considered by many observers of different political convictions to be bourgeois in nature, was abandoned by many workers in 1944-1945 in favor of the only existing alternative through which class cleavage could be more clearly expressed.[7] Developments since 1945 have not lessened, to any substantial degree, this discontent over the orientation of the Social Democratic Party. After Väinö Tanner was elected chairman of the Social Democratic Party in April 1957 by one vote, defeating K.-A. Fagerholm, who in the opinion of Hertta Kuusinen is a conciliator *(sovittelija)*,[8] a number of prominent Socialists broke with the party and entered the 1958 parliamentary election as a group separate from the Social Democratic Party. Shortly before the 1966 election, at which time these dissident Socialists, led by Aarre Simonen, joined with the SKDL in an election bloc and increased their representation from 2 to 7, the Social Democratic Party was described by Simonen as a petit bourgeois *(poroporvarillinen)* party.[9] This con-

---

dealing with Communism in the province of Kuopio. Jaakko Nousiainen, *Kommunismi Kuopion läänissä* (Joensuu: Pohjois-Karjalan kirjapaino, OY, 1956), pp. 69-70, 127-130.

[7] Allardt, "Patterns," p. 109, notes that Communist voters have a higher sense of class consciousness than Social Democratic voters.

[8] *Uusi Suomi*, March 31, 1966.

[9] *Ibid.*, March 7, 1966.

tention, as well as the hypothesis that of Finland's major political parties dissatisfaction is most characteristic of the Social Democratic Party, draws support from the study by Pesonen of voting behavior in Tampere.[10] Applicable to Finland is the argument advanced some years ago by Gabriel Almond in a comparison of French and Italian Communism, which, with Finnish Communism, are the strongest radical left movements in Western and northern Europe, that the weakness and ineffectiveness of Socialism as a political alternative leads to a strengthening of Communism.[11]

What can one expect in the foreseeable future? Based on the evidence at hand, one should stress the theme of continuity. The SKDL will probably continue to receive around one fifth of the popular vote, although the degree of electoral success will vary. Changes in Communist strength, reflecting either an increase or decrease in support, will no doubt be relatively modest and will be caused by internal as well as external forces. Probably of most importance internally is the factor of "insecurity," defined by Allardt as unemployment and housing conditions.[12] Pesonen in his study calls attention to the fact that in the spring of 1958, just before the election which brought the SKDL its greatest number of parliamentary seats to date, unemployment was exceptionally high.[13] Although Pesonen, with emphasis on the economic factor, concludes that foreign policy had little impact on the voters in 1958, one should not dismiss foreign events in interpreting Finnish voting behavior. For example, the Communist take-

[10] Pesonen, *op.cit.*, pp. 129, 131, 147.

[11] Gabriel A. Almond, *The Appeals of Communism* (Princeton: Princeton University Press, 1954), pp. 234-235, 366, 387-388.

[12] Allardt, "Social Sources," p. 71.

[13] Pesonen, *op.cit.*, pp. 88, 127.

over in Czechoslovakia, Hertta Kuusinen's public statement in March 1948 praising the path followed by the
Czechs, and the known existence within the Finnish
Communist Party of a "barricade group" surely should
be considered a causal factor in the worst electoral defeat,
that of 1948, ever suffered by the Finnish People's Democratic League.

While stressing continuity when projecting into the
future, one should not overlook the element of change.
Already there are signs that Finnish Communism today
is different from what it was twenty years ago. In 1965
a non-Communist, Ele Alenius, was elected general secretary of the SKDL for the first time in the history of
that organization. Following the 1966 parliamentary
election Hertta Kuusinen relinquished to Paavo Aitio,
a left-wing Socialist who joined the Communist Party
in 1948,[14] the post of chairman of the SKDL parliamentary group, a post which she had held throughout
the postwar period. At the Fourteenth Communist Party
Congress, which took place early in 1966, Aarne Saarinen, leader of the powerful Building Workers' Union
(Rakennustyöläisten liitto), was elected chairman of the
party. His election represented the first change in
chairmanship since 1944, when the Communist Party
was established for the first time as a legal political
organization. Ville Pessi remains general secretary of
the party, although there are indications that he too
will be replaced in the near future by a younger man
less tainted with events of the past. Most striking of the
recent changes is the inclusion in a Finnish Cabinet,
following the 1966 election, of three SKDL representatives. For eighteen years, since their refusal in 1948 to
enter a Finnish Cabinet on terms set forth by the Social-

[14] *Päivän Sanomat*, quoted in *Uusi Suomi*, April 7, 1961, p. 8.

ist Premier, K.-A. Fagerholm, Communists had been excluded from the government.[15] In May 1966, however, Alenius and two Communists were given relatively minor posts in a four-party, fifteen-member Cabinet headed by Rafael Paasio, chairman of the Social Democratic Party since the retirement in 1963 of Väinö Tanner. The program of the coalition government has been called by Paasio "a compromise of compromises," and for this reason one should not expect the new government to remain in office any longer than previous Finnish Cabinets—which have not been noted for their longevity. But Finnish Communists are no longer so isolated from the policy-making process, and it is hoped, perhaps with some justification, that Cabinet responsibility will speed the evolution which is now occurring within the Finnish Communist Party.

[15] One of the demands considered impossible by Fagerholm was Communist insistence that they be given either the post of Minister of the Interior or the Foreign Minister portfolio. K.-A. Fagerholm to author, February 8, 1963.

SELECT BIBLIOGRAPHY

Allardt, Erik. "Patterns of Class Conflict and Working Class Consciousness in Finnish Politics," in Erik Allardt and Yrjö Littunen, eds., *Cleavages, Ideologies and Party Systems: Contributions to Comparative Political Sociology.* Turku: Transactions of the Westermarck Society, Vol. x, 1964, pp. 97-131.

———. "Social Sources of Finnish Communism: Traditional and Emerging Radicalism," *International Journal of Comparative Sociology,* Vol. v, No. 1 (March 1964), pp. 49-72.

———. "Traditional and Emerging Radicalism," Draft.

Almond, Gabriel A. *The Appeals of Communism.* Princeton: Princeton University Press, 1954.

Ampuja, Mikko. *Pajasta parlamenttiin.* Helsinki: Tammi, 1947.

Antikainen, T., ed. *SKP:n taistelun tieltä: Muistelmia, kuvauksia ja aineistoa SKP:n 15-vuotistaipaleelta.* Leningrad: Kirja, 1934.

Baltiiskie moriaki v podgotovke i provedenii velikoi oktiabr'skoi sotsialisticheskoi revoliutsii. Moscow-Leningrad: Izdatel'stvo Akademii Nauk SSSR, 1957.

Billington, James H. "Finland," in Cyril E. Black and Thomas P. Thornton, eds., *Communism and Revolution: The Strategic Uses of Political Violence.* Princeton: Princeton University Press, 1964, pp. 117-144.

Bol'shaia sovetskaia entsiklopediia, Vol. lvii. Moscow: Ogiz, 1936.

Bol'shaia sovetskaia entsiklopediia, Vol. xxxi. Moscow: Ogiz, 1937.

Bol'shaia sovetskaia entsiklopediia, Vol. IX. Moscow: Gosudarstvennoe slovarno-entsiklopedicheskoe izdatel'-stvo "Sovetskaia entsiklopediia," 1934.

Bonsdorff, Göran von. *Suomen poliittiset puolueet.* Helsinki: Tammi, 1957.

————. "Suomi-Neuvostoliitto-Seura ja sen edeltäjät," in *10 vuotta Suomen ja Neuvostoliiton ystävyyttä.* Pori: Satakunnan Yhteisvoima Oy, 1954, pp. 35-58.

Borg, Olavi. *Suomen puolueideologiat.* Porvoo: WSOY, 1964.

Borkenau, Franz. *European Communism.* New York: Harper & Brothers, 1953.

Brzezinski, Zbigniew K. *The Permanent Purge.* Cambridge: Harvard University Press, 1956.

Carr, Edward Hallett. *The Bolshevik Revolution 1917-1923,* Vol. III. New York: The Macmillan Company, 1953.

Castrén, Arthur. "Kun senaatti aiottiin vangita," *Itsenäinen Suomi,* No. 12 (December 6), 1927, pp. 207-209.

Degras, Jane, ed. *The Communist International 1919-1943. Documents,* Vol. I. London: Oxford University Press, 1956.

Donner, Kai, Th. Svedlin, and Heikki Nurmio, eds. *Suomen vapaussota,* Vols. I, V. Jyväskylä: K. J. Gummerus Oy, 1921, 1925.

Dybenko, P. E. *Miatezhniki.* Moscow: Izdatel'stvo Krasnaia nov', 1923.

Enckell, Carl. *Poliittiset muistelmani,* Vol. 1. Porvoo: WSOY, 1956.

Eskola, Seikko. "Suomen kysymys vuonna 1917 Ruotsin sisäpolitiikassa," in *Uusi Suomi,* February 7, 1966, pp. 4, 8.

Finliandskaia revoliutsiia, sbornik statei. Moscow: Gosudarstvennoe izdatel'stvo, 1920.

Gummerus, Herman. *Jääkärit ja aktivistit*. Porvoo: WSOY, 1928.

Gylling, Edvard. "Ensimäinen Sosialististen tasavaltain välinen sopimus," *Kommunisti*, No. 1 (37), January 15, 1928, pp. 25-33.

Hakalehto, Ilkka. "Kommunistinen liike," in Päiviö Tommila, ed., *Kaksi vuosikymmentä Suomen sisäpolitiikkaa 1919-1939*. Porvoo: WSOY, 1964, pp. 89-119.

————. *Suomen kommunistinen puolue ja sen vaikutus poliittiseen ja ammatilliseen työväenliikkeeseen 1918-1928*. Porvoo: WSOY, 1966.

Halonen, A., ed. *Suomen luokkasota—Historiaa ja muistelmia*. Superior, Wisconsin: Työmies Society Print, 1928.

Hannula, J. O. *Suomen vapaussodan historia*. Porvoo: WSOY, 1956.

Hiitonen, Ensio. *Vääryyttä oikeuden valekaavussa*. Hyvinkää: Hyvinkään kirjapaino, 1953.

Hirvikallio, Paavo. *Tasavallan presidentinvaalit Suomessa 1919-1950*. Porvoo: WSOY, 1958.

Hodgson, John H. "Finland's Position in the Russian Empire, 1905-1910," *Journal of Central European Affairs*, Vol. xx, No. 11 (July 1960), pp. 158-173.

————. "The Paasikivi Line," *The American Slavic and East European Review*, Vol. xviii, No. 2 (April 1959), pp. 145-173.

Hoglund, A. William. *Finnish Immigrants in America 1880-1920*. Madison: University of Wisconsin Press, 1960.

Huttunen, E. *Sosialidemokraattinen puoluejohto ja kansalaissota*. Helsinki: Kansanvalta, 1918.

Idman, K. G. *Maamme itsenäistymisen vuosilta*. Porvoo: WSOY, 1953.

————. "Öinen neuvottelu sotalaivalla," *Suomen vapaussota*, December 6, 1932, pp. 78-80.

Ingul'skaia, L. A. - "Rabochii klass finliandii i demokratizatsiia strany (1944-1948 gg.)," in I. M. Maiskii, ed., *Rabochee dvizhenie v skandinavskikh stranakh i finliandii*. Moscow: Izdatel'stvo Nauka, 1965, pp. 128-169.

Iuvenalii, Iu. *Bor'ba klassov v Finliandii*. Moscow-Leningrad: Gosudarstvennoe Sotsial'no-Ekonomicheskoe izdatel'stvo, 1931.

"Iz istorii natsional'noi politiki Vremennogo Pravitel'stva," *Krasnyi arkhiv*, Vol. 5 (30), 1928, pp. 46-79.

Jääskeläinen, Mauno. *Itä-Karjalan kysymys*. Porvoo: WSOY, 1961.

Jakobson, Max. *The Diplomacy of the Winter War*. Cambridge: Harvard University Press, 1961.

Jansson, Jan-Magnus. "Post-war Elections in Finland," *Bank of Finland Monthly Bulletin*, Vol. xxxvi, No. 4, (April 1962), pp. 22-27.

Juva, Einar W. *Suomen kansan aikakirjat*, Vol. ix. Helsinki: Otava, 1937.

K.-A. Fagerholm, mies ja työkenttä—mannen och verket. Helsinki: Oy Tilgmann, 1961.

Kennan, George F. *Russia and the West under Lenin and Stalin*. New York: Mentor Books, 1962.

Key, V. O., Jr. *Politics, Parties, and Pressure Groups*. New York: Thomas Y. Crowell Company, fourth edition, 1958.

Kheimo, M. and A. Tivel', eds. *10 let Kominterna v resheniiakh i tsifrakh*. Moscow-Leningrad: Gosudarstvennoe izdatel'stvo, 1929.

Kholodkovskii, V. M. "Revoliutsiia v Finliandii v 1918 g. i interventsiia germanskogo imperialisma," *Novaia i noveishaia istoriia*, No. 4, 1957, pp. 116-136.

Kilpi, Sylvi-Kyllikki. *Päiväkirjamuistiinpanot. Kipinästä tuli syttyi.* Helsinki: Yhteistyön kirjapaino, 1958.

Knoellinger, Carl Erik. *Labor in Finland.* Cambridge: Harvard University Press, 1960.

Kolmannen yleiskarjalaisen työläisten, talonpoikain ja puna-armeijalaisten neuvostojen edustajakokouksen pöytäkirja. Kokous pidetty Petroskoissa lokakuun 2-7 p:nä v. 1922. Petroskoi: Aluekirjapaino, 1922.

Kommunaardien muistojulkaisu: kommunismin puolesta kaatuneille elokuun 31 p:nä 1920 veriteon uhrien muistolle. Leningrad: SKP:n KK, 1926.

Kommunisticheskii internatsional pered VII vsemirnym kongressom. Moscow: Partizdat TsK VKP (b), 1935.

"Kommunistinen vaalilippu," *Vapaus*, February 20, 1919, pp. 2-3.

Korhonen, Arvi. *Barbarossa-suunnitelma ja Suomi.* Porvoo: WSOY, 1961.

Korpimaa, Timo. *Salaisilla poluilla.* Rauma: O. Y. Länsi-Suomen kirjapaino, 1934.

Krosby, Hans Peter. "The Communist Power Bid in Finland in 1948," *Political Science Quarterly*, June 1960, pp. 229-243.

Kuusinen, O. W. "Anarkia ja vallankumous," *Sosialistinen Aikakauslehti*, No. 17-18 (October), 1906, pp. 388-399.

―――. "Eduskuntakomitean ehdotus valtiopäiväjärjestykseksi," *Sosialistinen Aikakauslehti*, No. 5 (March 1), 1906, pp. 99-103.

―――. "Eduskuntauudistuksen viimeiset vaiheet," *Sosialistinen Aikakauslehti*, No. 11-12 (June), 1906, pp. 242-247.

―――. "Kuntoon salaiset järjestöt Suomessa!," *Kumous*, No. 21-24 (January 18, 1919), pp. 79-84.

————. "Suomen Sosialidemokratian johtajille," *Sosialistinen Aikakauslehti*, April 16, 1920, pp. 98-106.

————. *Suomen työväenliikkeen opetuksia*. Lappeenranta: SKP:n puoluetoimikunta, 1949.

————. *Suuri vuosisatamme*. Helsinki: Yhteistyön kirjapaino, 1961.

————. "Venäjän vallankumousliike ja Suomen sosialidemokratia," *Sosialistinen Aikakauslehti*, No. 14 (August), 1906, pp. 314-324.

————, and Yrjö Sirola. *Suomen työväen tulikoe*. Superior, Wisconsin: Työmies Print, 1923.

Kuusisto, Allan A. "The Paasikivi Line in Finland's Foreign Policy," *The Western Political Quarterly*, Vol. XII, No. 1 (March 1959), pp. 37-49.

Kymmenen vuotta Neuvosto-Karjalaa 1920-1930. Petroskoi: AKSNT:n Toimeenpaneva Keskuskomitea, 1930.

Kymmenvuotias liitto. Helsinki: SKDL, 1954.

Laine, Y. K. *Suomen poliittisen työväenliikkeen historia*, Vols. I-III. Helsinki: Tammi, 1946, 1951.

Laitinen, Olli and Matti Nieminen, eds. *Kuin kallioon hakattu*. Helsinki: KK:n kirjapaino, 1956.

Latukka, J. E., ed. *Lenin suomalaisten muistelmissa*. Leningrad: Kirja, 1925.

Leino, Yrjö. *Kommunisti sisäministerinä*. Helsinki: Tammi, 1958.

Lekhen, T. "Proletariat Finliandii v bor'be za vlast'," *Istoriia proletariata SSSR*, sbornik 3 (19), 1934, pp. 3-25.

Lenin, V. I. *"Left-Wing" Communism, An Infantile Disorder*. New York: International Publishers, 1940.

————. *Sochineniia*, Vol. XXVI. Moscow: Gosudarstvennoe izdatel'stvo politicheskoi literatury, fourth edition, 1949.

Letonmäki, L. *Karjalan historia*. Leningrad: Kirja, 1931.

Lindström, Lenni. *Mitä ryömäläisyys tarjoaa Suomen työväenluokalle?*

Louhikko, E. K. *Teimme vallankumousta.* Helsinki: OY Suomen Kirja, 1943.

Lumivuokko, J. *Kommunisti ammatillisessa liikkeessä.* Kuopio: Savon Kansan kirjapaino, 1921.

Lundin, C. Leonard. *Finland in the Second World War.* Bloomington: Indiana University Press, 1957.

Luostarinen, Antti J. "Murhenäytelmä Leningradissa," in *Kevättervehdys.* Helsinki: Sosialidemokraattinen puoluetoimikunta, 1941.

Maizel', M. *Stranitsy revoliutsionnoi istorii finliandskogo proletariata.* Leningrad: Priboi, 1928.

Mannerheim, G. *Muistelmat,* Vol. I. Helsinki: Otava, 1953.

Mazour, Anatole G. *Finland between East and West.* New York: D. Van Nostrand Company, Inc., 1956.

"Mitä tahtoo Suomalainen Kommunistinen Puolue?" *Suomalaisten kommunistien sarjajulkaisu,* No. 5. Pietari: SKP:n KK, 1918.

Nekotorye dannye o rabote karel'skogo pravitel'stva. Petrozavodsk: Gos. Tipografiia im. P. F. Anokhina, 1929.

Norrmén, P. H. "Punaisten sotavalmistelut," in Kai Donner, Th. Svedlin, and Heikki Nurmio, eds., *Suomen vapaussota,* Vol. I. Jyväskylä: K. J. Gummerus Oy, 1921, pp. 404-449.

Nousiainen, Jaakko. *Kommunismi Kuopion läänissä.* Joensuu: Pohjois-Karjalan kirjapaino OY, 1956.

Nurmio, Yrjö. *Suomen itsenäistyminen ja Saksa.* Porvoo: WSOY, 1957.

Oittinen, R. H. *Työväenkysymys ja työväenliike Suomessa.* Helsinki: Tammi, 1954.

Paasikivi, J. K. *Paasikiven linja*, Vol. I. Porvoo: WSOY, 1956.

———. *Toimintani Moskovassa ja Suomessa 1939-41*, Vols. I-II. Porvoo: WSOY, 1958.

Paasivirta, Juhani. *Ensimmäisen maailmansodan voittajat ja Suomi*. Porvoo: WSOY, 1961.

———. *Suomen itsenäisyyskysymys 1917*, Vols. I-II. Porvoo: WSOY, 1947, 1949.

———. *Suomen poliittisen työväenliikkeen kehitys*. Porvoo: WSOY, 1949.

———. *Suomi vuonna 1918*. Porvoo: WSOY, 1957.

Pervyi kongress kommunisticheskogo internatsionala. Protokoly zasedanii v Moskve so 2 po 19 marta 1919 goda. Petrograd: Izdatel'stvo Kommunisticheskogo internatsionala, 1921.

Pesonen, Pertti. *Valtuutus kansalta*. Porvoo: WSOY, 1965.

Puntila, L. A. "Vapaussota-Kapina-Kansalaissota," in *Neljän vuosikymmenen takaa*. Porvoo: WSOY, 1958, pp. 9-20.

"Rabochaia revoliutsiia v Finliandii v 1918 g.," *Proletarskaia revoliutsiia*, No. 8 (79), August 1928, pp. 167-195.

Räikkönen, Erkki. "Suomen kohtalonyö 1917," *Helsingin Sanomat*, November 7, 1959, pp. 6, 10.

"Raivaajat" kutsuu Sinua rakentamaan yhteisvoimin 'hengen ja käden' työllä vapaata ja voimakasta Suomea. Helsinki: Työväen kirjapaino, 1940.

Rauanheimo, U. V. "Venäläiset joukot Suomessa maailmansodan 1914-18 aikana; niiden yleisryhmitykset ja toimintasuunnitelmat," *Tiede ja Ase*, No. 8. Helsinki: Otava, 1950, pp. 151-170.

Renvall, Pentti. "Neuvosto-Karjalan suomalaisuuden

kriisin alkuvaiheista," *Historiallinen Aikakauskirja*, 1944, pp. 77-106.

Rintala, Marvin. "An Image of European Politics: The People's Patriotic Movement," *Journal of Central European Affairs*, Vol. xxii, No. 3 (October 1962), pp. 308-316.

———. "The Politics of Gustaf Mannerheim," *Journal of Central European Affairs*, Vol. xxi, No. 1 (April 1961), pp. 67-83.

———. "The Problem of Generations in Finnish Communism," *The American Slavic and East European Review*, Vol. xvii, No. 2 (April 1958), pp. 190-202.

———. *Three Generations: The Extreme Right Wing in Finnish Politics*. Bloomington: Indiana University Press, 1962.

———. "Väinö Tanner in Finnish Politics," *The American Slavic and East European Review*, Vol. xx, No. 1 (February 1961), pp. 84-98.

Roos, Sigurd. *Suomen kansallislakko*, Vols. i-ii. Helsinki: Alex F. Lindberg'in kirjapaino, 1907.

Roshal', M. G. "Bol'sheviki gel'singforsa v dni revoliutsii 1917 g. (mart-iiul')," *Istoricheskii arkhiv*, No. 5 (September-October), 1956, pp. 149-168.

———. *Na putiakh revoliutsii*. Moscow: Voennoe izdatel'stvo ministerstva oborony soiuza SSR, 1957.

Rovio, K. "Kielikysymys Neuvosto-Karjalan kansallisuuspolitiikassa," *Kommunisti*, No. 8 (80), August 1931, pp. 376-385.

———. "Problema iazyka v natsional'noi politike AKSSR," *Karelo-Murmanskii krai*, No. 1-2 (January-February), 1931, pp. 16-21.

Rozdorozhnyi, I. "40 let Kompartii Finliandii," *Agitator*, No. 17 (September), 1958, pp. 33-36.

Schapiro, Leonard. *The Communist Party of the Soviet Union.* New York: Random House, 1960.

Seimovyi ustav Velikogo kniazhestva Finliandskogo, s prilozheniiami. St. Petersburg: 1913.

Seton-Watson, Hugh. *From Lenin to Malenkov.* New York: Frederick A. Praeger, 1956.

Sirola, Yrjö. "Industrialismista-kommunismiin," *Kumous,* No. 14 (October 26, 1918), pp. 149-151.

————. "Järjestynyt työväki ja järjestymättömät," *Sosialistinen Aikakauslehti,* Näytenumero 4 (February), 1906, pp. 54-57.

————. "Kehittyykö tilanne vallankumoukselliseksi?" in *Työmies,* January 12, 1918, pp. 4-6.

————. *Kommunisticheskaia partiia Finliandii.* Moscow-Leningrad: Moskovskii Rabochii, 1929.

————. "Kun se selkeni. Muistelma SKP:n perustamisajoilta," *Proletaari,* No. 6 (69), October 1933, pp. 6-11.

————. "Miksi ei Suomessa ollut bolshevikkipuoluetta?" *Kommunisti,* No. 1 (37), January 15, 1928.

————. "Millä tavoin vallankumous on tapahtuva?," *Säkeniä,* Vol. viii, No. 7 (July 1914), pp. 273-282.

————. "Puolueemme itsekritiikkiä," *Proletaari,* No. 5 (55), May 1931, pp. 15-22.

————. "Sosialistiherrasta herrassosialistiksi." Työväen Arkisto: 92 Sirola III.

————. "Suomen kommunistinen puolue," *Kommunisti,* No. 7 (43), July 1928, pp. 290-309.

————. "Suomen sosdem. puoluehallinnon suhtautumisesta Viaporin kapinaan," in V. N. Sokolov, *Viapori. Sotilaskapina v. 1906.* Petroskoi: Kirja, 1935, pp. 215-223.

————. "Suomen vv. 1905-1906 opetuksista," *Kommunisti,* No. 10 (147), October 23, 1935.

241

————. *Tilanteen arvioiminen ja toiminnan määrittely* (*alustus*). Työväen Arkisto: 323.2 (471) "1918."

————. "Työväen Vallankumouksellisen Keskusneuvoston toiminta." *Vapaussodan arkisto* I A 2.

————. "Valtiokäsitteen selvittelyä," *Säkeniä*, September 1912, pp. 315-324.

————. "Valtion säilyttäjät," *Säkeniä*, December 1912, pp. 441-447.

————. "Vospominaniia o Lenine," *Proletarskaia revoliutsiia*, No. 1 (96), January 1930, pp. 78-84.

Siukiiainen, I. I. "Gel'singforsskii seim rabochikh organizatsii v 1917-1918 gg.," in *Skandinavskii sbornik*, Vol. v. Tallinn: Estonskoe gosudarstvennoe izdatel'stvo, 1962, pp. 115-134.

————. *Revoliutsiia 1918 goda v Finliandii. Avtoreferat dissertatsii*. Petrozavodsk: 1958.

————. *Revoliutsionnye sobytiia 1917-1918 gg. v Finliandii*. Petrozavodsk: Karel'skoe knizhnoe izdatel'stvo, 1962.

SKP taistelujen tiellä, Vols. i-xi. Helsinki: Yhteistyön kirjapaino, 1945-1955.

Smirnov, V. *Iz revoliutsionnoi istorii Finliandii 1905, 1917, 1918 gg.* Leningrad: Leningradskoe oblastnoe izdatel'stvo, 1933.

Smith, C. Jay, Jr. *Finland and the Russian Revolution 1917-1922*. Athens: University of Georgia Press, 1958.

————. "Russia and the Origins of the Finnish Civil War of 1918," *The American Slavic and East European Review*, December 1955, pp. 481-502.

Soikkanen, Hannu. "Sosiaalidemokraatti vai kommunisti?," *Suomalainen Suomi*, Vol. xxix, No. 3 (March 1961), pp. 147-152.

————. *Sosialismin tulo Suomeen*. Porvoo: WSOY, 1961.

SELECT BIBLIOGRAPHY

——. "Sosialististen aatteiden sisältö ja leviäminen," *Historiallinen Aikakauskirja*, No. 4, 1961, pp. 280-285.

——. "Työväenliikkeen jakautumisongelma itsenäisyyden alkuvuosina," *Turun Historiallisen Yhdistyksen julkaisu*, Vol. xv, pp. 261-289.

Sosialistinen Kalenteri vuodelle 1935. Leningrad: Kirja, 1935.

Sovetskaia Kareliia: ocherki partiinogo, sovetskogo i kul'turnogo stroitel'stva AKSSR. Moscow-Leningrad: Ogiz, 1933.

Statistical Picture of the Finnish Social Democratic Party and the Various Fields of Activity of the Workers' Movement. Helsinki: Työväen kirjapaino, 1950.

Statisticheskii obzor 1923-1924 g.: Tilastollinen katsaus v. 1923-1924. Petrozavodsk: Izdanie statisticheskogo upravleniia AKSSR, 1925.

Stenberg, Elli. "Yrjö Sirola," in *Suomalaisia sosialisteja*, Vol. III. Helsinki: Työväen Sivistysliitto, 1947, pp. 67-156.

Ström, W. "Kun suomalainen jääkäri varoitti punaisten pääjohtajia tarttumasta miekkaan isänmaata vastaan," *Suomen vapaussota*, No. 5, May 16, 1934, pp. 86-88.

Suomen Ammattijärjestön kahdeksannen Helsingissä toukokuun 10-16 p:nä 1929 pidetyn edustajakokouksen pöytäkirja. Helsinki: Oy Työn kirjapaino, 1929.

Suomen Ammattijärjestön seitsemännen Helsingissä toukokuun 3-8 p:nä 1926 pidetyn edustajakokouksen pöytäkirja. Helsinki: Oy Työn kirjapaino, 1926.

Suomen Ammattijärjestön viidennen Helsingissä toukokuun 25-29 p:nä 1920 pidetyn edustajakokouksen pöytäkirja. Kotka: Kyminlaakson Työväen kirjapaino, 1920.

Suomen Ammattijärjestön v. 1917 pidetyn edustajako-

243

kouksen pöytäkirjaluonnos. Työväen Arkisto: 331.88 (471) (063) "1917."

Suomen kansanvaltuuskunnan pöytäkirjat.

Suomen kommunistinen puolue. Puoluekokousten, konferenssien ja keskuskomitean plenumien päätöksiä, Vol. 1. Leningrad: Kirja, 1935.

Suomen Metalliteollisuustyöntekijäin Liiton kahdeksannen Helsingissä joulukuun 4-11 p:nä 1917 pidetyn edustajakokouksen pöytäkirja. Helsinki: Työväen kirjapaino, 1919.

Suomen sosialidemokraattinen työväenliike 1899-1949. Helsinki: KK:n kirjapaino, 1949.

Suomen sosialidemokraattisen eduskuntaryhmän pöytäkirjat, 1917-1945.

Suomen sosialidemokraattisen puolueen kahdennenkymmenennen edustajakokouksen pöytäkirja. Helsinki: Työväen kirjapaino, 1948.

Suomen sosialidemokraattisen puolueen kahdennentoista edustajakokouksen pöytäkirja. Helsinki: Tampereen työväen kirjapaino, 1920.

Suomen sosialidemokraattisen puolueen kuudennen edustajakokouksen pöytäkirja. Kotka: Kyminlaakson työväen kirjapaino, 1909.

Suomen sosialidemokraattisen puolueen kymmenennen edustajakokouksen pöytäkirjaselostus. Turku: Sosialistin kirjapaino Oy, 1925.

Suomen sosialidemokraattisen puolueen neljännen edustajakokouksen pöytäkirja. Tampere: Työväen puoluehallinto, 1906.

Suomen sosialidemokraattisen puolueen neljännentoista edustajakokouksen pöytäkirja. Helsinki: Sosialidemokraattinen puoluetoimikunta, 1926.

Suomen sosialidemokraattisen puolueen seitsemännen

SELECT BIBLIOGRAPHY

edustajakokouksen pöytäkirja. Helsinki: Sosialidemokraattinen puoluetoimikunta, 1912.

Suomen sosialidemokraattisen puolueen viidennen edustajakokouksen pöytäkirja. Helsinki: Sosialidemokraattinen puoluetoimikunta, 1906.

Suomen sosialidemokraattisen puolueen viidennentoista edustajakokouksen pöytäkirja. Helsinki: Sosialidemokraattinen puoluetoimikunta.

Suomen sosialidemokraattisen puolueen yhdeksännentoista edustajakokouksen pöytäkirja. Helsinki: Työväen kirjapaino, 1946.

Suomen sosialidemokraattisen puolueneuvoston pöytäkirjat, 1909-1945.

Suomen sosialidemokraattisen puoluetoimikunnan pöytäkirjat, 1918-1945.

Suomen työväen vallankumous 1918. Arviota ja itsekritiikkiä. Leningrad: Kirja, 1928.

Suomen työväen vasemmistoryhmän Helsingin työväentalolla joulukuun 7 p:nä 1929 pidetyn kokouksen pöytäkirja.

Suomen työväen vasemmistoryhmän keskustoimikunnan pöytäkirjat.

Suomen vapaussota vuonna 1918, Vols. II-III, VI. Helsinki: Otava, 1921-1922, 1925.

Suurlakkovuosi 1905. Kuopio: Kansankulttuuri, 1955.

Svechnikov, M. S. *Revoliutsiia i grazhdanskaia voina v Finliandii 1917-1918 gody.* Moscow-Petrograd: Gosudarstvennoe izdatel'stvo, 1923.

Syyttäjistön arkisto (Valtionarkistossa).

Taimi, A. *Sivuja eletystä.* Petroskoi: Karjalais-Suomalaisen SNT:n Valtion kustannusliike, 1954.

Tanner, Väinö. *Itsenäisen Suomen arkea.* Helsinki: Tammi, 1956.

————. *Kuinka se oikein tapahtui.* Helsinki: Tammi, 1957.

————. *Olin ulkoministerinä talvisodan aikana.* Helsinki: Tammi, 1951.

————. *Suomen tie rauhaan 1943-44.* Helsinki: Tammi, 1952.

"Tezisy TsK KPF," *Proletarskaia revoliutsiia,* No. 8 (79), August 1928, pp. 170-195.

Toiset valtiopäivät 1917 pöytäkirjat, Vol. I. Helsinki: Valtioneuvoston kirjapaino, 1918.

Tokoi, Oskari. *Maanpakolaisen muistelmia.* Helsinki: Tammi, 1959.

Tommila, Päiviö, ed. *Venäläinen sortokausi Suomessa.* Porvoo: WSOY, 1960.

TsK KPF. "40 let rabochei revoliutsii v Finliandii," *Novaia i noveishaia istoriia,* No. 2, 1958, pp. 115-128.

Tuominen, Arvo. *Kremlin kellot.* Helsinki: Tammi, 1957.

————. *Maan alla ja päällä.* Helsinki: Tammi, 1958.

————. *Neuvostoliitto Leninin perinnön vartijana.* Stockholm: Tryckeriaktiebolaget tiden, 1941.

————. "The Northern Countries and Communism," *The Norseman,* Vol. XII, No. 4 (July-August 1954), pp. 217-229.

————. *Sirpin ja vasaran tie.* Helsinki: Tammi, 1957.

Upravlenie Narodno-Khoziaistvennogo Ucheta Karel'skoi ASSR (Karjalan ASNT:n Kansantalouden Luettelointihallinto). *Perepis' naseleniia AKSSR (Karjalan ASNT:n väenlasku) v. 1933 g.,* vypusk III julkaisu. Petrozavodsk: Izdanie UNKhU AKSSR, 1935.

Upton, Anthony F. *Finland in Crisis 1940-1941: A study in small-power politics.* Ithaca: Cornell University Press, 1965.

Valtiopäivät 1926 pöytäkirjat, Vol. II. Helsinki: Valtioneuvoston kirjapaino, 1927.

Valtiopäivät 1930 pöytäkirjat. Helsinki: Valtioneuvoston kirjapaino, 1930.

Valtiopäivät 1940 pöytäkirjat, Vol. I. Helsinki: Valtioneuvoston kirjapaino, 1940.

Valtiopäivät 1944 pöytäkirjat, Vol. III. Helsinki: Valtioneuvoston kirjapaino, 1945.

Valtiopäivät 1956 pöytäkirjat, Vol. I. Helsinki: Valtioneuvoston kirjapaino, 1957.

Vanha vasemmistolainen. *Avoin kirje Sasu Punaselle, K. H. Wiikille, Johan Helolle ym. Vapaan Sanan toimitusneuvoston jäsenille.* Helsinki: Työväen kirjapaino, 1940.

Vapaussodan arkisto (Valtionarkistossa).

Vilkuna, Kustaa. *Sanan valvontaa. Sensuuri 1939-1944.* Helsinki: Otava, 1962.

Wälläri, N. *Myrskyssä ja myötätuulessa.* Helsinki: Oy Kodaprint Ab, 1951.

Waltari, Mika. *Neuvostovakoilun varjossa.* Helsinki: Otava, 1942.

Wiik, K. H. *Aktivismen och socialdemokratin.*

———. *Dagboksanteckningar från åren 1917 och 1918.*

———. *Kovan kokemuksen opetuksia.* Helsinki: Kansanvalta, 1918.

———. *Kuka hajoittaa? Kuka yhdistää?*

———. "Mistä johtui vuoden 1918 Suomen sota," in *Kuoleman kentiltä.* Hämeenlinna: Osakeyhtiö Hämeen Kansan kirjapaino, 1924, pp. 9-24.

———. *Miten Suomen itsenäisyys saatiin tunnustetuksi.* Työväen Arkisto: 327 (47:471) "1917."

———. *Näkökohtia sos.-dem. puolueessa v:n 1941 alussa vallitsevasta tilanteesta.*

Zinov'ev, G. "Lenin i iiul'skie dni," *Proletarskaia revoliutsiia,* No. 8-9 (67-68), August-September 1927, pp. 55-72.

247

SELECT BIBLIOGRAPHY

JOURNALS AND NEWSPAPERS

Ajan puntari
The Communist International
Helsingin Sanomat
International Press Correspondence
Izvestiia
Izvestiia gel'singforsskago soveta deputatov armii, flota i rabochikh
Kansan Lehti
Kansan Työ
Kansan Voima
Karelo-Murmanskii krai
Kommuna
Kommunisti
Krasnaia Kareliia
Kumous
Kustaa Vaasa
Neuvosto-Karjala
Pohjolan Sanomat
Pravda
Proletaari
Punainen Karjala
Rintamamies
Säkeniä
Savon Työ
SKP:n Tiedonantaja
Soihtu
Sosialisti
Sosialistinen Aikakauslehti
Sosialistisen eduskuntaryhmän kirjeitä
Sovetskaia Kareliia (Neuvosto-Karjala)
Suomen Ammattijärjestö
Suomen Kansanvaltuuskunnan Tiedonantoja

SELECT BIBLIOGRAPHY

Suomen Kuvalehti
Suomen Punainen Ammattijärjestö
Suomen Sosialidemokraatti
Suomen Työläinen
Suomen Työmies
Toveri
Työ
Työkansan Sanomat
Työmies
Työmies (SKP:n äänenkannattaja)
Työmies (Superior, Wisconsin)
Työväenjärjestöjen Tiedonantaja
Työväen Vallankumouksellisen Keskusneuvoston Tiedon-
antolehti   *Vapaa Sana*
Uusi Aika   *Vapaus* (Leningrad)
Uusi Suomi   *Viesti*
Vapaa Pohjola   *Ylioppilaslehti*

INTERVIEWS

President Urho Kekkonen   Väinö Meltti
Hugo Ahokanta   Uno Nurminen
J. O. Arjanne   Antti Ojala
Tuomas Bryggari   Emil Paajanen
K.-A. Fagerholm   Betty Peltonen
Johan Helo   Santeri Saarikivi
Sylvi-Kyllikki Kilpi   Lauri Sulander
Jaakko Kivi   Väinö Tanner
K. L. Kulo   Vilho Toivari
Jalmari Kuusela   Emil Tuomi
Hjalmar Långström   Arvo Tuominen
Tuure Lehén   Jussi Tuominen
Kalle Lehmus   U. U. Utrio
Antti Luostarinen   Niilo Wälläri
                 Anna Wiik

249

INDEX